A MORE PERFECT UNION

YOUR GUIDE TO THE U.S. CONSTITUTION

Samuel P. Nielson

PUBLIUS

Mission Viejo, California

PUBLIUS
23456 Madero, Suite 170
Mission Viejo, California 92691

International Standard Book Number: 978-0-9967768-0-6

Library of Congress Control Number: 2015952799

Printed in the United States of America.

For my wife, Chanell, who made this possible,
and my children, who made this necessary.

CONTENTS

> Let reverence for the [Constitution and its] laws, be
> breathed by every American mother, to the lisping
> babe, that prattles on her lap—let it be taught in
> schools, in seminaries, and in colleges;—let it be
> written in Primmers, spelling books, and in
> Almanacs;—let it be preached from the pulpit,
> proclaimed in legislative halls, and enforced in courts
> of justice. And, in short, let it become the *political
> religion* of the nation . . . .
> — Abraham Lincoln,
> January 27, 1838[1]

Abraham Lincoln desired the Constitution to be America's political religion. Its framework would be the basis for the nation's political discourse; public officials and the people they served would know its contents and actively live by its rules.

Yet the nation today seems far afield from achieving Lincoln's goal, or even considering the document as something to be respected and obeyed. Instead, this is an era when countless elected politicians and many judges, who have all taken oaths to support and defend the Constitution, cast aside its provisions to pursue their own ambitions. Numerous professors and teachers naïvely denigrate the document. Pundits ascribe false notions to the Constitution to claim that it supports their point of view. I even observed a tour guide at Independence Hall in Philadelphia, where the Constitution was written, improperly condemn the Constitution to unsuspecting visitors. All the while, people go along with and adopt these distorted views without pausing to consider the document for themselves.

This book is designed to change that. It is written as a concise guide to the United States Constitution, with easy to understand language and current, relevant examples of its application. The purpose is to make it so that you can understand the Constitution independently, without relying on anyone else's interpretation. The expectation is that you will ask questions for yourself, come to your own conclusions, and then apply your knowledge as you act in the public square.

Too many "Constitution guides" are slanted in presentation based on the author's political preference, be it conservative or liberal. Such guides thus risk misinforming their readers. Not so here. My sole purpose is to inform you about the Constitution. This book cuts across party lines and political ideologies with its examples of public officials following or disregarding the Constitution.

Here, you have just the basics to help you form your own opinions and become constitutionally literate. In this way, you and I can engage in the public square and elect leaders who we individually believe follow the Constitution and who will safeguard our liberty (or become those leaders ourselves). If not, we need only blame ourselves since preserving our form of government rests with "we the people." And in applying our constitutional knowledge in the public square, we will advance Lincoln's goal of the Constitution becoming our political religion.

Individual knowledge and understanding is one reason why this book does not simply rely on Supreme Court interpretations to determine the Constitution's meaning. Abraham Lincoln expected as much. During his first inaugural address, Lincoln challenged what he called "the position assumed by some that constitutional questions are to be decided by the Supreme Court." In taking the opposite point of view, he said, "if the policy of the government upon vital questions affecting the whole people is to be irrevocably fixed by decisions of the Supreme Court, the instant they are made …[,] the people will have ceased to be their own rulers, having to that extent practically resigned their government into the hands of that eminent tribunal."[2] In other words, blind acceptance of Court decrees as binding for everyone makes a small, unelected, and unrepresentative body leader over the people rather than the people being leaders over their government.

Viewpoints from Supreme Court interpretations will of course be discussed, but not being directly identified as coming from the Supreme Court. The reason is that the Supreme Court can – and does at times – err in interpreting the document, just as Lincoln suggested. For example, Article IV, section 2, makes clear that the states "shall deliver" fugitives within their borders to the state where the fugitive committed his or her crime (a process known as "extradition"). In 1860, the Supreme Court ruled that extradition was not required if the governor refused to return the fugitive.[3] The Supreme Court then reversed course in 1987 and concluded that the Constitution mandated extradition. Basically, the Court concluded in 1987 that "shall" means "shall."[4] Nothing about the relevant constitutional provision changed during this time; the only change was the Court's composition. The same occurred regarding racial segregation, with the Court in 1896 giving its blessing to the practice only to reverse course in 1954.[5] So this book presents various sides of the issues and leaves it to you to make your own decision about which interpretation, if any, is correct.

As you read the following pages, my hope is to transform the way you think about the United States Constitution. I hope that you recognize the Constitution as a protector of rights, not as a source of rights. I hope that you question what politicians, pundits, and courts claim about the Constitution. Above all, I hope that you never again rely on anyone other than yourself to tell you what is in the Constitution and how to interpret it. That way we will work together to form a more perfect union.

— Samuel P. Nielson

CHAPTER 1 – THE BASICS

So where did the United States Constitution come from? Why did over 50 of America's best and brightest spend the summer of 1787 in the sweltering Philadelphia heat to create a four-page written constitution? And what is the Constitution's philosophical basis? Briefly answering these questions is essential to appreciating the Constitution's actual text.

1.   Historical Basis and Context

The Constitution's Framers were deeply familiar with America's long history of having one document embody the relationship between the people and their government. The Pilgrims, originally from England, created the Mayflower Compact in 1620. Many of the colonies operated under charters outlining their basic form of government. Most of the colonists were British-born and so had some familiarity with the Magna Carta and various parliamentary laws governing the government's relations with its citizens. Amid the Revolutionary War in 1781, the states adopted the Articles of Confederation as the governing document for the new nation. So a written constitution was simply a continuation of the Framers' experience.

The Articles of Confederation, however, contained severe defects. They required a two-thirds majority to pass any national legislation, for instance. There was no executive branch to enforce any of the laws that did pass. Nor was there the ability to raise a national army. This final issue became acute in 1786 when the national government was incapable of sending a force to put down Shays' Rebellion in western Massachusetts. These and other defects made it clear that the new nation needed a more robust, better-functioning national government if it was to endure. Continued existence was a key consideration for all because of their collective sacrifice in securing independence.

Many of those who had helped achieve independence, including George Washington and Benjamin Franklin, convened at the Pennsylvania State House in Philadelphia in the summer of 1787 in an effort to remedy the Articles'

1

defects. Creating an entirely new governing document was not many attendees' initial intention. (It became known as the "Constitutional Convention" only after the fact.) But as many discovered during the gathering's early debates, simply reforming the Articles would not ensure a properly functioning government that would adequately address the nation's interests while adhering to their philosophical belief of government.

2.   Philosophical Basis

Part of the Framers' governing philosophy was put in writing eleven years before the Constitutional Convention. On July 4, 1776, the Second Continental Congress adopted the Declaration of Independence, which proclaimed the basic government philosophy that people "are endowed by their Creator with certain unalienable rights," including life and liberty, and that government exists to preserve those rights. This idea of people inherently possessing "natural rights" and government existing to protect those rights came from English philosopher John Locke's *Two Treatises on Government*, first published in December 1689.

2.1   Popular Sovereignty

Locke's philosophy of rights resting with the people rather than the government, and the government's authority coming from the consent of the people, represents the principle of "popular sovereignty." It stands in contrast to "parliamentary sovereignty" or "personal sovereignty" where all rights rest with a governing legislative body or a single person (a monarch), and the body or person grants certain rights to the people. All rights not granted to the people then remain with the governing body or monarch. Parliamentary sovereignty was the prevailing philosophy in the United Kingdom and other European countries at the time of the Convention. It still is the prevailing concept in many countries across the world, particularly those subject to monarchy, dictatorships, or communism.

The United States Constitution is the world's first national implementation of popular sovereignty. Its effect is apparent in Article I, for example, where the people grant certain, enumerated legislative (law making) powers to Congress. The Ninth Amendment then makes clear that all powers not granted to Congress remain with the people, or with the state governments.

2.2 Separation of Powers

Separation of powers is another philosophical concept the Framers adopted in the Constitution. Borrowed from the French philosopher Baron de Montesquieu, separation of powers is the idea of dividing political power into three separate branches of government—a legislature, an executive, and a judiciary:

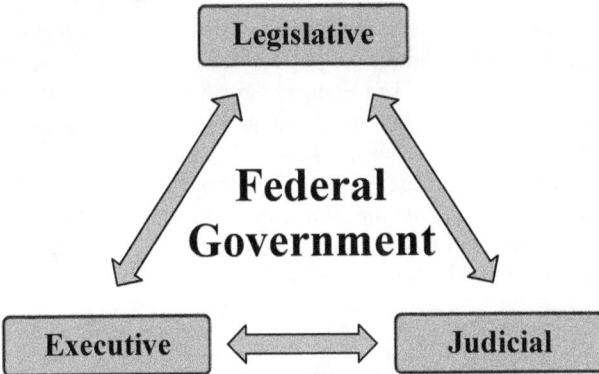

Each branch operates independently from the others and, through a series of checks and balances, limits the other branches' power. For example, the executive branch (the president) appoints members of the judicial branch, subject to the legislative branch's approval. The judicial branch then operates independently, but the legislative branch may limit the judicial branch's size and authority to hear certain matters. The legislative branch may also remove the president and judges from office. (Consistent with the idea of popular sovereignty, the people have the ultimate check because they may remove members of the legislative branch through elections.) And as will be seen, the Constitution secures complete separation of the branches by prohibiting all persons from simultaneously serving in more than one branch of government.

The separation of powers adopted in the Constitution contrasts with what the Framers observed in the United Kingdom and other parliamentary systems that did not have full separation of powers. Executive officers in the United Kingdom, such as the Prime Minister and other cabinet members, are also members of the legislature (Parliament). Further, the House of Lords, a part of Britain's legislative branch, also serves as the nation's highest court.

2.3   Federalism

A third philosophical concept in the Constitution is that of federalism, or a division of power between the nation and the several states. Unlike the two previous concepts of popular sovereignty and separation of powers, federalism was a unique American innovation. The Framers gave limited powers to the national government, but permitted the national government to operate exclusively in those spheres. State governments would then operate in other areas where the people of the states had given them power. And the people retained the rights not granted to the states or the federal government. This concept can be illustrated by the following diagram:

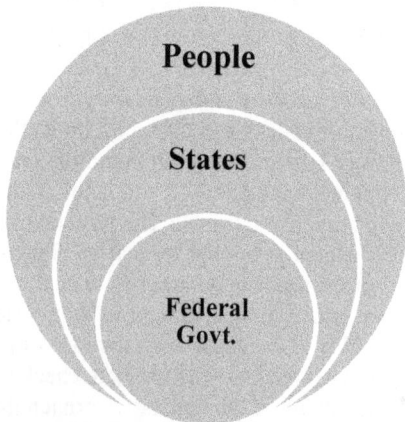

Those who favored granting certain powers to the national government alone became known as "Federalists"

during the debates on ratifying the Constitution; those who opposed the principle were known as "anti-Federalists." Federalists, including James Madison and Alexander Hamilton, wrote a series of 85 essays supporting the Constitution. These essays were later compiled into a two-volume work called *The Federalist Papers*; many refer to this work for an understanding of the Constitution by those who wrote it. This book does the same with references to various essays within *The Federalist Papers*.

3. Examining the Text

With this background on the Constitution's historical context and philosophical basis, we can now examine its text. To aid in reviewing the text, the following chapters set forth the Constitution's various articles, sections, and clauses individually. The Constitution's actual text is in **bold** (with its original spelling modernized), and an underlined heading describes the article/section/clause's content. The underlined language does not appear in the Constitution; it is included here for convenience. Language that has been changed by amendments is in brackets. Explanatory notes and examples related to the text then immediately follow. So that you can see the Constitution's contents at a glance, here is a brief outline summary:

Article I – The Legislative Branch: Article I creates a national legislature (Congress), grants it certain powers, prohibits others, and places some limits on states' powers.

Article II – The Executive Branch: Article II creates a national executive (the president) and grants him or her power to implement/execute the laws passed by Congress.

Article III – The Judicial Branch: Article III creates the judiciary, including one supreme court, guarantees trial by jury for all criminal trials, defines treason, and provides limits on the punishment of treason.

Article IV – States' Relations and Rights: Article IV establishes a basic framework for states' relations with one another, with citizens, and with the federal government.

Article V – Amending the Constitution: Article V sets out the method for amending (modifying) the Constitution.

Article VI – Constitutional Supremacy: Article VI makes the federal Constitution preeminent, provides for assuming debts incurred under the Articles of Confederation, and prohibits religious tests for public office.

Article VII – Ratification: Article VII provides the process by which the Constitution took effect.

Amendments I through X – The Bill of Rights: These particular amendments protect a number of personal freedoms, limit the government's power in judicial and other proceedings, and make clear that powers not granted to the federal government are reserved to the states and the people.

Amendments XI through XXVII – Other Amendments: These most recent amendments concern issues related to the presidency, voting, prohibition of alcohol, or they otherwise modify the rules set forth in the Constitution.

The Preamble

We the people of the United States, in order to form a more perfect Union, establish justice, insure domestic Tranquility, provide for the common defense, promote the general Welfare, and secure the Blessings of Liberty to ourselves and our Posterity, do ordain and establish this Constitution for the United States of America.

The preamble sets forth six primary reasons for drafting the Constitution and the reasons for its existence. Yet the preamble does not confer any authority on any branch of government. Nor does it secure any rights. Rather, it explains what the people are to expect from the express powers they granted to the federal government within the Constitution. So all laws created from the powers contained in the Constitution should achieve one of these six stated purposes:

- *Form a more perfect union*
- *Establish justice*
- *Insure domestic tranquility*
- *Provide for the common defense*
- *Promote the general welfare*
- *Secure the blessings of liberty to the people and their posterity*

Consider these purposes in examining the Constitution's text, particularly Articles I through IV. Some of these phrases even appear directly in the Constitution's text; "general welfare" and "common defense" are in Article I, section 8, in connection with a direct power granted to Congress.

This being said, there are some important aspects of the preamble that should be addressed. First is the phrase "We the people." The phrase reminds us of popular sovereignty—the federal government's source of power is the *people*. The government does not grant rights to the people; the people grant rights to the government.

The "people" referred to is *not* the nation's population as a single whole. James Madison pointed out in *Federalist No. 39* that the popular consent establishing the Constitution's authority was "given by the people, not as individuals composing one entire nation, but as composing the distinct and independent States to which they respectively belong." This is consistent with the preamble's original wording. The preamble draft submitted to the Constitution Committee of Style listed each of the states' names individually ("We the people of the States of New-Hampshire, Massachusetts, Rhode-Island and Providence Plantations, Connecticut," and so forth until Georgia). The 1778 Treaty of Alliance with France and the Articles of Confederation similarly listed the states this way. But the format presented a problem because no one knew exactly which of the thirteen states would be the nine needed to ratify the Constitution. So Gouverneur Morris, the preamble's primary drafter, substituted the introduction with today's familiar phrase "We the people of the United States." The people do ultimately have the authority over the federal Constitution through the states. The people also have the power over the states because the states too derive their power from the people in each state.

A second aspect from the preamble to consider is Constitution's intent to form "a more perfect Union." The Framers did not believe the Constitution to be perfect. But it certainly was better than any previous form of government. Benjamin Franklin, the Constitutional Convention's oldest delegate, said that he was astonished "to find this system [of government] approaching so near perfection as it does."[6] One hundred years later, British Prime Minister William Gladstone called the U.S. Constitution "the most wonderful work ever struck off at a given time by the brain and purpose of man."[7]

ARTICLE I—The Legislative Branch

Article I is the longest of the Constitution's seven articles. It creates Congress, meaning both the Senate and the House of Representatives. It also vests legislative powers (*i.e.,* the power to make laws) in Congress, lists the powers

Congress has (called *enumerated* powers), and grants the power necessary to exercise the enumerated powers (known as *implied* powers). Finally, Article I lists the powers specifically denied to Congress.

Section 1—<u>The Federal Congress</u>

All legislative Powers herein granted shall be vested in a Congress of the United States, which shall consist of a Senate and House of Representatives.

Simple and straightforward, section 1 gives the powers to create and pass laws, *i.e.* "all legislative powers," to a federal Congress. This section also establishes the federal Congress as a bicameral (two-chamber) legislature. "Herein granted" means that the powers are given to Congress from the states and, ultimately, from the people. Section 8 contains these enumerated powers. Section 9 specifically denies Congress other powers, making clear that the Constitution does not give Congress unlimited power.

The Framers conceivably limited the new Congress's powers because, as James Madison noted in *Federalist No. 53*, "Wherever the supreme power of legislation has resided, has been supposed to reside also, a full power to change the form of the government."[8]

Establishing a bicameral Congress was not a new concept. In fact, at the time of the Convention, all of the states except Pennsylvania had bicameral legislatures. Edmund Randolph of Virginia suggested at the Convention's outset that a new, bicameral national legislature be created. He proposed allocating membership in both chambers based on each state's population. The lower house, he suggested, would be filled by representatives nominated and elected by the people of each state. Conversely, the national government's upper house would be filled with representatives nominated by state legislatures and elected by each state's lower house. Such an approach of having representatives selected by different groups (the people and another entity) was readily found in Great Britain where the people elected members of the lower house (the House of Commons) while the monarch selected

9

members of the upper house (the House of Lords). In this way, the new national legislature would represent both the people and the states.

Randolph's proposal came from the Virginia Plan. Delegates from populous states like Virginia and Pennsylvania liked the concept. But states with smaller populations opposed the proportional-representation arrangement. They feared that, with fewer voices than the larger states, their interests would be marginalized. Just over two weeks after the Virginia plan's introduction, William Paterson of New Jersey proposed the small states' alternative known as the New Jersey Plan.

The New Jersey Plan called for a unicameral (single-chamber) legislature in which each state would receive one vote regardless of population. Small and large states alike would be considered equal in the national government. The plan essentially left the Articles of Confederation in place but granted the new body the power to regulate trade and to tax foreign goods.

After approximately one month of debates between the New Jersey and Virginia Plans, and as the Convention risked collapse, Roger Sherman of Connecticut put forth the "Great Compromise." The proposal incorporated aspects of both plans—proportional representation in the lower chamber and equal representation in the upper. Additionally, the compromise required that all laws generating revenue (*i.e.,* tax laws) start in the lower chamber. Delegates debated the issue for eleven days before the compromise passed by a vote of five to four.

Section 2—The House of Representatives

The House of Representatives is the legislative branch's first or "lower" chamber. Often referred to simply as "the House," it is the larger of the two chambers created by the Great Compromise.

Clause 1: Elections

The House of Representatives shall be composed of Members chosen every second Year by the People of the several States, and the Electors in

each State shall have the Qualifications requisite for Electors of the most numerous Branch of the State Legislature.

This clause explains why *all* members of the House of Representatives face reelection every two years (*i.e.*, 2016, 2018, 2020, etc.). The purpose of such short terms was to keep the representatives accountable to the people. If the representative did not act in accordance with the people's wishes, then the people could remove him or her from office fairly quickly (*i.e.*, within than two years). The clause makes the term of office unalterable by those in power.

The selection of a two-year term was somewhat of a compromise. Many at the Constitutional Convention shared the sentiment that "where annual elections end, tyranny begins."[9] That's why 10 of the 13 states held annual elections for their state legislatures. Two states, Connecticut and Rhode Island, held elections every six months. South Carolina was the exception, holding elections for its state legislature biennially. In justifying the selection of two-year terms, James Madison stated in *Federalist No. 53* that "it would be not easy to show that Connecticut or Rhode Island is better governed, or enjoys a greater share of rational liberty than South Carolina . . . ."[10]

Other reasons for the two-year term included competency for the office, ensuring legitimacy in elections, and travel. Of competency, Madison noted that "No man can be a competent legislator who does not . . . [have] a certain degree of knowledge of the subjects on which he is to legislate." At least part of this knowledge, Madison argued, "can only be attained, or at least thoroughly attained, by actual experience in the station which requires the use of it." So a two-year term affords a representative both the experience necessary to acquire knowledge for his or her office and the opportunity to effectively use that knowledge while in office to legislate on matters of foreign trade, interstate commerce, taxes, and militia regulations, what Madison termed the "principal objects of federal legislation."[11]

The two-year term continues to have an impact on representatives' accountability to their constituents. The 2010 Congressional elections are a notable example. The

Democratic Party held a majority of the seats in the House of Representatives and passed the unpopular Affordable Care Act (better known as "Obamacare") in March 2010. Voter anger and frustration resulted in Democratic candidates facing a massive electoral defeat in November 2010, with Democrats suffering the highest loss by a party in a House election since 1938,[12] and the largest House swing since 1948.[13]

One effect of the clause today is that some members of Congress seem to only live from one election to another; it's as if they seek more to maintain the office through incessant campaigning than actively legislating.

This clause delegates the qualifications for electors (voters) to the states. While the principle of voting in federal elections arises out of the Constitution, the requirements for doing so remain primarily with the states. Here, the Constitution makes clear that the qualifications required to vote in a federal election are to be the same as the requirements a state sets to vote for members of the largest house of its legislature.

Because states set up the qualifications to vote, there have historically been great variances in who could vote. For example, women had the right to vote in New Jersey at the time of the Constitution's ratification. After New Jersey revoked that right in 1807, however, no state permitted women to vote until several decades later. State prohibitions based on sex in federal elections continued in some states until the Nineteenth Amendment's passage in 1920. Other amendments to the Constitution prohibited states from imposing voting qualifications based on race, color, sex, or age.

Clause 2: <u>Legal Qualifications</u>

No Person shall be a Representative who shall not have attained to the Age of twenty five Years, and been seven Years a Citizen of the United States, and who shall not, when elected, be an Inhabitant of that State in which he shall be chosen.

This second clause lays out three legal qualifications for persons seeking office in the House of Representatives. First, an individual has to be at least twenty-five years old to hold the office. Second, he or she must have been a United States citizen for at least seven years. Third, the representative must be an inhabitant of the state that he or she represents.

Age
While the minimum age is twenty five, the average age for representatives is often much older. For instance, the average age of the House at the beginning of the 115th Congress that convened in 2017 is more than double that. In fact, it is one of the oldest Congresses ever with an average age of approximately 58 years old.[14]

There are nevertheless young representatives not far removed from age 25 in every Congress. All but 11 of the 115 Congresses have had at least one representative start his or her term while in his or her twenties. Among the younger members in history is Thomas Downey from New York, who was elected at age 25 in 1974. Others have been elected even before turning age 25. For example, John Brown was elected to Congress from Kentucky in 1859 but did not take his seat until he reached the minimum age the next year. The youngest Representative in the 115th Congress was Elise Stefanik of New York, who was 32 years old at the start of 2017. She was also the youngest member of the 114th Congress, assuming office in 2015 at age 30. Before Ms. Stefanik, the youngest member was Representative Patrick Murphy of Florida. He was first elected in 2012 at age 29.

Citizenship
The only citizenship requirement for Congress is that the person be an American citizen for at least seven years prior to taking office. As such, naturalized citizens are as eligible to serve in Congress as those born here. There have been several naturalized members in recent years from a broad range of countries. Stephanie Murphy, born Đặng Thị Ngọc Dung in Vietnam, began representing Florida in 2017. Other naturalized members who first took office in 2017 include: India natives Pramila Jayapal, representing Washington state, and Raja Krishnamoorthi of Illinois; Mexico-born Ruben Kihuen and Salud Carbajal, representing Nevada and California, respectively; and Adriano Espaillat, originally

from the Dominican Republic, representing New York. Ted Lieu, a naturalized citizen from Taiwan, began representing California in 2015. Albio Sires, originally from Cuba, has represented New Jersey since 2006. Anh "Joseph" Quang Cao, born in Saigon, South Vietnam, was elected to the House from Louisiana's second district in 2008 and served until 2011. Japanese-born Mazie Keiko Hirono represented Hawaii in Congress from 2007 to 2013. David Wu, born in Taiwan, represented Oregon from 1999 to 2011. Cuban-born Ileana Ros-Lehtinen has represented Florida since 1989.

Inhabitant

The Constitution only requires a representative to be an *inhabitant* of the state that he or she is elected from and not a legal *resident*. The technical difference between the two terms has a practical effect in how this clause plays out. To be a "legal resident" one often has to have a residence within the state and meet certain other criteria, such as having an intention to permanently reside there. Conversely, an "inhabitant" of a state can be a person who has a physical presence there.

Out-of-state college students and military personnel are good examples of this distinction. They are legal residents of the states from which they came, being registered to vote there and claiming that state as their residence. But the students and military members are considered inhabitants of the state where they are studying or serving. This distinction means that a person may be elected from a state of which he or she is not even a legal resident. While this would be rare, it has happened. In 1806, Philip Barton Key moved from Washington, D.C., to a partially completed home in Maryland to run for Congress. He moved to Maryland so close to the election that he didn't even meet the requirements to be an official resident and consequently could not vote for himself in the election, which he won. The House seated him because he was an "inhabitant" of Maryland even though he was not a legal resident of that state.[15]

The inhabitant/resident distinction has caused contention in the past and in fact cost a representative his seat. In 1822, Massachusetts elected John Bailey to serve in the House. Bailey had been living in Washington, D.C., while working as a State Department clerk prior to being elected. The House, as judge of its elections under Article I, section 5, subsequently concluded that Bailey was a legal resident of Massachusetts but that he was not an "inhabitant" of the state at the time of the election as required by the Constitution. So the House refused to seat him.[16] Bailey contested this decision by pointing out that Representative John Forsyth from Georgia, also elected in 1822, did not live in Georgia when he was elected but that he lived in Spain where he was an American diplomat. The House responded that it still considers those serving abroad for the government to be inhabitants of their home states and so seated Forsyth.[17]

Beyond the Constitutional requirement that a representative be an inhabitant of the state from which he or she is elected, there is no requirement that the representative reside in the district that he or she represents. Representative Parren Mitchell of Maryland represented a Baltimore district from 1971 to 1987 despite clearly living outside of its borders. He chose that district because he worked there as a poverty director and so believed that he was "closer to its problems." Representative Paul Gillmor of Ohio served in Congress for 18 years (1989 to 2007) without truly living within the Bowling Green district that he represented. He claimed his father's home as his official residence and voting address until he purchased a condominium within the district in 2006. Gillmor made the purchase under pressure from constituents who were upset that he lived elsewhere. But he was never really at the condo; his family lived in a Columbus suburb where his wife worked and located some 90 minutes away from his district. Gillmor spent his time either there or in Washington where he owned another home.[18]

In the 21st century, Mimi Walters began representing California's 45th Congressional district in 2015 despite living four miles from her district's nearest boundary.[19] In a more extreme example, Maxine Waters represents California's 43rd Congressional while living approximately 530 feet outside of its boundaries. Waters lived within her district for her first 22 years in office, but redistricting effective for the 2012 election moved her residence into a new district a mere three-minute walk away from the one she had historically represented.

Clause 3: <u>Apportionment of Representatives and Direct Taxes</u>

[Representatives and direct Taxes shall be apportioned among the several States which may be included within this Union, according to their respective Numbers, which shall be determined by adding to the whole Number of free Persons, including those bound to Service for a Term of Years, and excluding Indians not taxed, three fifths of all other Persons.] The actual Enumeration shall be made within three Years after the first Meeting of the Congress of the United States, and within every subsequent Term of ten Years, in such Manner as they shall by Law direct. The Number of Representatives shall not exceed one for every thirty Thousand, but each State shall have at Least one Representative; and until such enumeration shall be made, the State of New Hampshire shall be entitled to choose three, Massachusetts eight, Rhode-Island and Providence Plantations one, Connecticut five, New-York six, New Jersey four, Pennsylvania eight, Delaware one, Maryland six, Virginia ten, North Carolina five, South Carolina five, and Georgia three.

The brackets in this clause surround a sentence that has been changed by amendment. Specifically, the 13th, 14th, and 16th amendments changed this portion by altering: (1) the status of slaves (referred to here as "three fifths of all other persons") in Congressional apportionment, and (2) the method of taxation allowed regarding incomes.

Prior to being changed, the first sentence (beginning "Representatives and direct taxes shall ...") restricted Congress's ability to raise revenue. That is, direct taxes had to be apportioned based on a state's population. While neither the Constitution nor the Constitutional Convention's notes define "direct tax," in practice a direct tax is a fixed tax amount per person in the state. This represented a compromise of sorts regarding representation in Congress. Since states with large populations would have more representatives in the federal Congress due to the Great Compromise, so too would these states have to pay greater taxes because this clause required the taxes to be apportioned based on population.

The phrase "three fifths of all other Persons" also reflects a compromise among the Framers. The "other Persons" referred to are slaves. Slave states did not allow slaves to vote; if slaves were counted the same as the free inhabitants in each state, then slave states would have had increased representation in Congress and so an incentive to import even more slaves. Non-slave states opposed counting slaves *at all* for representation; slave states understandably supported their inclusion in the population count. As a compromise to bring the union together, slaves were counted as three-fifths of a person for both representation purposes and taxes. Since slaves would be counted as less than a whole person for population, they would also count less towards the southern states' direct-tax liability. Later, the Fourteenth Amendment's adoption made the three-fifths number obsolete; all former slaves were counted as whole persons.

> *The actual Enumeration shall be made within three Years after the first Meeting of the Congress of the United States, and within every subsequent Term of ten Years, in such Manner as they shall by Law direct.*

This small sentence in clause 3 explains why the federal government allocates substantial resources to the census every ten years (2000, 2010, 2020, etc.). The government must perform a census to determine how many representatives each state gets in Congress and also the number of electors to the Electoral College. (The Electoral College is the body that elects the president. Its creation occurs in Article II, section 1.) Since the federal government now relies primarily on income taxes rather than direct taxes, apportionment of representatives is the principal reason for taking the census.

The first census occurred in 1790, one year after Congress's first meeting and less than the three years allowed by the Constitution. The most recent census occurred in 2010. While the 2010 census was one of the shortest in history, it still asked questions regarding race, gender, date of birth, ownership of the residence, and phone number. Many people opposed answering census questions beyond the number of people in their household. They argued that doing so exceeded the census's constitutional objective of counting citizens. But they failed to appreciate a purpose of the additional questions in ensuring the accuracy of the number of persons given.

> *The Number of Representatives shall not exceed one for every thirty Thousand, but each State shall have at Least one Representative;*

Here we find the maximum number of representatives possible under the Constitution (no more than one for every 30,000 people) and the minimum number guaranteed to each state (at least one). The provision declares that a representative has to represent *at least* 30,000 people, not that there has to be one representative for every 30,000. It is essentially left to Congress to fix the number of persons that a representative will represent. Hypothetically speaking, Congress could declare that one representative will represent one million people and still be in accordance with the Constitution, provided that states without one million people had at least one representative. Oddly enough, one million people per representative is not too far off from where we are today. There is one representative for every 710,767 people according to the 2010 Census.[20]

Today seven states—Alaska, Delaware, Montana, North Dakota, South Dakota, Vermont, and Wyoming—have only one representative. These representatives serve their states "at large" rather than from a single district. And they range in size from one representative for approximately 550,000 people in Wyoming to one representative for approximately 995,000 in Montana. Rhode Island has only 60,000 more people than Montana but has two representatives. California, the most populous state, has 53 representatives.

The total number of representatives today stands at 435. Again this means that there is one representative for an average of every 710,000 people. This is a far cry from the number for the first six apportionments (one for every 50,000 or less), or even from the last time that Congress increased the number of representatives to 435 (one for every 210,000) in 1913.

Why did we reach this disparity? In 1921 a recently elected Republican majority in Congress refused to reapportion the representatives as required by the Constitution (possibly out of fear of reapportionment's effect on future election prospects). Congress ultimately capped the number at 435 in 1929. Other than for a period of four years when Hawaii and Alaska joined the Union in 1959 and the number temporarily increased to 437, House membership has remained steady at 435 ever since, despite the United States' population more than tripling in size since then!

The arbitrary fixing of Congress to 435 members is not without opposition. Several groups advocate for an increase in House membership according to the Constitution's original numbers so that the House be more representative of the people. The maintenance of a fixed number also means that several states lose representatives in Congress every ten years simply because their populations did not grow as fast as another state's, while other states gain seats or have no change. This explains why, following the 2010 census, Texas gained four new representatives, Florida gained two, Arizona and five other states gained one, while eight states lost one representative, with two others, New York and Ohio, each losing two. The determination of which states gain and lose seats is made by U.S. Census Bureau, which relies on a mathematical formula. These new representative districts became effective for the 2012 elections.

> *and until such enumeration shall be made, the State*
> *of New Hampshire shall be entitled to choose three,*
> *Massachusetts eight, Rhode-Island and Providence*
> *Plantations one, Connecticut five, New-York six,*
> *New Jersey four, Pennsylvania eight, Delaware*
> *one, Maryland six, Virginia ten, North Carolina*
> *five, South Carolina five, and Georgia three.*

This provision was temporary. It provided representation in Congress until the required enumeration was taken to determine the proper basis for representation. Following the enumeration in 1790 and the subsequent apportionment, this provision became irrelevant. It has historical significance today in that it provides the Framers' estimate of the original thirteen states' populations at the time of ratification.

Clause 4: <u>Vacancies</u>

When vacancies happen in the Representation from any State, the Executive Authority thereof shall issue Writs of Election to fill such Vacancies.

This clause mandates that the governor of each state order a special election (the "writ of election" referred to here) to fill any House vacancies rather than appointing someone to the position. This helps ensure that the House truly be representative of the people.

Writs of election to replace a representative are fairly common. Ron Estes won a special election in April 2017 to complete the remainder of Mike Pompeo term from Kansas's 4th District after Pompeo resigned two months earlier to become the CIA Director. Colleen Hanabusa was elected in November 2016 to serve the last eight weeks of Mark Takai's term from Hawaii's 1st District. Takai died in office in July 2016.[21] All told, seventy-six representatives entered the House by special elections between 1997 and 2016,[22] or an average of four per year.

Some governors have nevertheless refused to issue writs of election if the representative would serve less than one year, believing that the cost of an election did not outweigh the potential benefit. Governor Richard Ogilvie of Illinois did this in 1969 and Governor Robert Taft of Ohio did the same in 2002. Voters took both governors to court for depriving them of their constitutional right to representation and the voters prevailed both times.

Clause 5: <u>Officers and Impeachment</u>

The House of Representatives shall choose their Speaker and other Officers; and shall have the sole Power of Impeachment.

The Speaker of the House is the only House officer mentioned in the Constitution. This clause makes clear that the House selects its Speaker independent of *all* other bodies. But the Constitution is silent on the Speaker's responsibilities. They are left to historical practice and so may vary according to the Congress. Historically, the Speaker's duties include setting the agenda, presiding over debate, preserving order, and participating in committee appointments.

The Constitution also does not specify that the Speaker must be a member of the House. So, in theory, the Speaker could be an individual selected by House members but not by regular citizens. The House has nevertheless always selected its Speaker from its members. And the Speaker traditionally selects some of the House officers including the House Historian, General Counsel, and Inspector General. Most recently, the House selected Representative Paul Ryan of Wisconsin as its Speaker.

The "other Officers" selected by members of the House include the Clerk, Sergeant-at-Arms, Chief Administrative Officer, Pages, House Parliamentarian, and the Chaplain. This section also covers the House's selection of majority and minority party leaders and whips.

Impeachment

The House has the sole power of impeachment. "Impeachment" is popularly misunderstood to mean the removal of an official from office. But impeachment really means the power to formally accuse and bring charges against government officials for wrongdoing.

The Senate then tries those impeached by the House (*i.e.,* determines their guilt or innocence) under the power granted it in Article I, section 3. That same section sets forth the procedures for the trial and the punishment for those who are found guilty. Article II, section 4, outlines the basis for impeaching an official and those officials that are subject to impeachment.

Impeachment is rare. In fact, the House has impeached only 19 federal officers in its entire history. This number includes two presidents (Andrew Johnson and Bill Clinton), one cabinet member, one senator (although senators aren't technically subject to impeachment), one Supreme Court

21

justice, and fourteen federal judges. The most recent impeachment occurred in March 2010 when the House unanimously impeached federal district court judge Thomas Porteous. (The Senate convicted 7 of the 19 impeached federal officers.)

One official who was close to impeachment but who was never actually impeached is President Richard Nixon. In July 1974 the House Judiciary Committee voted to impeach him for his role in the Watergate scandal. But President Nixon resigned before the full House voted. The House then dropped the issue.

Section 3—The Senate

The Senate is the legislative branch's second chamber, or "upper" chamber. The term "senate" comes from the Latin "senatus," meaning "council of the elders." It was the name given to the ancient Roman republic's highest legislative, judicial, and religious authority. Because the Framers adopted the word to describe one of the Constitution's legislative chambers, the term is now generally used to describe a body possessing only legislative functions.

Clause 1: Elections

The Senate of the United States shall be composed of two Senators from each state, [chosen by the Legislature thereof], for six years, and each Senator shall have one Vote.

As discussed in section 1, the Great Compromise incorporated aspects of both the Virginia and New Jersey Plans. The Virginia Plan called for representation based on population. That proposal resulted in section 2, which established the House of Representatives. Here, in section 3, is the implementation of the New Jersey Plan's call for equal representation between the states. Each state has two senators, no matter how large or small the state is. Article V will show that this equal representation of the states in the Senate is the only part of the Constitution that cannot be changed by amendment.

The original Constitution called for the state legislatures to choose their senators. One reason to do this was to make sure that the states' interests were represented in the federal legislature. The House would represent the people directly, while the Senate would represent the states. James Madison noted this in *Federalist No. 62* when he said: "No law or resolution can now be passed without the concurrence, first, of a majority of the people [*i.e.,* the House of Representatives], and then, of a majority of the States [*i.e.,* the Senate]."[23] The Seventeenth Amendment changed this legislative election to make senators elected by popular vote, the same as the representatives.

Additionally, this clause sets out a six-year term of office for senators. The longer term allows senators to consider lasting effects of legislation that could impetuously pass through the House without having to worry about immediate reelection. Thus it allows legislation to "cool" in the Senate.

Finally, the single vote accorded to each senator, and the equal voting power per state, recognizes the sovereignty remaining in each state.

Clause 2: Senate Classes and Voting

Immediately after they shall be assembled in Consequence of the first Election, they shall be divided as equally as may be into three Classes. The Seats of the Senators of the first Class shall be vacated at the Expiration of the second Year, of the second Class at the Expiration of the fourth Year, and of the third Class at the Expiration of the sixth Year, so that one third may be chosen every second Year; [and if Vacancies happen by Resignation, or otherwise, during the Recess of the Legislature of any State, the Executive thereof may make temporary Appointments until the next meeting of the Legislature , which shall then fill such Vacancies.]

By creating three Senate classes with different starting points for their terms, this clause means that every two years one-third of the Senate will have served their six-year terms and so face election. Put differently, only one third of the Senate is elected every two years rather than the entire body like the House. This arrangement ensures continuity and stability in the Senate. It also ensures that no two senators from the same state have the same term of office since a state's senators are assigned to different classes (although this clause does not explicitly require them to be).

When new states have been admitted to the Union, their senators were separated into these established classes in a way that was designed to keep each class of senators roughly the same size. Class III is the largest class, with thirty-four senators. This class's term ends in January 2023. The term for Class I's thirty-three senators will end in January 2019. The term for the thirty-three senators in Class II will end in January 2021.[24]

The Seventeenth Amendment changed the bracketed portion of this clause. The change is that two senators from the same state may face election at the same time *if* a special election occurs to fill a vacancy (since the legislature would no longer be filling the vacancies as they occurred). This occurred in California 1992 when Dianne Feinstein was elected to the Senate in a special election to replace Pete Wilson. Wilson had resigned his seat in 1991 after being elected California's governor. The special election occurred in November 1992, at the same time as the regular election for California's other Senate seat. Consequently, Ms. Feinstein was elected to serve the remaining two years of Wilson's term in Senate Class I, while Barbara Boxer was elected at the same time for the full six year term in Senate Class III.

Clause 3: <u>Legal Qualifications</u>

No Person shall be a Senator who shall not have attained to the Age of thirty Years, and been nine Years a Citizen of the United States, and who shall not, when elected, be an Inhabitant of that State for which he shall be chosen.

Section 3, clause 3, lays out three legal qualifications of office for the Senate just as section 2, clause 2, does for the

House. Other than a few changes accounting for age and citizenship, the requirements are the same for a representative as outlined in the following diagram:

Congressional Qualifications

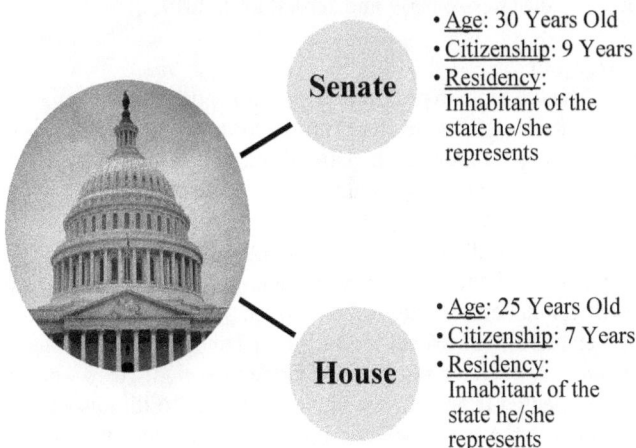

Senate
- Age: 30 Years Old
- Citizenship: 9 Years
- Residency: Inhabitant of the state he/she represents

House
- Age: 25 Years Old
- Citizenship: 7 Years
- Residency: Inhabitant of the state he/she represents

Age

The Senate has a higher age requirement than that of the House by five years. James Madison commented in *Federalist No. 62* that this distinction "is explained by the nature of the senatorial trust, which, requiring greater extent of information and stability of character, requires at the same time that the senator should have reached a period of life most likely to supply these advantages." In other words, the Framers believed that age brought maturity.

Based on this reasoning, today's senators should be quite mature. The average senator's age at the beginning of the 115th Congress in January 2017 was 61.8.[25] The average age at inauguration for the newly elected senators was 54.8 years, roughly 25 years above the Constitutional requirement![26]

A person need not be thirty years old to be *elected* to the Senate, but only needs to reach that age *before* being sworn in when the individual would actually serve as a senator. West Virginia's Rush Holt was elected to the Senate in 1934 at the age of 29. Holt promised to wait six months until he reached his thirtieth birthday to take the oath and assume the office; he took the oath in June 1935. More recently, Delaware voters elected Joseph Biden to the Senate in 1972 at age 29. He turned 30 just two weeks after the election and before taking the oath of office. Biden became the 47th Vice-President of the United States in 2009 and served until 2017.

Citizenship

The citizenship period is longer for senators than for representatives. This results from the Framers' desire for greater understanding of the United States and also to try allegiance to the nation, as James Madison explained in *Federalist No. 62*.

Similar to the House, the Senate has had several naturalized citizens serve in it throughout history. In fact, there have been dozens of naturalized-citizen senators.[27] In 1848, the Senate refused to seat Ireland-born James Shields because he had only been a United States citizen for eight years when he was elected from Illinois. Shields returned to Illinois and prevailed in the special election to replace him because the election occurred shortly after his being a nine-year United States citizen. The Senate ultimately seated Shields. He later served as a senator from two other states—Minnesota and Missouri.[28]

Naturalized citizens have served in the Senate on a fairly regular basis. Cuban-born Mel Martinez served as one of Florida's senators from 2005 until resigning in July 2009. The most recent naturalized-citizen senator is Japanese-born Mazie Keiko Hirono. She began serving as a senator from Hawaii in January 2013.

Inhabitant

As with members of the House, a senator needs to only be an "inhabitant" of the state and not even a legal resident. One of the most famous individuals to take advantage of this flexible language for the Senate was the late Robert Kennedy. He moved to New York in September 1964 to run for the Senate. Kennedy ultimately won the election in spite of not being able to vote for himself because he did not meet New York's residency requirement for voter registration.[29]

The resident/inhabitant distinction and voting came up again in early 2012 when the Marion County Election Board in Indiana ruled that Senator Richard Lugar of Indiana, first elected to the Senate in 1976, was ineligible to vote in the primary election because he did not have a physical address in the voting precinct. Lugar sold his Indiana home in 1977 to move to the Washington, D.C. area, and he had lived there ever since. Lugar said that moving there was the only way that he could afford to keep his family together and also remain involved in his son's school activities.[30]

Today, Senator Orrin Hatch of Utah takes advantage of the "inhabitant" requirement to be elected from Utah in spite of his primary residence being in Virginia, a home that he purchased shortly after his election to the Senate in 1976. But Hatch differs from Lugar in that he owns a condominium in Salt Lake City, Utah, where he can claim residence for voting and other purposes. A more extreme example that is akin to Lugar's not maintaining a residence in his state is Pat Roberts of Kansas. During his 2014 campaign, Roberts claimed as his "residence" a home owned and occupied by campaign donors as Roberts had not lived in Kansas since first being elected to Congress 33 years earlier.[31]

Senators Lugar and Hatch, and other like them, may believe that they are better able to serve their states by living close to the nation's capital. They may be right. Lugar boasted a 98% attendance record during his years in office (1977 to 2013).[32] Through the end of the 114th Congress in January 2017, Hatch's attendance was over 96%, having missed fewer than 500 out of 14,443 roll-call votes.[33]

Clause 4: President of the Senate

The Vice President of the United States shall be President of the Senate, but shall have no Vote, unless they be equally divided.

This clause is fairly straightforward—the vice president is the president of the Senate and he or she only gets to vote if the Senate is tied. It is the only clause in the Constitution to state the vice president's responsibilities. So what does it mean to be "President of the Senate" and what are the duties that go along with the office?

This issue arose in the 2008 vice-presidential debates between Alaska Governor Sarah Palin and then-Senator Joseph Biden. Ms. Palin came under fire for suggesting that the Constitution allowed the vice president to have an important role working in the Senate as a legislative official. Some thought that she was incredibly misinformed. But Ms. Palin was right. The vice president is described in this clause as a legislative official, namely the Senate's presiding officer.

The Framers understood this distinction. The first two vice presidents, John Adams and Thomas Jefferson, consistently presided over the Senate during their terms in the office. Each did a great deal to shape the vice president's role. In fact, John Adams used the office to persuade senators to vote against legislation that he opposed, and he frequently lectured the Senate on policy matters. He also performed his only constitutionally defined function, voting in the event of a tie, a record 29 times. (By comparison, Vice President Dick Cheney voted only eight times between 2001 and 2009, and Vice President Joseph Biden never voted during his two terms as vice president from 2009 to 2017). Jefferson said that he considered the office "constitutionally confined to legislative functions."[34] Vice presidents from John Adams in 1789 to Richard Nixon in the 1950s regularly presided over the Senate; presiding in the Senate was their primary function and they rarely attended executive meetings.[35] Also, the vice president still keeps offices at the capitol.

In any event, the directive for the vice president to vote only in the event of a tie prevents a stalemate. The Senate will always either outright pass or reject proposed legislation because there will be no ties.

Ironically, before taking office, and in the same vice presidential debates that resulted in Ms. Palin's criticism, then-Senator Biden incorrectly stated that the vice president presides over the Senate "only in a time when in fact there's a tie vote"[36] (despite the fact that the vice president can always preside over the Senate and did until Lyndon Johnson ended the practice in 1961 and his successors followed his example).[37] Mr. Biden also said that "Article I" defines the vice president's role in the "Executive Branch" (even though

the Executive Branch is created and outlined in Article II).
Finally, he stated that the idea that the vice president "is part
of the Legislative Branch is a bizarre notion invented by
[Dick] Cheney."[38]

Clause 5: Officers of the Senate

**The Senate shall choose their other Officers, and
also a President pro tempore, in the Absence of
the Vice President, or when he shall exercise the
Office of President of the United States.**

Like the House, the Senate selects its own officers. Its
current elected officers include a Chaplain to provide spiritual
care and counseling for Senate members and their families, a
Secretary to supervise Senate offices and services, a
Parliamentarian to advise the Senate on its rules and
procedures, and a Sergeant at Arms who serves as sort of a
chief law enforcement and administrative officer in the
Senate.[39] Committee Chairmen can also be considered officers
of the Senate since they have leadership roles.

This clause also points out that there needs to be a
presiding officer in the vice president's absence (further
supporting the idea mentioned in the last clause that the vice
president is a legislative role) or if the vice president serves as
president. *Pro tempore* is a Latin phrase meaning "for the time
being" or "temporarily," and the president pro-tempore is the
Senate's presiding officer in the vice president's absence. The
practice today is for the majority party to choose its longest-
serving member to serve as the president pro tempore. Since
1947, the president pro tempore is by law designated as the
third in line to the presidency, after the vice president and the
Speaker of the House. The president pro tempore for the 115th
Congress beginning in 2017 was Senator Orrin Hatch of Utah.
Hatch also served as the president pro tempore for the 114th
Congress, while Patrick Leahy of Vermont held the position
for the 113th Congress from 2013 to 2014.

29

Clause 6: <u>Trial of Impeachments</u>

The Senate shall have the sole Power to try all Impeachments. When sitting for that Purpose, they shall be on Oath or Affirmation. When the President of the United States is tried, the Chief Justice shall preside: And no Person shall be convicted without the Concurrence of two thirds of the Members present.

Here lies the Senate's power to try those impeached by the House. Only the House can impeach (accuse) an individual. Once it does, only the Senate acts as a court and puts the impeached on trial. Since the Senate has this power alone, it also has the power to make the rules for the trial with a few exceptions mandated by the Constitution. These mandatory rules are also contained in this clause.

The first unchangeable rule is that the senators be under oath or affirmation when trying an impeachment. This is no different than when citizens serve as jurors in a courtroom and promise to be honest in evaluating the case. Senators must do the same when trying impeached officers.

The second fixed rule is that the Chief Justice of the Supreme Court must preside when the president is on trial. This rule prevents a conflict of interest for the vice president who normally presides over the Senate and thus impeachment trials. Since the vice president would have a substantial interest in the outcome of the president's trial (namely the possibility of becoming president), the act of presiding might call into question his or her impartiality. This is why Chief Justice William Rehnquist presided over President Clinton's impeachment trial in 1999.

The third fixed rule is that the Senate cannot convict anyone without a two-thirds vote of the senators present (67 senators in today's Senate if all 100 are present) voting to convict. The Senate failed to convict President Johnson by one vote in 1868. In 1999, the Senate failed to convict President Clinton by 22 votes on his perjury charge and 17 votes on his obstruction of justice charge. In total, the Senate has convicted seven of the nineteen individuals ever impeached by the

House. The other impeachments resulted in acquittals or the person resigning prior to trial in the Senate.

Clause 7: <u>Judgment in Impeachment Cases</u>

Judgment in Cases of Impeachment shall not extend further than to removal from Office, and disqualification to hold and enjoy any Office of honor, Trust or Profit under the United States: but the Party convicted shall nevertheless be liable and subject to Indictment, Trial, Judgment and Punishment, according to Law.

This clause places limits on the penalties the Senate can impose on the impeached officers that it convicts. There are only two penalties. First, the Senate can remove the offender from office. Second, it can prohibit the offender from ever again holding any public office, elected or appointed. The Senate cannot do any more than this. But this clause makes clear that an impeached officer can still face charges and punishment in criminal courts for any criminal offense just as an ordinary citizen may be.

To better understand what this means, it is interesting to consider the example of former Illinois governor Rod Blagojevich's impeachment trial and the subsequent judgment in January 2009. (This was not a federal impeachment, but the concept is the same.) The Illinois House of Representatives impeached Mr. Blagojevich for abuses of power. The Illinois State Senate then acted as a trier of fact on the impeachment and unanimously voted to remove Mr. Blagojevich from office. It then voted to prevent him from ever again holding any public office in Illinois. The state Senate did nothing else to Blagojevich and, like the United States Senate, could do nothing further. Officials filed criminal charges against Blagojevich four months after his removal of office, just as criminal charges can be brought against any impeached officers. (Blagojevich was subsequently convicted of corruption and sentenced to 14 years in federal prison.[40])

In 1989, the Senate removed federal judge Alcee Hastings from office after his impeachment in the House. But his impeachment and removal did not bar him from any future office. As a result, Mr. Hastings ran for, and was elected to, the United States House of Representatives from the state of Florida in 1992. He still serves in that position as of 2017. The most recent official removed from office by the Senate was federal district court judge Thomas Porteous. The Senate removed and disqualified him from office on December 8, 2010, after finding him guilty of perjury, accepting bribes, and other conduct considered "incompatible with the trust and confidence placed in him" as a federal judge.[41]

Section 4—Congressional Elections

Clause 1: Elections

The Times, Places and Manner of holding Elections for Senators and Representatives, shall be prescribed in each State by the Legislature thereof; but the Congress may at any time by Law make or alter such Regulations, [except as to the Places of choosing Senators].

States have the right to make the procedural rules regarding elections just as they do under Article I, section 2, regarding the qualifications for voting in federal elections. Each state could thus set its own election day. So why then are all federal elections held on the same day nationwide? The answer lies in this clause's second part. Congress is given the power to alter state rules or make its own procedural rules in the place of the state rules on the time, place, and manner of elections. And Congress did so in 1872 when it required that federal elections occur on the first Tuesday after the first Monday in November in the even-numbered years.[42] The Seventeenth Amendment, which provides for direct election of senators, effectively altered the portion of this clause shown in brackets so that senators face election on the same day as representatives. (Remember, state legislatures selected senators until the Seventeenth Amendment's ratification; this clause as written ensured that the states retained control over their senators' elections.)

32

Clause 2: Meetings

The Congress shall assemble at least once in every Year, [and such Meeting shall be on the first Monday in December, unless they shall by Law appoint a different Day.]

This simple clause ensures that Congress meets at least once each year. This requirement redresses an abuse the Framers had suffered during colonial times. Prior to independence, King George III repeatedly dissolved the colonies' representative bodies and refused to reconvene them for extended periods of time. (These injuries were among those listed in the Declaration of Independence.) Mandating that Congress convene each year is an easy solution to avoid similar problems.

The Twentieth Amendment changed the time of the meeting to January 3rd but still allowed Congress to appoint a different day.

Section 5—Congressional Rules and Procedures

Clause 1: Congressional Organization

Each House shall be the Judge of the Elections, Returns and Qualifications of its own Members, and a Majority of each shall constitute a Quorum to do Business; but a smaller number may adjourn from day to day, and may be authorized to compel the Attendance of absent Members, in such Manner, and under such Penalties as each House may provide.

Section 5 makes both the House and the Senate judges of their respective members. This includes the authority to verify that an individual meets the Constitutional qualifications for office and that the election was proper. That's why Rush Holt and Joseph Biden were both able to be elected to the Senate at age 29. The Senate, using the power given here, determined that the thirty-year age requirement applied to the date that the senator takes the oath, not to the date of election.

33

Both chambers sometimes acted under this power to exclude members, albeit sometimes for political reasons rather than constitutional violations. In 1794, the Senate declared Albert Gallatin's election void because he did not meet the Constitution's citizenship requirement and so excluded him from the office.[43] (Gallatin eventually was elected to the House and also served as Jefferson's Treasury Secretary.) From 1903 through 1907, the Senate refused to seat Reed Smoot because of his religious affiliation. Smoot was a Mormon (member of the Church of Jesus Christ of Latter-day Saints) and held a leadership post in his church.[44] In 1919, the House refused to seat Victor Berger of Wisconsin because of a felony conviction stemming from his opposition to war, specifically World War I. The Senate refused membership to Frank Smith of Illinois in 1928 because of improper campaign contributions and alleged corruption.[45] In late 2008 and early 2009, the Senate threatened to not seat Roland Burris of Illinois under this section. The reason: he was appointed to the position by the publicly disgraced governor Rod Blagojevich. Ultimately the Senate consented to Burris's nomination and he assumed office in January 2009.

There have also been instances in which Congress possibly abused its power under this section. In 1927, Congress seated Representative James Beck of Pennsylvania in spite of his not being a resident of that state. A national magazine reported that Beck lived in Washington, D.C., and summered in New Jersey. When he decided to run for Congress, however, the magazine reported that Beck "promptly rented a sleazy apartment in a poor district of Philadelphia, which he never actually occupied." When his election was challenged on the grounds that he did not live in Pennsylvania, the same magazine reported that, "A cocky Republican majority in the House overrode the evidence against him, (and) seated him regardless."[46] But a representative need only be an "inhabitant" to qualify for the office. So if Congress considered simply renting an apartment to make one an "inhabitant," then Congress had that right under this clause to seat Representative Beck for being an "inhabitant" of Pennsylvania.

The second part of this clause specifies that, for either chamber to do business, a majority of its members (a quorum) must be physically present. This translates to 218 members in the House of Representatives and 51 members of the Senate. But these members do not need to vote on every issue in order for the matter to be valid. This is because a small minority could otherwise block legislation simply by refusing to vote. In the House of Representatives, once it is established, a quorum is presumed to continue until a present member makes a point of no quorum. So if a quorum is present at the start of the day, then business may be conducted throughout the day, even if members leave. If members leave, essentially leaving less than a quorum present while work is being transacted, then the final part of this clause permits remaining members in both Houses to compel absentee colleagues to return and reassemble a quorum before business can continue.

Clause 2: Rules of Conduct

Each House may determine the rules of its proceedings, punish its members for disorderly behavior, and, with the concurrence of two thirds, expel a member.

Here we find the reason behind different procedures between the Senate and the House. In short, this clause allows each the opportunity to establish its own procedural rules free from interference from the other. There are significant differences, as detailed in the following chart:

House Rules	Senate Rules
• Debate time *always* restricted • No individual filibusters[*] • Debate on a measure ends by a simple majority vote	• No time limit for debate • Individual filibusters permitted • Debate on a measure ends when 60 senators agree to close the issue

---

[*] A "filibuster" is an act, such as an extended speech or series of speeches, that blocks action by prolonging debate and prohibiting voting on an issue.

Even though Senate rules require approval by 60 senators to end debate and vote on a bill, [47] a bill still only needs a simple majority to pass, just as it does in the House.

The Senate rule requiring a 60-vote threshold became a hot topic in early 2010 amidst debate on health care bills (more commonly known as "Obamacare" bills). The House and the Senate stood at a gridlock on how to proceed with health care legislation as each had passed its own bill but the two bills conflicted. Once the people of Massachusetts elected Scott Brown in a January special election to fill a vacant Senate seat, it became clear that the House version could not get the 60 votes necessary in the Senate to end debate on the bill and to allow a vote. (Brown had promised during his campaign to be the forty-first vote to filibuster health care legislation in the Senate.) Many in the House did not desire the Senate bill. As such, Congressional leaders moved to use a Senate rule called "reconciliation" to bypass traditional rules requiring 60 votes to end debate and move to a vote. Reconciliation is a Senate rule that limits debate in the Senate to twenty hours before a vote is taken, and requires only a simple majority to pass, essentially prohibiting a filibuster. The Senate pursued this approach even though the reconciliation rule is, by definition, limited to budget bills. Senator Robert Byrd of West Virginia stated as much when, speaking about using the reconciliation rule for health care legislation, he said that "The misuse of the arcane process of reconciliation—a process intended for deficit reduction—to enact substantive policy changes is an undemocratic disservice to our people and to the Senate's institutional role."[48] The Senate nevertheless went ahead with the process and passed the Health Care and Education Reconciliation Act on March 25, 2010, as an "amendment" to the Patient Protection and Affordable Care Act.

The Senate's 60-vote rule came under pressure again in 2013. That year, a Democratic-led Senate employed a parliamentary procedure known as the "nuclear option" to change the Senate rules to prohibit filibusters on executive branch and federal judicial nominations other than those to the Supreme Court. A Republican-led Senate then employed the same procedure in April 2017 to prohibit filibusters on Supreme Court nominees.

36

This clause also gives Congress the right to punish its members for improper conduct. In the House, punishment can be in the form of a reprimand, censure, or expulsion. Censures and reprimands are near synonymous in that they both are formal disapproval by the House of a member's conduct. Either occurs by a majority vote. The difference between censure and reprimand is that when a member is censured, he or she must stand in the well of the House (the center of the room) while the censure is read; reprimanded members do not need to stand in the well. The House censured Representative Charles Rangel of New York in December 2010 for several ethics violations. The most recent use of the reprimand occurred in 2012 when the House voted to reprimand Representative Laura Richardson of California for compelling official congressional staff to work on her political campaign. Three years earlier, the House reprimanded Representative Joe Wilson of South Carolina for yelling "You lie!" during a speech to Congress by President Obama. Overall the House has censured or reprimanded 33 members.[49] Conversely, the Senate has done so only eight times.[50] The procedure is similar in both chambers.

Finally, because members of Congress are not subject to impeachment, this clause allows each chamber to expel members. Because it requires a two-thirds vote, however, expulsion is rare. In 1797, William Blount of Tennessee became the first senator to be expelled from the Senate due to his involvement in a conspiracy to help the British capture parts of Spanish Florida. Besides Blount, the Senate expelled fourteen other senators during the Civil War for supporting the Confederacy. Expulsion in the House is likewise rare; it has expelled only five members in its history. Three members were expelled for treason during the Civil War. The other two expulsions resulted from criminal convictions against the members. The most recent expelled representative was James Traficant of Ohio. The House expelled Traficant in 2002 after he was convicted of accepting bribes. Unlike impeachment in which the removed officer may be prohibited from again holding office, this section does not prohibit expelled members from again holding office. This explains why Traficant ran for Congress again in 2010 following his release from prison. (Traficant lost.)

Clause 3: <u>Record of Proceedings</u>

Each House shall keep a Journal of its Proceedings, and from time to time publish the same, excepting such Parts as may in their Judgment require Secrecy; and the Yeas and Nays of the Members of either House on any question shall, at the Desire of one fifth of those Present, be entered on the Journal.

This clause mandates that Congress keep track of its proceedings. Consequently, the House and the Senate each publish journals that provide a summary of each day's activities including the bills passed, motions made by members, and votes taken. The actual record on the journals is relatively sparse. Individual members' yea or nay votes on a bill are not recorded on the journal unless it is requested by the necessary one-fifth of members present threshold stated in this section (so at least 20 senators must request that the votes be recorded if all senators are present; 87 representatives must make the request if all House members are present).

While the journals do not record actual floor debates, Congress nevertheless publicizes its debates in a separate publication called the *Congressional Record*. Congress began the *Congressional Record* in 1873 to contain floor speeches and other proceedings. But since Congress controls its contents, the record may be altered and the *Congressional Record* is not always the best for accuracy. For example, if a member of Congress who wanted to speak in a debate but did not, then the member can add his or her words to the record. Similarly, if a member regrets saying something, then he or she can retract the remark before publication. Congress also deposits video recordings of its proceedings, like those seen on C-SPAN, with the National Archives. (C-SPAN is *not* a government-run network. It is owned and operated by the cable industry.)

Clause 4: <u>Temporary Adjournment</u>

Neither House, during the Session of Congress, shall, without the Consent of the other, adjourn

**for more than three days, nor to any other Place
than that in which the two Houses shall be
sitting.**

This clause prohibits one chamber from holding up the
legislative process by simply refusing to meet. The two bodies
must coordinate. And they always have. Legislators adjourn
sine die (without fixing a date for a new meeting) at the end of
a congressional session, by each chamber adopting a
resolution to adjourn. However, if the House and Senate do
not agree on a date to adjourn, the president could adjourn
them as will be seen in Article II, section 3.

To preserve independence and avoid having to ask the
other body for permission to adjourn for longer than three
days, the Senate and the House sometimes hold *pro forma* (as
a matter of formality) sessions. These are brief meetings, often
lasting less than a minute, of only a few members of a
chamber and with no formal business being conducted. These
sessions' purpose is to fulfill this clause's requirement to not
adjourn for more than three days without the other body's
consent.

The second part of this clause provides for flexibility in
Congress's meeting place. Essentially, each chamber can alter
its designated meeting location from the Capitol building in
Washington provided that it has the other's consent. Congress
has done so in the past. In the 1790s, the legislative bodies met
in Trenton, New Jersey, due to yellow fever outbreaks. Later,
during the War of 1812, Congress fled from Washington. In
each circumstance, both chambers were still able to meet to
conduct business because of the other's consent.

Section 6—Congress Members' Compensation, Privileges and Immunities, and Prohibitions

Clause 1: Compensation and Travel to Legislative Sessions

**[The Senators and Representatives shall receive
a Compensation for their Services, to be
ascertained by Law, and paid out of the
Treasury of the United States.] They shall in all**

39

Cases, except Treason, Felony and Breach of the Peace, be privileged from Arrest during their Attendance at the Session of their respective Houses, and in going to and returning from the same, and for any Speech or Debate in either House, they shall not be questioned in any other Place.

Although only two sentences long, this is an important clause and is broken down below, phrase by phrase.

[The Senators and Representatives shall receive a Compensation for their Services, to be ascertained by Law, and paid out of the Treasury of the United States.]

The federal government, by means of the Treasury, pays members of Congress. Individual states do not. This helps keep members independent of the political whims of the states in performing their duties. For example, if states paid the salaries, then a state legislature could essentially tie compensation to its own approval.

This clause also presents a problem in that members set the amount that they receive with really no oversight. Because compensation is "to be ascertained by Law" and Congress is the one to make the law, Congress essentially sets its own pay. The Twenty-seventh Amendment altered this predicament by prohibiting any pay increases from taking effect until after the next election. In 2017, Congressional pay stood at $174,000 per year for rank and file members, unchanged from its level in 2009 but nearly double its amount from 1990.[51] Beyond salary, senators and representatives have granted themselves compensation in the form of various benefits including health insurance and retirement plans. At the beginning of 2012, one in six of the retired lawmakers who were still living (79 of 463) received annual pensions greater than $100,000.[52] As of October 2015, 620 former senators and representatives were receiving pensions under two different plans. More than half (344) received average annual pensions of $74,136; the remaining 276 received average pensions of $41,316.[53]

They shall in all Cases, except Treason, Felony and
Breach of the Peace, be privileged from Arrest
during their Attendance at the Session of their
respective Houses, and in going to and returning
from the same;

This clause prohibits members of Congress from being arrested while attending, or traveling to or from, a session of Congress with certain exceptions. The exceptions listed— treason, felony, and breach of the peace—are all criminal activities. So this clause prohibits the practice of *civil arrest*, which was common when the Constitution was adopted.[54] Civil arrest permitted the physical detention of an individual if there was a civil lawsuit against him or her. Without this privilege from arrest, one individual could disrupt the legislative process by filing lawsuits against members of Congress and then detaining them by civil arrest. But since civil arrests are rarely used in modern times, this phrase has little practical application today.

Members of Congress can be and are arrested for criminal activities. One example is Idaho Senator Mike Crapo being arrested in late 2012 for driving under the influence. In early 2017, police arrested Representative Luis Gutierrez of Illinois for disruptive behavior at an Immigrations and Customs Enforcement office in Chicago.[55] Washington D.C. police arrested Representatives Keith Ellison of Minnesota, John Lewis of Georgia, Raul Grijalva of Arizona, Al Green of Texas, Joseph Crowley and Charles Rangel of New York, and Luis Gutierrez and Jan Schawkowsky of Illinois, for disruptive behavior during an immigration rally in 2013.[56] Police also arrested three other representatives in March 2012 for their actions in a protest outside of the Sudanese Embassy.[57]

and for any Speech or Debate in either House, they
shall not be questioned in any other Place.

Known as the "Speech and Debate Clause," these eighteen words provide members of Congress with immunity for anything that they say during official business such as a committee hearing or while speaking on the chamber floor. The purpose behind this protection is to guarantee that lawmakers can speak free from fear of reprisal for their remarks. This was an explicit change from England where the king could fine members of parliament for slander if he didn't like their speeches. Hence, if a senator or representative makes a false accusation during a debate in the House or Senate (as Senator Harry Reid did in 2012 about presidential candidate Mitt Romney not paying taxes), the only recourse for the accused is to ask for the opportunity to deny the remark. He or she cannot sue the defaming legislator for slander or invasion of privacy. If so, being questioned in court would violate the prohibition on questioning the lawmaker about the remarks "in any other place." But if the remark is made elsewhere, such as at a news conference or during a television interview, then the lawmaker may be sued for defamation. This exact situation occurred in 2007 when Marine Corps staff sergeant Frank Wuterich sued Representative John Murtha of Pennsylvania for libel and invasion of privacy after Murtha made several critical comments to the news media about actions taken by Wuterich's Marine squad in Haditha, Iraq. (A federal court of appeals eventually dismissed the suit in April 2009 under a law protecting federal employees from tort claims for statements made while in the course of the employee's official duties. The dismissal was not based on this clause.[58])

Clause 2: Prohibitions

> **No Senator or Representative shall, during the Time for which he was elected, be appointed to any civil Office under the Authority of the United States which shall have been created, or the Emoluments whereof shall have been increased during such time; and no Person holding any Office under the United States, shall be a Member of either House during his Continuance in Office.**

In sum, this "Emoluments Clause" prohibits all representatives and senators from serving in any appointed office if Congress created that office or increased the office's salary and/or benefits (emolument) during that senator or representative's term. An election has to occur in the meantime. Or at least this is what is supposed to happen under this clause.

In practice, however, presidents and the senators that confirm their appointments have contravened this clause for the past century. President Barack Obama did so in 2009 when he nominated Senator Hillary Clinton of New York to be Secretary of State. After Ms. Clinton's 2006 Senate reelection, Congress increased the Secretary of State's salary from $186,600 to $191,300.[59] So her nomination violated this clause. Why then did Ms. Clinton serve as secretary from 2009 to 2013?

The answer lies in a provocative procedure originating in 1909 when President William Taft nominated Senator Philander C. Knox of Pennsylvania to be Secretary of State. Knox previously voted during his term, which was set to expire in 1911, to increase all Cabinet members' salaries by $4,000. This clause, as applied to Knox, would have prevented him from serving until 1911, the end of his term. But to allow for his pick to go through, Taft asked Congress to put the salary back to its previous level. Congress complied by passing a bill that reduced only the Secretary of State's salary to the level it was at prior to Knox's term.

Congress repeated the procedure of rolling back the salary in 1973 when President Nixon nominated Senator William Saxbe of Ohio to be Attorney General. This procedure became known as the "Saxbe Fix" after this incident.

President Jimmy Carter and the Senate followed suit in using the Saxbe Fix seven years later by appointing and confirming Senator Edmund Muskie of Maine to be Secretary of State in 1980. (Ironically, Muskie voted against using the Saxbe Fix for Senator Saxbe.) President George H.W. Bush signed Saxbe legislation that helped President Clinton appoint Senator Lloyd Bentsen of Texas as Treasury Secretary. And after President Obama's election in late 2008, President George W. Bush signed Saxbe legislation for Senator Clinton to become Secretary of State and for Senator Ken Salazar of Colorado to become Secretary of the Interior.

Some have argued that the Saxbe fix violates the spirit of the Constitution. Senator Robert Byrd's statements during the Saxbe confirmation hearings in 1973 are some of the clearest on the issue. He said that the prohibition is "so clear that it can't be waived" and that the Senate "should not delude the American people into thinking a way can be found around the constitutional obstacle." He then added that President Nixon "should have explored this (constitutional) matter further before presenting Mr. Saxbe for confirmation."[60]

> *and no Person holding any Office under the United States, shall be a Member of either House during his Continuance in Office.*

This final phrase of section 6 is known as the "Incompatibility Clause." It states clearly that an individual cannot "double-up" in public service by being both an elected representative in Congress and an official in the executive branch. This ban on double service maintains a separation of powers and is a break from the English tradition where the Prime Minister is both an executive and legislative official, and the Prime Minister's cabinet is made up of members of Parliament. This phrase explains why Ryan Zinke and Tim Price resigned as representatives in 2017 to join President Trump's Cabinet, just as Rahm Emmanuel had left the House to serve as President Obama's chief of staff. It also is the reason why Hillary Clinton, Jeff Sessions, and John Kerry (among others) resigned as senators to serve in presidential Cabinets.

Section 7—The Legislative Process

Clause 1: Origination of Revenue Bills

All bills for raising Revenue shall originate in the House of Representatives; but the Senate may propose or concur with Amendments as on other Bills.

This "Origination Clause" reflects the Framers' adoption of the English parliamentary requirement that legislation to raise money must start in the House of Commons, the representatives seen as closer to the people. Because the House of Representatives is directly elected by the people (and would thus be more responsive to their wishes), the Constitution gave it "power over the purse." So all revenue-raising bills (taxes) as well as appropriations bills (those authorizing the government to spend money) must originate in the House.

In practice, however, the Senate at times evades this requirement by simply substituting the text of any previously passed House bills with the text of the Senate's own revenue bill. The Senate treats this substitution as an "amendment" to the bill since the Senate is allowed to amend under this clause. The Senate used this stratagem to pass the Emergency Economic Stabilization Act of 2008 (better known as the "Wall Street bailout"). The House first rejected a bailout bill by a vote of 205 to 228 on September 29, 2008.[61] Two days later, the Senate substituted the entire text of its own bailout bill to an entirely separate piece of legislation that the House passed before the bailout issue ever arose. The Senate then passed this "amended" House bill 74-25 and returned it to the House for consideration.[62] The House ended up passing the bill by a vote of 263-171.[63]

When the Senate sends its own appropriations bill to the House, the House traditionally rejects the bill and asserts its power to initiate legislation raising revenue. It does so by returning the bill to the Senate accompanied by a notice of formal rejection known as a "blue slip."[64] This blue slip essentially kills the bill because it cannot pass the House.

Clause 2: Presenting Legislation to the President

Every Bill which shall have passed the House of Representatives and the Senate, shall, before it become a Law, be presented to the President of the United States; If he approve he shall sign it, but if not he shall return it, with his Objections to that House in which it shall have originated, who shall enter the Objections at large on their Journal, and proceed to reconsider it. If after such Reconsideration two thirds of that House shall agree to pass the Bill, it shall be sent, together with the Objections, to the other House, by which it shall likewise be reconsidered, and if

45

approved by two thirds of that House, it shall
become a Law. But in all such Cases the Votes of
both Houses shall be determined by Yeas and
Nays, and the Names of the Persons voting for
and against the Bill shall be entered on the
Journal of each House respectively. If any Bill
shall not be returned by the President within ten
Days (Sundays excepted) after it shall have been
presented to him, the Same shall be a Law, in
like Manner as if he had signed it, unless the
Congress by their Adjournment prevent its
Return, in which Case it shall not be a Law.

More commonly known as the "Presentment Clause,"
clause 2 spells out the steps necessary for a bill to become a
law. First, it mandates that the House and the Senate, by a
majority vote, each pass legislation that is identical in form.
Then, before that legislation can become law, it must be
submitted to the president for approval. At that point the
president has 10 days to pursue one of the following options:

1) <u>Sign the bill.</u> The bill then becomes law. Nothing else
is required.

2) <u>Hold the bill for 10 days (not including Sundays).</u> If
Congress is *still* in session, the bill becomes law without the
president's signature. But if Congress *adjourns* during that
time, then the bill does not become law. The president is said
to have put the bill in his or her pocket until Congress
adjourns, making this action more commonly known as a
"pocket veto." ("Veto" is a Latin phrase meaning "I forbid.")

3) <u>Reject the bill outright.</u> This rejection is popularly
referred to as a "regular veto." If the president rejects the bill,
then he or she must return it along with the reasons for
rejection to the chamber in which the bill originated. The
reason behind the veto may be that the president believes the
law to be unconstitutional, as was the case with President
Washington's first veto, or the president may disagree with the
law. President Grover Cleveland regularly rejected bills during
his first term in office. He vetoed 304 laws outright, and used

the pocket veto for 110 more, thus giving him the record for most vetoes in a four-year period. On the other hand, seven presidents, including Thomas Jefferson never vetoed a single bill. In the 21st century, George W. Bush vetoed a total of 12 bills, all during the final two years of his second term. President Obama vetoed two bills in his first term, and ten more during his second term.[65]

If the president rejects the bill by veto, then Congress has three options. It may:

1) <u>Accept</u> the rejection and take no further action on the bill.

2) <u>Amend</u> the bill to resolve the president's objections and then send it back to the president for approval. (The amended version must still pass both chambers by a majority vote before being sent back to the president.)

3) <u>Override</u> the veto by a two-thirds vote. When the president rejects a bill, he or she must send a message stating the objections to the chamber in which the legislation originated. That chamber then records the president's objections on its house journal and reconsiders the bill. If two-thirds of a quorum in that chamber approves the bill, then it is sent to the other chamber for reconsideration. If two-thirds of a quorum in the second chamber also approves the legislation, then it becomes law. In these situations, each member's vote for or against the bill *must* be recorded. In pocket-veto situations, however, Congress may not override the veto or amend the bill because it is no longer in session. Congress's only option is to reintroduce the bill in the next Congress.

Overriding a veto is rarely successful. Between George Washington's first term starting in 1789 and the end of Barack Obama's second term in January 2017, Congress overrode approximately seven percent of regular vetoes. Including pocket vetoes, which cannot be overridden, the number drops to four percent (111 of 2,574 vetoed bills).[66]

Clause 3: Presidential Veto

Every Order, Resolution, or Vote to which the Concurrence of the Senate and House of Representatives may be necessary (except on a question of Adjournment) shall be presented to the President of the United States; and before the Same shall take Effect, shall be approved by him, or being disapproved by him, shall be repassed by two thirds of the Senate and House of Representatives, according to the Rules and Limitations prescribed in the Case of a Bill.

This clause is a near repeat of the last clause. So why is it in the Constitution and what is its effect? In short, this clause prevents Congress from avoiding a veto by calling a bill a "resolution" or some other name. It ensures that any action Congress takes that has the force of law is passed in the manner outlined in clause 2. This includes public bills (laws of general application), private bills (those providing specified benefits to named individuals), and joint resolutions. A joint resolution is similar to a public bill but differs in that the former deals with only one subject while the latter may involve multiple issues. Examples of joint resolutions include those to declare war, abrogate treaties, annex territories without a treaty (such as Texas), adjust the debt limit, and alter the dates for Congress to meet.[67] Congress also uses joint resolutions to propose amendments to the Constitution. But these proposed amendments need not be submitted to the president because they are dealt with under a separate procedure set forth in Article V.

Orders or simple resolutions by one chamber dealing with internal matters do not need to be submitted to the president. Nor do concurrent resolutions. Concurrent resolutions are those agreed upon by both chambers that deal with issues affecting both chambers alone. Examples of concurrent resolutions include those: adjournment *sine die*; Congressional budget resolutions; a recess of more than three days (as required by Article I, section 5); and providing for a joint session of Congress, such as those called to hear the State of the Union address. Since none of these has the force of law, this clause does not require the president to approve them.

Section 8—The Powers of Congress

Section 8 is extremely important since it enumerates most of the powers that are granted to Congress in the Constitution. Section 8 contains 18 clauses. Each clause grants a specific power to the federal Congress. Two clauses concern financial powers, seven grant regulatory powers, one concerns powers on the high seas, six govern military powers, one covers jurisdictional powers, and one provides "necessary" powers.[68]

Financial Powers

Clause 1: Power to Tax and Spend

The Congress shall have Power To lay and collect Taxes, Duties, Imposts and Excises, to pay the Debts and provide for the Common Defense and General Welfare of the United States; but all Duties, Imposts and Excises shall be uniform throughout the United States;

This is known as the "Spending Clause" and it gives Congress the power to tax and the power to spend the money raised by taxes. Both are necessary powers for an effective government. In granting these powers, the Framers limited the spending of money to two purposes: (1) paying the United States' debt and (2) providing for the common defense and general welfare of the United States.

But what exactly do the terms "the common defense and general welfare of the United States" mean? Alexander Hamilton believed these terms should be broad in meaning and should permit Congress to spend according to what it believed to be in the nation's best interests.[69] James Madison, Thomas Jefferson, and others interpreted these terms to mean that Congress could only spend in connection with the other powers granted in the Constitution to fulfill the objectives specified in the Constitution.[70] President Washington favored

Hamilton's view during his administration, while subsequent presidents, including Jefferson and Madison, adopted a more limited view.[71] It also could be said that the "general welfare" meant the welfare of the several states rather than the welfare of the nation's people generally (as suggested by "we the people" in the preamble). Regardless, presidents were divided in their interpretations, although Madison's and Jefferson's viewpoints generally held sway, until the 1930s when Congress and the courts adopted Hamilton's perspective.[72] Today, Congress spends money for whatever purposes it deems are in the "general welfare."

The taxing power specifically permits Congress to collect "Duties, Imposts and Excises." These are all types of taxes. Duties and imposts are a type of tax on exports or imports. A better known name for them is a "tariff." Tariffs were actually the federal government's leading source of income from the 1790s through World War I.[73] An excise is a tax on the manufacture, consumption, or sale of goods. Excises are fairly common and can be levied (imposed) on different items. The basic example is the federal gasoline tax. One pays a federal excise of approximately 18 cents for every gallon of gasoline purchased. It's 18 cents whether one purchases the gas in Alabama, Hawaii, Maine, or anywhere else because the last part of this clause requires that the excise be the same no matter where it occurs in the United States. A second example is a $4.00 federal excise tax per person per domestic flight segment (takeoff and landing) as well as a 7.5% tax on the base ticket price.[74]

Clause 2: <u>Power to Borrow Money</u>

To borrow money on the credit of the United States;

Here, Congress has the power to borrow money with the promise that the federal government will pay it back with interest. Congress borrows money by issuing treasury bills (T-Bills), notes, and savings bonds to anyone who will buy them. A lot of the purchasers are foreign governments, with Japan and the People's Republic of China leading the list at the beginning of the year 2017.[75]

Federal debt is not a recent issue. In 1791, soon after the Constitution's inception, the United States' debt stood at approximately $75 million, mostly as a result of Revolutionary War debts. The debt briefly shrank to zero in 1835 before increasing again. At the end of World War I the debt was roughly $22 billion. It dipped to $16 billion in 1929 (from $33 billion in 1921)[76] before ballooning to $260 billion following World War II.[77] Total debt in 1990 was approximately $3.2 *trillion*. In 2010, the total exceeded $13 trillion, more than thirteen times the total debt in 1980. In 2013, the federal debt stood at $16 trillion.[78] In early 2017, the debt totaled nearly $20 trillion.[79]

Congress by law sets the limit of public debt that the federal government will have. In February 2010, Congress set the statutory limit on all debt at $14.294 trillion. It raised it again the following year to $16.394 trillion, effective January 2012.[80] In 2013, Congress raised the limit to $16.699 trillion.[81] The limit increased again in 2014 to $17.2 trillion.[82] Between 1960 and 2014, Congress acted 78 separate times to permanently raise, temporarily extend, or revise the definition of the debt limit.[83] In late 2015, Congress suspended the debt limit through March 2017.[84]

Regulatory Powers

Clause 3: Power over Foreign and Interstate Commerce

To regulate Commerce with foreign Nations, and among the several States, and with the Indian Tribes;

Clause 3 is often known as the "Commerce Clause." It gives Congress the right to make rules for business dealing with foreign nations (*i.e.*, international trade), between states, and with Indian tribes. Indian tribes are listed separately because early colonists and the Framers treated them as sovereign governments. The federal government likewise considered Indian tribes to be separate, sovereign governments until 1871. (American Indians did not receive United States citizenship until 1924.)

51

The power to make rules for foreign commerce, or international trade, coincides with Article I, section 8, clause 1. For example, clause 3 allows Congress to set the rules for dealing with foreign businesses and governments, such as what goods may be imported or exported, while clause 1 allows Congress to levy tariffs on various imported goods. Acting under this power, Congress prohibits the importation of certain substances like opium and more illicit drugs like cocaine and heroin.

Commerce "among the several states" means what or who (persons, products, or services) moves across state lines for business purposes and how the movement occurs (by rail, street, air, or water, or even electronically). This clause gives Congress the power to regulate these interstate activities. And Congress does. For example, Congress passed the Sherman Antitrust Act in 1898 to limit monopolies acting in interstate commerce. Today it regulates, among other things, the sale of securities, prohibits the manufacture or sale of armor-piercing handgun ammunition, and prescribes the minimum safety requirements for automobiles sold in the United States. This section foresees such regulation provided the items cross state lines.

Clause 4: <u>Power over Naturalization and Bankruptcy</u>

To establish an uniform Rule of Naturalization, and uniform Laws on the subject of Bankruptcies throughout the United States;

Clause 4 gives Congress two very different powers. The first is the power over naturalization, or the acquisition of citizenship. The second is power over bankruptcy, or the elimination of debt.

<u>Naturalization</u>
Congress has exclusive power in making the laws for people born in other countries to become "naturalized" American citizens. So it may change the rules for acquiring citizenship from time to time. In 1882, for example, Congress passed a law prohibiting Chinese persons from becoming

naturalized citizens.[85] The law remained until 1943. Further, persons born in U.S. territories do not always have U.S. citizenship. It wasn't until 1917 that Congress granted citizenship to Puerto Ricans, almost twenty years after Puerto Rico became a U.S. territory. Congress did the same in 1927 for those living in the U.S. Virgin Islands and in 1950 for residents of Guam. Even today, residents of American Samoa are U.S. nationals but not U.S. citizens. This means that they can legally live and work in the United States but they cannot vote or exercise other rights of citizenship unless they become naturalized citizens.

To become a naturalized citizen under current laws, an individual must:

1. Be age 18 or older;
2. Have been a legal resident in the United States for five years (or three years if married to a citizen);
3. Be of good moral character;
4. Pass a naturalization test on U.S. history and government;
5. Be able to read, write, and speak English (with few exceptions for disabilities or age);
6. Support the principles of the Constitution; and
7. Swear allegiance to the United States.[86]

Similarly, a person may *not* become a naturalized citizen if he or she has been affiliated with or supports any organization that advocates for totalitarian government or any violent or other unconstitutional overthrow of the United States government.[87]

This clause allows Congress to change these requirements at any time. In November 1986, for example, Congress made it so that immigrants who had previously entered the United States illegally could become citizens if, at that time, they had been in the country continuously since before January 1, 1982.[88] One of the more recent changes to naturalization laws occurred in 2001 when Congress made it easier for children adopted overseas to acquire U.S. citizenship.

As permitted by this section, Congress also has laws concerning the *forfeiture* of citizenship. Both native-born and naturalized citizens may lose their United States citizenship by:

1. Becoming naturalized in a foreign state after turning 18 years old;
2. Taking an oath or affirmation or other formal declaration of allegiance to a foreign state after turning 18 years old;
3. Serving in the armed forces of a country at war with the United States or serving as an officer in that country's force;
4. Working for a foreign government if the person already has nationality in that country, or
5. Working for a foreign government if doing so requires an oath, affirmation, or declaration of allegiance to that country;
6. Making a formal renunciation of nationality at a U.S. consular office in a foreign country;
7. Formally renouncing citizenship to the U.S. Attorney General; or
8. Being convicted of committing treason.[89]

Singer Tina Turner, known as the "Queen of Rock 'n' Roll," relinquished her U.S. citizenship in 2013 after becoming a naturalized Swiss citizen. Turner had lived in Switzerland for nearly 20 years and had married a Swiss national.[90] Ms. Turner did not renounce her citizenship.

In 2016, approximately 5,411 individuals renounced their U.S. citizenship by one of the two means of renunciation described above (items 6 and 7 on the list).[91] That number represented an 80% increase increased from the 2,999 persons taking the same actions in 2013, compared to the 231 total renunciations in 2008. The sharp upswing in renunciation is largely attributed to U.S. tax laws, which seek income taxes from American citizens living abroad, and an increase in tax enforcement beginning in 2012.

Bankruptcy
This "Bankruptcy Clause" gives Congress complete power to make standardized bankruptcy laws in the United States. Bankruptcy is a process that allows an individual or

business that cannot pay off its debts to repay or eliminate all or a portion of that debt under court protection. A bankruptcy court decides what debts must be paid and which creditors will recover money.

Congress has enacted various laws throughout history dealing with bankruptcy. The most relevant laws on the subject today were passed in 1978 and 2005. The 1978 law established federal bankruptcy courts, meaning that bankruptcy cannot be filed in any state courts. The 2005 law made it more difficult for a debtor to completely eliminate debt. This means that more debtors have to repay at least a portion of their debt to their creditors.

High profile examples of bankruptcy include Lehman Brothers in 2008, General Motors Corporation in 2010, and Hostess Corporation (maker of "Twinkies" and other sweets) in 2012. Lehman's bankruptcy court ordered it to sell all of its assets, ultimately leading to the company ceasing to exist. By contrast, the bankruptcy court in General Motors's case allowed the company to restructure itself and eliminate much of its debt. Bankruptcy does not necessarily mean that a company ceases to exist.

Clause 5: Power over Money and Measurements

To coin Money, regulate the Value thereof, and of foreign Coin, and fix the Standard of Weights and Measures;

This clause, like the one before it, grants two powers to Congress: (1) power over the country's currency system; (2) power to set standard weights and measurements.

Power over Currency

Congress acted under this power in 1792 to establish the United States dollar as the national currency.[92] It chose the "dollar" rather than something similar to the British pound because the Spanish milled dollar (known as "pieces of eight" because it could be divided into eight pieces) was the most widely known form of currency in the Americas, including the 13 original states, at the time. In fact, Congress expressly based the new United States dollar's value on the Spanish dollar's then-existing value, which was based on the weight of silver in the dollar (currency was in coins, not paper).[93] And since the Spanish dollar was so popular, Congress permitted it to be legal tender in the United States until 1857.[94] (In 1793, Congress passed a law permitting gold and silver coins from Great Britain, France, Portugal, and Spain to be legal tender in the United States.[95])

Congress in 1792 also adopted a decimal system for money, meaning that it divided the dollar by tenths for smaller denominations. This explains the half-dollar, quarter-dollar, dime, nickel, and penny. Finally, Congress set up the United States Mint and gave it responsibility for producing coin. The Mint currently coins money in four locations across the United States (Denver, Philadelphia, San Francisco, and West Point). Every coin bears the "mint mark" of the location where it was minted (a "D," "P," "S," or "W").

Congress proceeded under this power in 1913 to establish the Federal Reserve System to regulate America's money supply.[96] Congress simultaneously assigned the Federal Reserve the authority to print as much paper money as the Federal Reserve sees fit. It used to be the Treasury Department that handled the printing of paper money, specifically United States Notes. But now it is the Federal Reserve that authorizes the printing of paper money. That's why the paper money in circulation says "Federal Reserve Note" rather than "United States Note" at the top of each bill. The Federal Reserve's place in the money system explains why the chair of the Federal Reserve, currently Janet Yellin and previously Ben Bernanke, is often in the news. Whether it was proper—or even constitutionally permissible—to create the Federal Reserve is a hot topic for some.

The power regarding foreign coin means that Congress has the power to specify the value of foreign coin in relation to the national currency, just as it did with the Spanish milled dollar when introducing the United States dollar in 1792.

Weights and Measurements

This clause permits Congress to adopt standard weights and measures for the United States as a whole. But Congress failed to act for years. As a result, many states defined their own standards, and essentially adopted a system similar to the

English imperial system. The use of "customary system" measurements like the gallon, quart, foot, inch, pound, ounce, and so forth became prevalent as a result.

Finally, in 1866, Congress gave legal recognition to the metric system. Congress passed the Metric Conversion Act in 1975 that made the metric system "the preferred system of weights and measures for United States trade and commerce."[97] The same legislation also permitted continued use of customary units. This is why highway distances, weather reports, and other common measurements are generally customary rather than metric, while medical, military, and scientific measurements are metric, not customary.

Clause 6: <u>Power to Punish Counterfeiting</u>

To provide for the Punishment of counterfeiting the Securities and current Coin of the United States;

Clause 6 gives Congress power to protect money by punishing those making counterfeit money or securities. This follows clause 2 giving Congress the power to borrow money, and clause 5 giving Congress power to coin money.

The initial penalty chosen by Congress to punish counterfeiters was death.[98] The 1825 Crimes Act replaced death with a penalty of a fine up to $5,000 and 10 years of hard labor in prison.[99] The penalty today is not nearly as severe. Congress's chosen penalty for making counterfeit money is a fine or imprisonment for up to 20 years, or both.[100] The penalty for simply possessing counterfeit money is the same but with a maximum sentence of 15 years in prison.[101]

In 1913, Congress assigned the Treasury Department the responsibility of designing currency in a way to prevent counterfeiting.[102] In 2010, the Bureau of Engraving and Printing, an agency within the Treasury, announced a redesign of the $100 bill for this purpose. The bill entered circulation in late 2013. In 2016, the Treasury announced a plan to redesign the $20, $10, and $5 bills by 2020, including a proposal to replace Andrew Jackson's portrait on the front of the $20 bill with that of abolitionist Harriet Tubman.[103]

Researchers have estimated that roughly 1 out of 10,000 notes in circulation (or about 80 cents to $1 per $10,000) is counterfeit.[104] In 2015, the Secret Service seized $58 million in counterfeit U.S. currency before it entered public circulation.[105]

Clause 7: <u>Postal Power</u>

To establish Post offices and post Roads;

Clause 7, the "Postal Clause," gives Congress the power to establish a nationwide postal system to "secure an easy communication between the States" and to give the nation a source of revenue.[106] The inclusion of this power preserved what already was a practice of the national government. The Continental Congress established a postal service in July 1775, almost one year before the Declaration of Independence, as an alternate to the British mail system[107] and one that facilitated communication during the American Revolution. The Continental Congress then appointed Benjamin Franklin to be the first Postmaster General.

Acting under this clause, Congress created the Post Office Department in 1792 with the Postmaster General as its head. In 1872, Congress made the Post Office a cabinet position (meaning that the Postmaster General was considered one of the president's most senior advisers that met regularly with the president). Congress disbanded the Post Office Department and replaced it with the United States Postal Service (USPS), an independent government agency, in 1970. In 2016, the USPS employed nearly 500,000 workers who processed 154.2 billion pieces of mail during the preceding year, or an average of 4,886 pieces of mail per second.[108]

Clause 8: <u>Power to Grant Patents and Copyrights</u>

To promote the Progress of Science and useful Arts, by securing for limited Times to Authors and inventors the exclusive Right to their respective Writings and Discoveries;

This "Copyright Clause" or "Patent Clause" gives Congress the power to make laws protecting authors' and inventors' works for a set amount of time. Copyrights and patents are direct results of Congress's actions under this clause. Copyrights refer to the exclusive right granted to "Authors" to protect their "Writings." Patents stand for the exclusive right granted to "inventors" to protect their "Discoveries."

Copyrights
Copyrights cover items such as books, movies (hence the FBI copyright warning shown at the beginning of movies on DVD), plays, dances, pictures, paintings, sculptures, sound recordings, and even architectural works. The "limited time" for these copyrighted works most recently set by Congress is the life of the creator plus 70 years. For corporate authorship (when a person creates a work on behalf of a client corporation, the company is still considered the creator), the exclusive period is 120 years after creation or 95 years after publication, whichever is earlier. Exclusive rights granted under current copyright law include: the right to reproduce the work; sell, lease, or rent copies of the work; publicly display or perform the work; and create derivatives of a work (*i.e.,* sequels, a movie based on the original book, etc.).[109]

Initial copyright legislation under this clause provided protection for 28 years. Congress had doubled that protection to 56 years by the 20th Century. In 1976, Congress again extended the copyright term to the period of a creator's life plus 50 years for individuals and 75 years for corporations. Congress passed the Copyright Term Extension Act (CETA) in 1998, which retroactively extended existing copyright protection an additional 20 years and set the term for new copyrights at its current levels (life plus 50, etc.).[110] The retroactive application caused CETA to be pejoratively known as the "Mickey Mouse Protection Act"[111] since it kept Disney Corporation's Mickey Mouse character from falling into the public domain until 2023 rather than 2003 as it would have under prior copyright law. Similarly, Disney's *Snow White and the Seven Dwarves* would have entered the public domain in 2013 rather than 2033.[112]

<u>Patents</u>

Patents come in three types: utility, design, and plant. "Utility patents" protect an inventor's "new and useful" machines, manufacturing techniques, composition of matter (chemicals, drugs, etc.), processes (ways to do something), or any improvements on any of these items that already exist.[113] In other words, they protect the way an article works and is used. "Design patents" protect the way an article looks.[114] They cover everyday items from cars to clothing/accessories to electronics to food. So it is that the Volkswagen Beetle, Rolex watches, the iPhone, and even Kellogg's Eggo Waffles are all patented in the way they look. "Plant patents" may be granted to anyone who invents or discovers and asexually reproduces any distinct and new plant variety.[115]

In order to secure a patent, the inventor must disclose all information relating to the invention to the U.S. Patent and Trademark Office (USPTO). The USPTO can issue a patent so long as an invention is novel, non-obvious, and useful. Consequently, countless products are patented including medical equipment, computer software, hybrid plants, food products, and even children's board games. The USPTO receives hundreds of thousands of patent applications each year and has issued over eight million patents![116] Utility patents filed on or after June 8, 1995, provide 20 years of patent protection from the date the patent is issued.[117] Design patents have a protection term of 14 years.[118]

The most recent change in patent laws took effect in March 2013 when the United States changed from a "first to invent" patent system (as it had been since the nation's founding) to a system known as "first inventor to file." Under the former system, a person was entitled to patent protection as the actual inventor on the date he or she conceived the invention and then diligently worked to make the conception a reality. The United States was unique in this process. Now, what matters for patent protection is who first files a patent application for that invention, not who first invents it.[119]

While patents offer legal protection, not everything is patented. For example, the formula for Coca-Cola soda is <u>not</u> patented. If it were, then the Coca-Cola Company would have to disclose the soda's formula to obtain the patent. Doing so would give Coca-Cola exclusive rights to use the formula for

20 years. Afterwards, the company's competitors could use the formula. So by not patenting the soda, Coca-Cola can keep the formula secret indefinitely.

After the expiration of the time set by law, both patented and copyrighted works enter the "public domain," meaning that they become freely available to the public to be used without the creator's permission or payment of a royalty. William Shakespeare's works are in the public domain, meaning no royalty has to be paid to print or perform them. This is perhaps a reason why performing Shakespeare in schools is so popular.

Clause 9: Power to Establish Inferior Courts

To constitute Tribunals inferior to the Supreme Court;

Congress is given the power here to create courts lower than the Supreme Court. (The Supreme Court is the only court named in the Constitution.) The tribunals created under this clause are most often referred to as "legislative courts" and they have finite powers directed towards accomplishing a specific purpose. For example, Congress used this power to create the bankruptcy courts mentioned in section 8, clause 4. Those courts can only hear bankruptcy issues and no other. Similarly, other legislative courts cannot rule on any subjects other than the ones for which Congress gives permission.

Another aspect of these legislative courts that differs from the Supreme Court is the fact that the judges for these inferior tribunals do not have life tenure and their salary can be reduced while they are in office.

Legislative court examples include: the United States Court of Appeals for Veterans Claims (hears appeals from veterans who are denied benefits); the United States Court of Appeals for the Armed Forces (designated to hear appeals from court-martial convictions); the United States Tax Court (adjudicating disputes over federal tax matters); and the United States Court of Federal Claims (hears monetary claims against the federal government).

In the early 21st century, Congress acted under this clause to create the Guantanamo military commissions in 2006 to try cases of non-citizens who are designated as "unlawful enemy combatants" for having fought against the United States.[120]

Powers on the High Seas

Clause 10: Power to Define and Punish Piracies and Felonies on the High Seas

To define and punish Piracies and Felonies committed on the High Seas, and Offenses against the Law of Nations;

This clause gives Congress power over actions done at sea and to punish piracy. Specifically, Congress has the ability to define what acts constitute piracy, as well as what acts are criminal when committed on American ships in the open ocean or within the territorial waters of another country. These crimes are the "felonies" stated in the clause.

One example of a crime being committed on the "high seas" (and so subject to the felonies created by Congress under this section) is a man's murder of his wife on a cruise ship off the coast of Mexico in 2009. Both the man and the woman were California residents returning to the United States. Because the killing occurred in international waters (which are within the federal government's territorial jurisdiction because of this clause), the FBI charged the man with murder on the high seas.[121] He pled guilty to second-degree murder and a federal judge sentenced him to life imprisonment in 2011.[122]

Piracy was a common problem in the Americas when the states adopted the Constitution; English pirates often attacked and robbed Spanish ships filled with gold. It remains a problem today in some areas of the world, such as the waters near the Horn of Africa, where pirates from Somalia regularly attack ships. In July 2013, a federal jury convicted three Somali men of piracy and other charges resulting from the men hijacking an American couple's boat in the Indian Ocean in 2011.[123] The current punishment in the United States for individuals convicted of committing piracy is mandatory life imprisonment.[124]

The *law of nations* refers to international treaties (signed agreements between countries), customs, and general principles of law used by countries in commercial and political dealings. Acting under this clause, Congress may make what is a crime under international law be a crime under federal law.

Military Powers

Clause 11: Power to Declare War

To declare War, grant Letters of Marque and Reprisal, and make Rules concerning Captures on Land and Water;

Power to declare war

This clause contains the first of the two "war powers" granted in the Constitution. Article II, section 2, contains the other. This clause gives Congress the power to *declare* war; whereas Article II, section 2, gives the president the power to *wage* war once Congress declares it. The Framers intentionally separated the powers so that one person alone could not engage the nation in war when it was otherwise at peace.[125] The words used in this clause reflect that. Rather than give Congress the power to "make war" James Madison suggested using the phrase "declare war" so that the president could have "the power to repel sudden attacks."[126] In such an instance, according to Alexander Hamilton, the country would already be in a state of war caused by another nation's act and, since the president would not be beginning the conflict, no declaration was needed.[127]

Formal declarations of war by Congress are rare. In over 220 years, Congress has formally declared war only 11 times in five separate wars as follows:

1. War of 1812: Declaration against the United Kingdom in 1812 to redress American grievances.
2. Mexican-American War: Declaration against Mexico in 1846 after Mexico invaded the United States following the annexation of Texas.

3. Spanish-American War: Declaration against Spain in 1898 following Spain's declaration of war against the United States.
4. World War I: Declaration against Germany, and later Austria-Hungary, in 1917 following the former's sinking of several American ships.
5. World War II: Declaration against Japan in 1941 as a result of Japan's attack on Pearl Harbor, and later declarations against Germany and Italy that same year because of their declarations of war against the United States. Declarations against Bulgaria, Hungary, and Romania in 1942 as part of the ongoing war with Germany and these nations' fighting and declaring war against the United States.[128]

Stopping short of formal war declarations, Congress also passed resolutions authorizing combat military operations in several instances, including:

1. The Franco-American War: authorized President John Adams to use force against France to protect American merchant ships in 1798, resulting in a quasi-war until 1800.
2. The Barbary Wars: authorized President Thomas Jefferson in 1802 to order Navy commanders to seize all Barbary goods and ships in the Bay of Tripoli and "to cause to be done all such other acts of precaution or hostility as the state of war will justify."[129] ("Barbary" referred to countries on the coast of North Africa from western Egypt to Morocco.)
3. Formosa: authorized President Dwight Eisenhower in 1955 to use military power to secure and protect Formosa (Taiwan) against armed attack. Congress repealed this authorization in 1974 without the United States ever acting on it.
4. Vietnam War: authorized President Lyndon Johnson in 1964 to use conventional military force to assist member states of the Southeast Asia Collective Defense Treaty.
5. Persian Gulf War: authorized President George H.W. Bush in 1991 to use U.S. armed forces to implement

United Nations Security Council Resolution 678,
which called for Iraq's withdrawal from Kuwait.

6. <u>War on Terror:</u> authorized President George W. Bush in 2001 to use military force against nations *and* organizations linked to the September 11, 2001, terror attacks on the United States. The war in Afghanistan resulted from this resolution.

7. <u>Iraq War:</u> authorized President George W. Bush in 2002 to use military force against Iraq to (1) defend the United States's national security against ongoing threats from Iraq and (2) enforce all United Nations Security Council resolutions regarding Iraq.[130]

Yet Congress never authorized numerous military campaigns directed by different presidents. These include the occupation of Nicaragua from 1909-1933;[131] the Korean War in 1950-1953; the 1983 invasion of Grenada; the 1989 invasion of Panama; the deployment of armed forces to Somalia, Haiti, Bosnia, and Serbia in the 1990s; and the attacks on Libya in 2011.[132]

Letters of Marque and Reprisal

A letter of marque is a formal document licensing a private citizen to attack and seize goods or citizens of other nations. A person with this license is thus known as a "privateer" while a person acting without it is known as a "pirate."

Congress granted some letters of marque against the United Kingdom in 1812. The idea of issuing letters of marque surfaced in Congress again after the September 11, 2001, terror attacks. A few suggested the method again in April 2009 as a way to deal with Somali pirates in the Indian Ocean.

Some believe that letters of marque are no longer valid following the 1856 Treaty of Paris when several countries agreed to no longer grant them. The United States signed the treaty, but the Senate never ratified it, meaning that the treaty has no effect.

Rules Concerning Captures

Congress has the power to set rules for what follows when the military or a privateer captures persons or goods.

This means that Congress can, by law, allow the military or the privateer to keep the property captured as a prize of war.

Clause 12: <u>Power to Create and Maintain Armed Services</u>

To raise and support Armies, but no Appropriation of Money to that Use shall be for a longer Term than two Years;

Congress is given the power to raise (create) and support armies. While much is made of the president being "Commander in Chief," this clause makes clear that Congress is given ultimate control over armies. Today that includes both the Army and the Air Force. Congress created the latter as a separate department from the Army in 1947 after it had previously been known as the Army Air Corps. If Congress decided to disband the Army or Air Force, it could do so under this clause.

The two-year limit on money spent for the army that this clause imposes essentially forces military leaders to report to Congress on the state of the military, such as its size and capabilities. The genius of this requirement is that it ensures continual civilian control and oversight of the military. It also ensures that no standing army can be built up without Congressional approval. This resolved a key concern for the Framers who viewed standing armies in peacetime as a threat to liberty.[133]

In 2016, the Army had approximately 475,000 active-duty soldiers and 198,000 soldiers in the reserve.[134] Concurrently, the Air Force had nearly 308,606 active-duty personnel, more than 68,000 reservists, and approximately 5,000 aircraft.[135]

Clause 13: <u>Power to Create and Maintain a Navy</u>

To provide and maintain a Navy;

This clause grants Congress a similar power to that of the last clause. The difference is that there is no two-year limitation on funding the Navy. Perhaps this was done because the Framers saw the Navy as less threatening to citizens' liberties, and because of the Navy's unique purposes.[136]

The Navy's focus is not only to engage in wars, but also to deter aggression and to promote freedom of the seas (*i.e.*, freedom for merchant ships to move about without the threat of piracy).[137] In fact, eliminating piracy against American merchant ships in the Mediterranean Sea was a central purpose for Congress acting under this power in 1794 to create a naval force.[138] Today, piracy is non-existent or significantly reduced in waters patrolled by the United States Navy.

The United States Navy was the largest in the world in 2016 with over 329,000 active-duty personnel, over 107,000 reserves, and a fleet of over 270 battle-ready ships and 3700-plus aircraft.[139]

The Marine Corps is considered an infantry unit created under this clause. Marines are "soldiers of the sea" and provide forces to Navy ships and shore operations.[140] That is why the Marine Corps is organizationally located within the Department of the Navy. The Corps had 182,000 active-duty Marines in 2016 along with roughly 38,500 reserves.[141] Among the Corp's more unique roles is providing security at United States embassies and consulates around the world.

Clause 14: Power to Control the Armed Services

To make Rules for the Government and Regulation of the land and naval Forces;

Congress here is given complete control over the rules and regulations for members of the armed services. Acting under this power, Congress created the Uniform Code of Military Justice (UCMJ).[142] The Code is called "Uniform" to imply that it uniformly applies to all members of the military, such that a sailor is as subject to the UCMJ as a soldier or a marine.

Part of the current rules is a separate court system from civil courts. Instead of a trial in civil courts, members of the military charged with violating the UCMJ face a military trial known as a "court-martial." Appeals from these tribunals go to the United States Court of Appeals for the Armed Forces, one of the "inferior tribunals" created by Congress under section 8, clause 9.

A well-known example of a military member facing a court-martial is the case of Sergeant Bowe Bergdahl. While fighting in Afghanistan in 2009, Bergdahl left his post. The Taliban captured him and held him prisoner for five years before releasing him in exchange for Taliban prisoners. After his return, the Army charged Bergdahl with desertion and misbehavior before the enemy. Bergdahl's court-martial was set to begin in late 2017. Another prominent example of a court-martial is that of Major Nidal Hasan. In November 2009, Hasan went on a shooting rampage at Fort Hood, a large army base in Texas. He killed 13 people and wounded 30 others. Hasan's court-martial occurred in July 2013; the military jury found him guilty and sentenced him to death. Had Hasan committed the same crime off of the military base, then he could have been charged in a regular criminal court even though he was a member of the military.

Clause 15: <u>Power to Call Forth the Militia</u>

To provide for calling forth the Militia to execute the Laws of the Union, suppress Insurrections and repel Invasions;

The Militia referenced here is civilian soldiers divided by Congress into two types: (1) the organized Militia, known today as the National Guard, and (2) the reserve Militia, which Congress defined under this power as every able-bodied man 17 to 45 years of age who is or intends to become a citizen, and female citizens if they are members of the National Guard.[143] Because all men are part of the reserve militia, they must register with the Selective Service at age 18 so that they can be drafted into service.

Congress acted on this clause to give the president the ability to call forth the Militia during George Washington's presidency. President Washington exercised the power in 1794 to suppress the insurrection known as the Whiskey Rebellion in Massachusetts. President Dwight Eisenhower summoned the National Guard in 1957 to prevent violence during school desegregation in Little Rock, Arkansas. President George W.

Bush ordered National Guard troops to the US-Mexico border to execute immigration and drug laws in 2006. President Barack Obama took the same action in May 2010.[144]

Clause 16: Power to Regulate the Militia

To provide for organizing, arming, and disciplining, the Militia, and for governing such Part of them as may be employed in the Service of the United States, reserving to the States respectively, the Appointment of the Officers, and the Authority of training the Militia according to the discipline prescribed by Congress;

Congress shares power over the Militia with the states. Under current law, the National Guard operates under state control, with the governor of each state appointing officers and overseeing the training of his or her state's National Guard unit. Nevertheless, Congress provides most of the funds.[145] It also established the National Guard Bureau to create rules concerning training and govern the members so that there is uniformity among the Militia members.[146]

Since state governors control their respective National Guard units, they may call them into service within their states for similar reasons to those listed in section 8, clause 15. Some examples include California's governor calling up the National Guard in 1992 to quell the Los Angeles Riots, Louisiana's governor calling up the National Guard in 2005 to respond to the destruction caused by Hurricane Katrina, and North Carolina's governor calling up the National Guard in 2016 to restore order in Charlotte, North Carolina, following violent protests and looting.

Territorial Powers

Clause 17: Power to Govern National Capital Area, Territories, and Governmental Places

To exercise exclusive Legislation in all Cases whatsoever, over such District (not exceeding ten

69

Miles square) as may, by Cession of particular States, and the Acceptance of Congress, become the Seat of the Government of the United States, and to exercise like Authority over all Places purchased by the Consent of the Legislature of the State in which the Same shall be, for the Erection of Forts, Magazines, Arsenals, dock-Yards, and other needful Buildings;—And

This clause gives Congress the power to create a federal district (a territory/an area of land) to be the national capital that is independent of all of the states. A purpose for creating a separate federal area, as James Madison explained in *Federalist No. 43*, was to ensure that no state was preferred over another by having the nation's capital in its borders.[147] Another was that having a separate federal territory forced the federal government to be responsible for its own security rather than being dependent on a state.

National Capital Area

Congress exercised the power granted here to pass the Residence Act in July 1790.[148] The act gave President Washington the power to select a site for the nation's capital along the Potomac River between Maryland and Virginia. The reason for the capital being in this particular location was a compromise between Northern and Southern states. Several Southerners agreed to support the federal government by assuming state debts from the Revolutionary War in exchange for the capital being located on land ceded by two Southern states.[149] This explains why the national capital is in its current location. The federal district became known as the District of Columbia. "Columbia" refers to Christopher Columbus.[150] The city within the district later became known as "Washington" in honor of President Washington.

Congress is given exclusive legislative control over the capital district. Throughout history, Congress has exercised its power over the district in different ways, ranging from directly making the district's laws to a more *laissez-faire* approach. Since 1973, Congress permits those living in Washington, D.C., to elect their own mayor and city council. The mayor and council legislate for the city. But Congress reviews all

legislation passed by the council before it can become law.
Because Congress has exclusive control, Congress may veto
any city council legislation that it does not like. Congress has
the final say.

Federal Enclaves

Clause 17 is also known as the "Enclave Clause" because
it gives Congress "like Authority" over places owned by the
federal government as it does regarding the district. In other
words, places owned by the federal government such as forts,
arsenals, and other "needful Buildings" are governed
exclusively by Congress. Examples today range from 125,000-
acre Camp Pendleton Marine Base in Southern California to
the local post office. Congress purchases these properties with
the respective state legislature's consent and then sets the rules
for these "enclaves" just as it does for the federal district
because the enclaves are federal territory. Since this clause
gives Congress control over federal territory (and these areas
are federal territory) crimes and other acts committed in them
are subject to federal laws rather than the state laws where
they are located.

General Power

Clause 18: Power to Make Necessary and Proper Laws

**To make all Laws which shall be necessary and
proper for carrying into Execution the foregoing
Powers, and all other Powers vested by this
Constitution in the Government of the United
States, or in any Department or Officer thereof.**

More commonly known as the "Necessary and Proper
Clause" or the "Elastic Clause," clause 18 gives Congress
power to make the laws needed to successfully execute the
powers listed in section 8 and elsewhere in the Constitution.
But how much power to legislate does this clause actually give
Congress?

Just as in section 8, clause 1, the Framers disagreed as to
what could be done under the power granted here. Nearly all

Framers believed that the Constitution needed this clause. James Madison even went so far in *Federalist No. 44* to say that without this clause, the Constitution would be a "dead letter." Still, the Framers lacked agreement as to how much power this clause gave Congress. One of the best examples to show this difference is the story of the First Bank of the United States.

In 1791, Congress passed a bill creating a national bank.[151] Treasury Secretary Alexander Hamilton strongly supported the idea and urged President Washington to sign the bill. In an opinion letter to Washington, Hamilton considered the bank's creation to be constitutional under this clause because he claimed the creation, "has a relation, more or less direct, to the power of collecting taxes, to that of borrowing money, to that of regulating trade between the States," and other specific, enumerated powers including coining money and regulating foreign coins.[152] So he reasoned that Congress had the power to incorporate a bank to oversee the nation's finances since this clause gives it power to make "all needful rules and regulations respecting the property of the United States." He continued, "These powers combined, as well as the reason and nature of the thing, speak strongly this language: that it is the manifest design and scope of the Constitution to vest in Congress all the powers requisite to the effectual administration of the finances of the United States."[153]

Attorney General Edmund Randolph and James Madison, who was serving in the House of Representatives, took a contrary view. So did Thomas Jefferson, who was serving as Secretary of State. Concerning the powers granted in clause 18, Jefferson expressed sentiments shared by Madison and others when he said, "The second general phrase is, 'to make all laws necessary and proper for carrying into execution the enumerated powers.' But they can all be carried into execution without a bank. A bank therefore is not necessary, and consequently not authorized by this phrase."[154] Jefferson added: "The incorporation of a bank, and the powers assumed by this bill, have not, in my opinion, been delegated to the United States, by the Constitution."[155] Regardless of his views in 1791, James Madison, as president in 1816, signed legislation that created the Second Bank of the United States.

72

An everyday example of action under this clause, regardless of which Framer's philosophy one espouses, is Congress's creation of the Secret Service in 1865. Congress created the Secret Service to stop the counterfeiting of U.S. currency.[156] Creating something like the Secret Service was "necessary and proper" to the powers granted Congress in section 8, clause 6 to punish counterfeiting.

Section 9—Powers Denied Congress

While section 8 grants Congress certain powers to act, section 9 specifically prohibits Congress from taking certain actions.

Clause 1: The Slave Trade

[The Migration or Importation of such Persons as any of the States now existing shall think proper to admit, shall not be prohibited by the Congress prior to the Year one thousand eight hundred and eight, but a Tax or duty may be imposed on such Importation, not exceeding ten dollars for each Person.]

This clause prohibited Congress from banning the trans-Atlantic slave trade until 1808, just over twenty years following the Constitutional Convention. It represents a compromise between the Northern states, many of which had already prohibited slavery, and the Southern states that depended on slave labor.

In 1807, Congress passed a law prohibiting slave importation that took effect January 1, 1808, the first possible day that such a ban was allowed under the Constitution. That ban remained in place until the Thirteenth Amendment, which prohibited slavery entirely, made this clause obsolete in 1865.

Some denigrate the Constitution because of this clause and others that permitted slavery. But those who belittle the Constitution for this ignore certain facts. First, without compromises on slavery such as the one in this clause, there could not have been a true United States. The Southern states would not have joined the Union. Without their support, the

Northern states would likely not have been strong enough to stand independent. Second, the Constitution made it possible to end slavery. And it did so *before* any similar actions by other countries, including both France and the United Kingdom. This clause in particular set a timeframe for ending the slave trade a full twenty years before the United Kingdom passed a law prohibiting the slave trade, and thirty years before France created a similar timeline that didn't even go into effect until 1826. Further, the amendment process outlined in Article V made it possible to prohibit slavery forever. So the Constitution is fundamentally the first document paving the way for slavery's abolition, not one institutionalizing it.

Clause 2: Suspension of Habeas Corpus

The Privilege of the Writ of Habeas Corpus shall not be suspended, unless when in Cases of Rebellion or Invasion the public Safety may require it.

This "Suspension Clause" preserves the right of habeas corpus. "Habeas corpus" is a Latin phrase meaning "you shall have the body." A writ of habeas corpus is a legal tool requiring a jailed/imprisoned person to be brought to court in front of a judge.[157] The judge determines whether the government can legally detain the person. If the judge determines that the person is being held illegally, then the judge can order the prisoner's release. So in practice, habeas corpus prevents someone from being imprisoned illegally (without formal charges, based on an unlawful arrest, insufficient evidence, etc.).

A writ of habeas corpus is such an important right that this "Suspension Clause" permits Congress to suspend the writ only in cases of rebellion or invasion. It was suspended during the Civil War and again in 1871 within nine counties in South Carolina as part of an effort to combat the Ku Klux Klan and their attacks on former slaves.[158]

This clause entered public discussion following the September 11, 2001, terrorist attacks. The federal government detained several persons connected to terrorists or terrorism, or suspected as terrorists or of terrorism connections, during the War on Terror and held them as prisoners at Guantanamo Bay Naval Base in Cuba. Many debated whether habeas protections applied to the detainees, almost all of whom were not U.S. citizens, and several advocacy groups filed habeas writs on the detainees' behalf.

Prisoners in both state and federal custody regularly bring habeas petitions in an attempt to get out of their sentences. In fact, until passage of the Anti-Terrorism and Effective Death Penalty Act (AEDPA)[159] in 1996, prisoners could file writs of habeas corpus as long as they were in government custody. They could file one right after another. In part to alleviate the burden on federal courts, the AEDPA restricted prisoners' ability to bring the writ by allowing only one writ without approval from a federal court of appeals. It also shortened the time period to request the writ. So today, prisoners have one chance to file a writ within one year of the end of their direct appeals to state courts for relief from their sentences. They may file an additional writ provided they meet certain requirements under the AEDPA.

Clause 3: <u>Bills of Attainder and Ex Post Facto Laws</u>

No Bill of Attainder or ex post facto Law shall be passed.

Bill of Attainder

A "bill of attainder" is a law that criminally punishes a named person or group of people without a judicial trial. For example, if Congress passed a law specifically calling out Tea Party supporters and ordering their arrest and imprisonment, the act would violate this clause of the Constitution.

Issues related to bills of attainder came up in 2009 when Congress passed a law prohibiting the Association of Community Organizations for Reform Now (better known as "ACORN") from receiving federal funding.[160] ACORN protested the act as a bill of attainder and sued the federal government. But the issue ended when a federal court of appeals determined that taking away funding was not "punishment."[161] Some similarly labeled Congressional efforts to defund Planned Parenthood in 2017 as bills of attainder.[162]

Ex Post Facto Law

An *ex post facto* law is one that is adopted after an act is committed but that applies retroactively. More specifically, it criminally punishes a person for an act that was legal when done. (Ex post facto literally means "after the fact" in Latin.)

The three types of ex post facto laws are those that: (1) make an act criminal that was not criminal when performed; (2) increase the punishment for crimes already committed; or (3) change the trial rules to make it easier to convict someone. For example, if the trial rules that are in place when a crime is committed require a unanimous jury to convict the individual of a crime, and then during the trial the law changes the number required to convict from unanimity to a simple majority, the change would be invalid as ex post facto because it would be easier to convict the accused.

An ex post facto law has to work *against*, not in favor of, the accused. So the inverse of the last example, from a simple majority of a jury to unanimity to convict, would not be ex post facto. Retroactive laws that *decriminalize* certain acts or reduce penalties are also not ex post facto.

Finally, ex post facto laws are retroactive *criminal* laws. Retroactive civil laws are legal. For example, Congress can pass a tax law in September that it makes effective as of the previous July. That is not an ex post facto law.

The Framers included these prohibitions because of their experience with Great Britain during colonial times, including the Revolutionary War. American colonists suffered bills of attainder and ex post facto laws and wanted to prohibit them in the new republic.

Clause 4: Direct Taxes

No Capitation, or other direct, Tax shall be laid, unless in Proportion to the Census or enumeration herein before directed to be taken.

This clause reiterates section 2's provision requiring direct taxes to be proportional to a state's population. Again, "direct tax" is undefined but presumed in practice to mean taxes on property and on people (*i.e.* a flat rate for each person in the state). This clause eliminated fears by Southern states that their slave populations would be subject to a specific tax.

The Sixteenth Amendment affected this clause because it allowed Congress to tax income without regard to the census.

Clause 5: Export Taxes

No Tax or Duty shall be laid on Articles exported from any State.

Congress cannot pass a law imposing taxes on exports. At the time of the Convention, the Southern states' economy relied upon agricultural exports. Those states did not want the new national government to hinder their economy, so the Framers included this clause, like the previous clause on direct taxes, to mollify concerns and bring the South into the new nation.[163]

Clause 6: Preferential Treatment to Ports

No Preference shall be given by any Regulation of Commerce or Revenue to the Ports of one State over those of another; nor shall Vessels bound to, or from, one State, be obliged to enter, clear, or pay Duties in another.

There are two prohibitions here. First, Congress cannot make laws under the commerce power (section 8, clause 3) that favor one port over another. For example, Congress could not pass a law making all goods shipped through Los Angeles and nowhere else free of importation duties. This would "prefer" Los Angeles over other ports, such as Seattle.

Second, a vessel (*i.e.*, a boat or a plane) cannot be forced to enter into certain states or to pay a tax when it does enter. A plane bound for Miami from Chicago, for instance, cannot be forced to land in Atlanta when it enters the airspace over Georgia. This encourages trade between the states because it is not more expensive to trade with states located greater distances from each other. More recently, the European Union has tried to emulate this second prohibition among its member states.

Clause 7: <u>Appropriations and Accounting</u>

**No Money shall be drawn from the Treasury,
but in Consequence of Appropriations made by
Law; and a regular Statement and Account of
the Receipts and Expenditures of all public
Money shall be published from time to time.**

This "Appropriations Clause" prohibits both the
legislative and executive branches from spending money at
will. All money is to be spent by "law," meaning that is must
be appropriated towards a specific purpose approved by both a
majority of Congress and the president. So even when the
federal government owes a legitimate debt, the government
cannot pay anything towards it without following the rule set
out in this clause.

The second part of this clause requires that Congress
publish the appropriations it makes. Accordingly, Congress
regularly publishes spending proposals, actual income, and
actual expenditures. The publication of these figures allows
for public debate. The clause requires publications from "time
to time" perhaps because of the cost associated with annual
publications and also partly to allow Congress discretion in
spending.

Since 1937, however, Congress has somewhat skirted
this clause by declaring certain items "off budget."[164] The
federal government does not count these off-budget items as
part of the regular federal budget. The off-budget spending is
isolated from the normal appropriations process and so the
open debate that normally accompanies spending bills. This
practice disguises the true cost of federal programs. In 2000,
off-budget spending was roughly $330 billion.[165] By 2017,
off-budget spending surpassed $800 billion and equaled an
estimated 20% of all federal expenditures.[166] Two prominent
off-budget items are Social Security and the United States
Postal Service. The Federal National Mortgage Association
(known as "Fannie Mae") and the Federal Home Loan
Mortgage Corporation (known as "Freddie Mac"), two
government-sponsored companies that the Treasury
Department took over in 2008, are also considered off-budget

items.[167] Other off-budget items include the wars in Iraq and Afghanistan.[168]

Clause 8: <u>Titles of Nobility and Awards from Foreign Officers or Countries</u>

No Title of Nobility shall be granted by the United States: And no Person holding any Office of Profit or Trust under them, shall, without the Consent of the Congress, accept of any present, Emolument, Office, or Title, of any kind whatever, from any King, Prince, or foreign State.

The final two powers prohibited Congress are found in this "Title of Nobility Clause" or "Emoluments Clause."

Titles of Nobility

The first prohibition found here is that the United States government cannot grant any titles of nobility. This marked a defining contrast to what occurred in Great Britain or France where a leader could have the title of "Duke," "Viscount," or "Baron." No country had done anything similar. The idea was truly revolutionary.

This clause also helps explain the origins of the expression "Mr. President" when addressing the President of the United States. With the Constitution prohibiting nobility titles, and with many wishing to make a clean distinction between the United States and European governments, sharp debate occurred during the first Congress over the appropriate title and manner to refer to the president. President Washington chose to use the simple term "Mr. President." The title stuck and is the appropriate title for the president today.

Emoluments and Other Awards

This clause's second prohibition applies to people in the government rather than to the government itself. Specifically, no person holding any office in the United States government, whether elected or appointed, can accept any award or emolument from a foreign leader or country without Congress's consent. "Emolument" is an old, technical term meaning "profit or gain arising from station, office of employment," as well as "reward, remuneration, salary."[169] The Framers included this provision specifically to prevent foreign influence and corruption from affecting the government.[170] So a person *can* receive and accept a gift or an award *if* Congress consents.

Congress does consent on occasion. In World War II, Congress passed a resolution allowing members of the armed services to accept "decorations, orders, medals, and emblems" from foreign governments for their service during the war.[171] Congress made the authorization specifically because of this Constitutional requirement. Its consent allowed Audie Murphy, America's most decorated soldier in history, to receive the *Croix de Guerre* 1940 Palm from Belgium and two *Croix de Guerre* medals from France as well as the Legion of Honor, France's highest honor.

This clause, or rather the disregard of it, became an issue with President Obama accepting the Nobel Prize in December 2009. The Nobel Committee, a five-member panel elected by the Norwegian Parliament, awards the Nobel Prize each year. Consequently, the award comes from a group representing the legislature of a sovereign foreign country. The prize itself is also an emolument. It compensates the winner with the award and with substantial prize money. The two together meet this clause's requirement for necessary Congressional consent. But President Obama never requested consent. And Congress never granted it.

Perhaps President Obama felt that he didn't need to request consent since he donated the prize money to charity. Yet the amount he donated, $1.4 million, could have given President Obama a significant income-tax reduction had he accepted the money first and then gifted it rather than taking advantage of tax laws to have the Nobel committee donate the money directly to the named charities so that it did not show up as his "income." To avoid issues with this clause, President Obama could have followed President Theodore Roosevelt's lead. Awarded the prize in 1906, Roosevelt did not accept the award or the money until 1910, more than one year after he left office.[172]

Accepting the Nobel Prize without Congressional consent was the second time in less than one year that

President Obama's actions ran contrary to this clause. In June 2009, President Obama accepted from King Abdullah, and even wore, the Collar of the King Abdul Aziz Order of Merit, Saudi Arabia's highest honor. Being a member of the Order confers a title or office in Saudi nobility. President Obama was not the first sitting American president to accept this particular honor. President George W. Bush accepted the award in January 2008, and he too failed to request or receive Congressional consent.

The issue arose again in 2017 when President Donald Trump assumed office yet maintained ownership in his business empire. Trump's businesses receive significant money from foreign states. The largest commercial tenant at the Trump Tower in New York City, for instance, is a bank owned by the Chinese government.

Section 10—<u>Powers Denied the States</u>

Just as section 9 specifically denies Congress certain powers, section 10 prohibits the States from exercising powers reserved for the federal government.

Clause 1: <u>Federal Exclusivity and Guarantee of Contracts</u>

No State shall enter into any Treaty, Alliance, or Confederation; grant Letters of Marque and Reprisal; coin Money; emit Bills of Credit; make any Thing but gold and silver Coin a Tender in Payment of Debts; pass any Bill of Attainder, ex post facto Law, or Law impairing the Obligation of Contracts, or grant any Title of Nobility.

This clause specifically prohibits states from taking certain actions in areas where power is granted to the federal government in section 8. This prohibition's net effect is to make those powers *exclusive* to the federal government.

First, the clause denies states the power to make any treaty, alliance, or any other agreement that creates obligations between a foreign nation and the state. So the federal government has complete power over foreign relations.

Second, states cannot issue letters of marque and reprisal, documents authorizing private individuals to wage war against foreign nations. Congress alone has that power under section 8, clause 11.

Third, states cannot coin or mint money. Section 8, clause 5 gives that power to Congress. Nor can states emit "bills of credit," meaning that they cannot make paper money that is not backed by gold or silver a valid means of exchange. The Framers included this provision because, in the period following the Revolutionary War, several state legislatures made laws permitting paper money to be acceptable payment for debts.[173] (Rhode Island even made a law fining persons refusing to accept its paper money at face value.) The legislatures then authorized the printing of more and more paper money, which reduced the paper money's value. The Continental Congress had done the same thing during the early part of the Revolutionary War when it issued "Continentals." Not backed by gold or silver, the Continentals quickly lost their value, resulting in the pejorative comparison that something was "not worth a Continental."

Just as section 9, clause 3 prohibited the federal government from enacting bills of attainder and ex post facto laws, this clause applies the same prohibition to the states. States are similarly forbidden from granting titles of nobility.

Finally, this clause is sometimes referred to as the "Contracts Clause" because it prohibits states from making laws that retroactively impair contract rights. A state cannot change the terms of a contract after the contract is made. This clause's initial impact was to encourage much-needed foreign investment in the new nation by its effectively prohibiting states from passing laws benefitting native debtors at the expense of foreign creditors. In a more modern context, this clause prohibits states from retroactively reforming their state pension systems since the pension system is a contract between the worker and the state itself or the local government.

Clause 2: <u>Taxes on Imports and Exports</u>

No State shall, without the Consent of the Congress, lay any Imposts or Duties on Imports or Exports, except what may be absolutely necessary for executing its inspection Laws: and the net Produce of all Duties and Imposts, laid by any State on Imports or Exports, shall be for the Use of the Treasury of the United States; and all such Laws shall be subject to the Revision and Control of the Congress.

Federal supremacy over interstate and international trade is found here. Congress is given power over cross-border trade in Article I, section 8, clause 3. This clause prohibits states from taxing imports or exports without Congressional approval. The sole exception to acting without approval is when a state taxes the amount necessary to carry out its inspection laws.

An example of this exception would be if California passed a tax on agricultural imports or exports to pay for its state border protection stations. California is a significant agricultural producer and is free from many invasive insects and weeds because of natural geographic barriers that pests cannot cross on their own (mountains in the north and east, the Pacific Ocean on the west, and deserts in the south).[174] To protect California agriculture and keep out invasive plants and insects, the state operates 16 border protection stations on the major highways entering California from neighboring states. The stations inspect vehicles and goods to ensure that they are pest free.[175] But the stations come at a cost. Each year, the 16 stations inspect nearly 30 million vehicles and remove scores of infested plant matter (fruits, vegetables, plants, etc.).[176] California could act independently to enact a tax on agricultural imports or exports to offset this inspection cost.

Even if California passed the law as it could, the latter part of this clause would require the state to pay the profits from the tax to the federal treasury. The last part of the clause also makes clear that Congress would have the power to revise California's law. The same standard applies for all other states.

Clause 3: <u>Compacts and Agreements</u>

No State shall, without the Consent of Congress, lay any Duty of Tonnage, keep Troops, or Ships of War in time of Peace, enter into any Agreement or Compact with another State, or with a foreign Power, or engage in War, unless actually invaded, or in such imminent Danger as will not admit of delay.

This "Compacts Clause" limits the increase of political power for individual states and also reaffirms federal supremacy over international commerce, foreign relations, and national defense.

A "duty of tonnage" is a charge imposed on commercial ships entering, remaining in, or exiting a port.[177] In other words, it is a tax for doing business in a port that is based on the ship's weight and cargo capacity (its "tonnage").[178] Congress retains control of trade in the nation's ports by not allowing states to lay duties of tonnage without Congressional consent.

The agreements and compacts referred to here are different from treaties and confederations. States are absolutely prohibited from entering in the latter under section 10, clause 1, but states may enter the former with Congress's approval. Congress may give approval either before the compact's creation or after. The agreements, or interstate "compacts," are official agreements, essentially contracts, between two or more states.[179] They are made for a variety of purposes. For example, in 1922 seven states in the Colorado River Basin signed the Colorado River Compact. The Compact related to distributing the Colorado's water among the seven member states. Congress approved the compact the year before.[180] Another compact is one between the District of Columbia, Maryland, and Virginia creating the Washington Metropolitan Area Transit Authority.[181] Fourteen states created the Emergency Management Assistance Compact to coordinate disaster relief efforts following Hurricane Andrew in 1992. Congress approved the compact in 1996.[182] All 50 states are members as of 2013. More recently, states have entered the Interstate Compact on Educational Opportunity for

Military Children beginning in 2008. The compact's purpose is to provide uniform treatment of military children who transfer between school districts and states in terms of transferring educational records, immunization requirements, and graduation-related issues such as exit exams and course waivers.[183] Twenty-six states joined the compact within its first 18 months.[184] All 50 states had joined by 2015.[185]

The remaining prohibitions in this clause relate to the military powers given to the federal government in Article I, section 8. Since the States gave up their powers of defense to the federal government, Congress must consent to a state engaging in war or keeping troops and warships in times of peace, as both actions relate to national defense.

ARTICLE II—The Executive Branch

Article II concerns the federal government's executive branch, the second of the three branches, and the one responsible for "executing" (carrying out/implementing) the laws passed by Congress. It creates the office of the president, sets out the qualifications for that office, delineates the president's powers and duties, and provides for the president's election. This article essentially defines the presidency.

Section 1—The President – Elections and Qualifications

Clause 1: Power and Term of Office

The executive Power shall be vested in a President of the United States of America. He shall hold his Office during the Term of four Years, and, together with the Vice President, chosen for the same Term, be elected, as follows

This clause assigns all executive power to one individual–the president. But neither this clause nor the rest of the Constitution defines what that power is exactly. This stands in contrast to the legislative power in Article I where "all legislative powers *herein granted*" are vested to Congress, meaning that the national government's legislative power is defined in the Constitution.

Because the executive power is undefined, there are various interpretations as to what it means. The debate started early on. In 1793, President Washington issued a proclamation declaring American neutrality in the war between France and the United Kingdom despite there being no express power to do so the Constitution. In defense of Washington's action, Alexander Hamilton wrote a series of essays on the power of the presidency. Using the pen name "Pacificus," Hamilton argued that the executive power vested in the president is limited only by the qualifications and express restrictions listed in the Constitution.[186] James Madison responded to Hamilton's arguments by writing several articles expressing his own view of the executive power. Writing as "Helvidius," Madison countered that the executive power given the president was limited to the powers specifically granted to the president in the Constitution or delegated to the president by Congress under one of its enumerated powers. Hamilton and Madison's essays were compiled and are known today as *The Pacificus-Helvidius Debates of 1793-1794*. Hamilton's view seems to be the prevailing view today.

Beyond vesting the executive power in the president, this clause sets a four-year term of office for both the president and vice president. This term is both longer than representatives' terms and shorter than senators' terms.

Clause 2: <u>Appointment of Electors</u>

Each State shall appoint, in such Manner as the Legislature thereof may direct, a Number of Electors, equal to the whole Number of Senators and Representatives to which the State may be entitled in the Congress: but no Senator or Representative, or Person holding an Office of Trust or Profit under the United States, shall be appointed an Elector.

This clause creates Electors and the Electoral College to elect the president and vice president rather than a direct election by the people. So while voters see a candidate's name on the ballot, by casting their vote for that candidate, they are really voting for an Elector pledged to vote for the candidate.

Electors may theoretically vote for any person eligible to be president. In most states, however, the Electors pledge to vote for the candidate winning that state's popular vote. So if a candidate wins the state's popular vote, even by only a few votes, then *all* Electors pledged to that candidate are elected. The Electors then vote for the president. This proved critical in the 2000 Presidential Election. George W. Bush won the Florida popular vote by 537 votes.[187] Yet under Florida law he received all 25 of the state's Electoral votes. This was enough to make Bush the Electoral College winner and thus president.

Two states, Maine and Nebraska, follow an alternative. There, state law distributes Electors based on the popular-vote winner in each Congressional district with the overall popular-vote winner receiving two additional electors representing the senators.

So why does America elect the president and vice president by the Electoral College? The Electoral College came about as a compromise between those Framers wanting a direct election by the people, those wanting election by the state legislatures, and those wanting election by Congress.[188] A direct, nationwide election by the people was seen as too impractical to carry out at that point in history. Election by state legislatures made the president too bound by the states and state interests. And an election by Congress would not make the branches truly separate. So the compromise was to elect the president by Electors selected in a method determined by the states.

There have been five elections where the person receiving the most popular votes did not win the presidency. The first occurred in 1824, when Andrew Jackson received 41% of the popular vote in a five-way race but did not receive a majority of the electoral votes. In 1876, Samuel Tilden received nearly 51% of the popular vote, but finished with one less electoral vote than Rutherford B. Hayes. The third instance happened in 1888 when Grover Cleveland received nearly 49% of the popular vote; his challenger, Benjamin Harrison, secured nearly 60% of the electoral votes despite receiving almost 96,000 fewer votes in the popular vote than Mr. Cleveland. In 2000, Al Gore received roughly 544,000 more votes that George W. Bush. But as mentioned above, Mr. Gore failed to secure a majority of the electoral votes because of the winner-take-all method most states used for awarding electors. The 2016 election resulted in Hillary Clinton receiving a larger share of the popular vote than Donald Trump (48% to 46%), although neither candidate achieved a majority of the popular vote. Mr. Trump received 304 electoral votes compared to 227 for Mrs. Clinton, with seven electoral votes going to other candidates. Those electoral votes going to candidates other than Mrs. Clinton or Mr. Trump occurred when some electors decided not to vote for the candidate who won their state's popular vote. These electors voting contrary to their state's popular vote are known as "faithless electors." Only in the 1876 election did a candidate receiving over 50% of the popular votes cast not win the electoral vote and thus the presidency.

In summary, this clause specifies that each state legislature sets up the process for selecting Electors in that state to be part of the Electoral College. Most states follow the winner-take-all format. The total number of Electors that a state has is equal to its total number of popularly elected representatives (representatives and senators). California has the most with 55; seven states have only 3 (Alaska, Delaware, Montana, North Dakota, South Dakota, Vermont, and Wyoming). Also, this clause prohibits any person holding federal office—appointed or elected—from becoming an Elector.

The total number of elected representatives today is 535 (435 representatives and 100 senators). Yet there are 538 electors. This is because the Twenty-third Amendment gave the District of Columbia Electors in the presidential election.

Clause 3: <u>Meeting of Electors</u>

[The Electors shall meet in their respective States, and vote by Ballot for two Persons, of whom one at least shall not be an Inhabitant of the same State with themselves. And they shall make a List of all the Persons voted for, and of the Number of Votes for each; which List they shall sign and certify, and transmit sealed to the Seat of the Government of the United States, directed to the President of the Senate. The

President of the Senate shall, in the Presence of
the Senate and House of Representatives, open
all the Certificates, and the Votes shall then be
counted. The Person having the greatest
Number of Votes shall be the President, if such
Number be a Majority of the whole Number of
Electors appointed; and if there be more than
one who have such Majority, and have an equal
Number of Votes, then the House of
Representatives shall immediately choose by
Ballot one of them for President; and if no
Person have a Majority, then from the five
highest on the List the said House shall in like
Manner choose the President. But in choosing
the President, the Votes shall be taken by States,
the Representation from each State having one
Vote; A quorum for this Purpose shall consist of
a Member or Members from two thirds of the
States, and a Majority of all the States shall be
necessary to a Choice. In every Case, after the
Choice of the President, the Person having the
greatest Number of Votes of the Electors shall be
the Vice President. But if there should remain
two or more who have equal Votes, the Senate
shall choose from them by Ballot the Vice
President.]

The Twelfth Amendment deleted this clause in 1804. But
before moving on, it is beneficial to briefly examine what this
clause did that prompted the change.

Clause 3 had Electors vote for two people, with the
person receiving the most Electoral votes becoming president
and the person finishing second becoming vice president. In
the event of a tie, the House of Representatives voted as states
rather than individually to determine the winner. A majority of
the states was needed to win. It seems simple enough. But in
practice it proved to be more complicated.

In the third presidential election, held in 1796, John
Adams received the most Electoral votes followed by Thomas
Jefferson. So Adams became president and Jefferson vice
president. But the two were from opposing parties and had

very different policies. As a result, Jefferson used his position as vice president (and thus as president of the Senate) to attack Adams and his policies rather than working effectively with him.

Then, in 1800, Jefferson again ran for president. This time, he tied for first with Aaron Burr who was a member of Jefferson's own party. So the election moved into the House of Representatives. Because of partisan deadlock, the House could not select a winner until casting ballots for the thirty-sixth time!

Due to these problems in two consecutive elections (the first two after Washington's unanimous Electoral victories), Congress moved swiftly to change this clause to avoid similar problems in the future. These changes will be addressed under the Twelfth Amendment.

Clause 4: <u>Election Day</u>

The Congress may determine the Time of choosing the Electors, and the Day on which they shall give their Votes; which Day shall be the same throughout the United States.

Congress acted under this power in 1845 to set the date for Presidential Elections (*i.e.,* choosing Electors) as the Tuesday after the first Monday in November in the year before the president's term expires.[189] This means that elections are held every four years in years evenly divisible by four (2016, 2020, 2024, etc.). In this pattern, November 2 is the earliest possible election date and November 8 is the latest possible election date.

Congress also set the day for Electors officially to cast their votes as the first Monday after the second Wednesday in the December immediately following their selection. [190] State legislatures dictate where the Electors meet to cast their votes.

Clause 5: <u>Eligibility for Office</u>

No Person except a natural born Citizen, or a Citizens of the United States, at the time of the Adoption of this Constitution, shall be eligible to

**the Office of President; neither shall any Person
be eligible to that Office who shall not have
attained to the Age of thirty five Years, and been
fourteen Years a Resident within the United
States.**

Here are the qualifications to be president:

- Be a natural born citizen of the United States
- Be at least thirty-five years old
- Be living within the United States for at least
  fourteen years

That's it! Note the similarities and differences to the
legislative qualifications set out in Article I in the following
diagram:

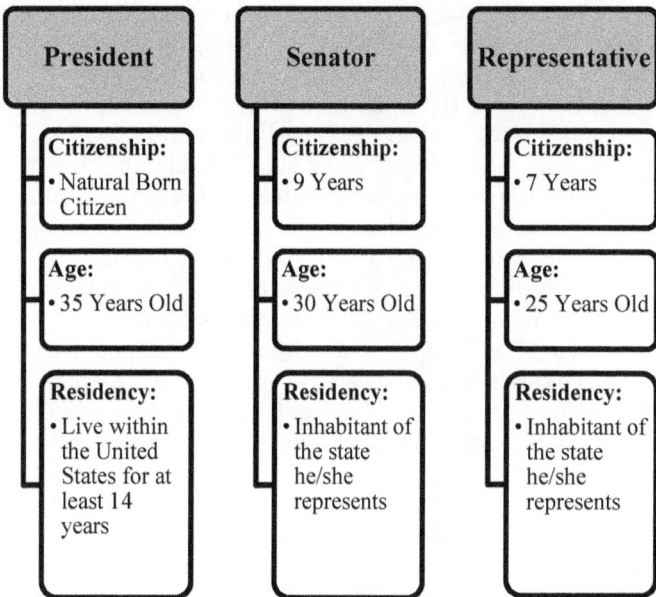

President	Senator	Representative
Citizenship: • Natural Born Citizen	**Citizenship:** • 9 Years	**Citizenship:** • 7 Years
Age: • 35 Years Old	**Age:** • 30 Years Old	**Age:** • 25 Years Old
Residency: • Live within the United States for at least 14 years	**Residency:** • Inhabitant of the state he/she represents	**Residency:** • Inhabitant of the state he/she represents

Citizenship

Perhaps the biggest difference between the qualifications
for president and those for Congress concerns citizenship.

Unlike members of Congress who can be naturalized citizens, presidents must be natural-born. Yet "natural born" is undefined in the Constitution and its meaning has been the subject of several debates. Everyone seems to agree that at the very least it means those born within the United States. But what about those born abroad to American parents? The First Congress, which included a number of the Framers, answered this in the Naturalization Act of 1790 which stated that "the children of citizens of the United States, that may be born beyond the sea, or out of the limits of the United States, shall be considered as natural born citizens...."[191] Since then, however, the language "natural born citizen" has not been used in legislation.[192]

Controversy over the natural-born citizen requirement arose during the 2008 Presidential Election and involved the two most popular candidates. Republican candidate John McCain was born in 1936 at the Coco Solo Naval Air Station in the Panama Canal Zone where his father was stationed as a naval officer. At the time of McCain's birth, the area was not considered U.S. territory. But a law passed in 1937 retroactively conferred citizenship to those born in the Canal Zone since 1904.[193] Many debated whether or not McCain qualified for the presidency as a natural born citizen[194] (even though the language used in the Naturalization Act of 1790 mentioned above should have resolved the issue). Meanwhile, scores of people similarly accused Democratic candidate Barack Obama of not being a natural born citizen and thus ineligible for the presidency. Some even filed lawsuits challenging his citizenship status. Most of these argued that Obama was not born in Hawaii. Others argued that Obama was not a natural born citizen since he had dual citizenship at birth, United States citizenship from his mother and British colonial citizenship from his father. In response, Obama's campaign posted a copy of his birth certificate online. Still, challenges continued even after Obama's 2008 election. The White House then posted a copy of the long-form version online in April 2011 in an attempt to erase doubts once and for all since Obama had just announced his reelection bid.

As an aside, the one exception to the natural-born requirement is no longer applicable. Listed in this clause, the exception stated that the natural-born requirement did not apply to those who were born prior to the American Revolution but who were American citizens at the time of the Constitution's adoption. The exception included the first several presidents and candidates who were born as British subjects during colonial times.

Age

Another difference with the legislative branch is that presidents have a higher age requirement than both representatives and senators. This age requirement came perhaps to ensure that the president has more experience and maturity. The youngest president was Theodore Roosevelt who assumed office at age 42 following the assassination of President William McKinley. President John Kennedy became the youngest elected president at age 43. Being sworn into office roughly five months before his 71st birthday, Donald Trump became the oldest person to begin service as president for the first time. (Ronald Reagan won reelection to his second term in 1984 at age 73.) The average age when first elected is just under age 55.

Residency

The president's residency requirement has never really been an issue. This is because a person could live abroad for years but have lived within the United States for 14 years at some point and could still qualify for the presidency under this clause.

Beyond the above qualifications, the Constitution has various clauses that disqualify certain persons from seeking the office, including:

- Those convicted of impeachment under Article I, section 3, clause 7
- Those who previously took an oath to support the Constitution but then rebelled against it (Fourteenth Amendment)
- Those who have already been elected to the office twice (Twenty-second Amendment)

These are the only disqualifications found in the Constitution.

Clause 6: <u>Presidential death, disability, and methods of succession</u>

[In Case of the Removal of the President from Office, or of his Death, Resignation, or Inability to discharge the Powers and Duties of the said Office, the Same shall devolve on the Vice President, and the Congress may by Law provide for the Case of Removal, Death, Resignation or Inability, both of the President and Vice President, declaring what Officer shall then act as President, and such Officer shall act accordingly, until the Disability be removed, or a President shall be elected.]

The Twenty-fifth Amendment replaced this clause. Before being superseded, this clause governed what would happen if the president died, became disabled, resigned, or was removed from office following impeachment. It provided that the vice president would assume the president's duties (without explicitly stating that the vice president would become president), and that Congress could create a law to determine what would happen if both the president and vice president died, were disabled, or removed from office.

Clause 7: <u>Compensation</u>

The President shall, at stated Times, receive for his Services, a Compensation, which shall neither be increased nor diminished during the Period for which he shall have been elected, and he shall not receive within that Period any other Emolument from the United States, or any of them.

The president receives compensation while holding office in an amount pre-set by Congress. This clause ensures that the president's compensation remains constant throughout his or her term of office by prohibiting any increase or decrease in the amount received. It also prohibits any additional compensation from the federal government or any

of the states. These prohibitions preserve the presidency's
independence from Congress and from the states.

The current compensation includes a $400,000 annual
salary, a tax-free $50,000 expense allowance, and free lodging
at the White House.[195] Not all presidents accepted their salary.
President George Washington initially refused his salary, just
as he had done while serving as the nation's top general during
the Revolutionary War. Yet the first Congress recognized that
this clause mandates pay to the president;[196] it insisted that pay
occur so as to ensure financial independence for the nation's
chief executive and leave him or her less susceptible to
corruption. So the first Congress set the president's pay at
$25,000.[197] Presidents Herbert Hoover and John Kennedy
accepted their salaries but donated them to charity.[198]
President Donald Trump pledged shortly after his election to
accept only $1 in compensation for his services.[199] In April
2017, he donated his first three months' salary to the National
Park Service.[200]

The last part of this clause, that the president not receive
any emolument from any state while serving as president,
became an issue regarding President Ronald Reagan. Reagan
has served as California's governor from 1967 to 1975. So he
received pension payments from the California state
government as a former state employee. Critics claimed this
ran afoul of this clause's emoluments prohibition. Reagan
ignored the complaints, with his advisors noting that he had
earned the pension more than six years prior to assuming the
presidency.[201]

Clause 8: Oath of Office

**Before he enter on the Execution of his Office,
he shall take the following Oath or
Affirmation:—"I do solemnly swear (or affirm)
that I will faithfully execute the Office of
President of the United States, and will to the
best of my Ability, preserve, protect and defend
the Constitution of the United States."**

The oath laid out here requires the president to make a
formal commitment to uphold the Constitution before

performing any executive responsibilities. Notice what the oath requires the president to preserve, protect, and defend. It's not the American people as one might think based on presidents often saying that their job is to "keep the American people safe."[202] Nor is it the president's job to further his or her political party, or even his or her personal ideology. The Framers set it up so that the president promises to preserve, protect, and defend the Constitution. Doing so protects the people by preserving their form of government and freedoms.

The president is only required to take the oath before assuming office. There is no requirement as to who administers the oath. Traditionally, it is the Supreme Court's Chief Justice.

President Franklin Pierce, the fourteenth President of the United States, was the first and, to date, only president to affirm rather than swear the oath of office.[203] "Swear" and "affirm" are legally the same. Both are formal promises to do something/act in a certain way. Often those who "affirm" rather than "swear" do so for religious reasons, as some religions forbid swearing oaths.

Section 2—<u>Powers of the President</u>

Clause 1: <u>Military, Administrative, and Clemency Powers</u>

The President shall be Commander in Chief of the Army and Navy of the United States, and of the Militia of the several States, when called into the actual Service of the United States; he may require the Opinion, in writing, of the principal Officer in each of the executive Departments, upon any Subject relating to the Duties of their respective Offices, and he shall have Power to Grant Reprieves and Pardons for Offences against the United States, except in Cases of Impeachment.

This clause gives the president military, administrative, and clemency powers.

Military Powers

The first part of this clause names the president as Commander in Chief of the armed forces. This means that he or she, as a civilian, controls the military and is able to send American forces throughout the world. President Theodore Roosevelt exercised this power to send the Navy's "Great White Fleet" on a tour around the world from 1907-1909.

But the presidency's power over the military is subject to control by Congress. Again, Congress alone has the power to declare war, build up and financially support the armed forces, and make the rules governing them.

Administrative Powers

The second part of this clause serves as the basis for what is known as the president's Cabinet. This is also where the president's administrative powers come from. The Cabinet consists of the principal officer from each of the executive departments created by Congress to carry out the laws. The president then oversees these officers as they fulfill their duties by requiring, if desired, each officer's written opinion on a matter concerning their own responsibilities. Today, each principal officer carries the title of "Secretary" with the exception of the Attorney General (Secretary of State, Treasury Secretary, etc.). The president regularly meets with Cabinet members.

The practice of requesting executive officers' opinions started in 1791, just two years into the republic, when President Washington asked for each Cabinet member's opinion concerning a bill chartering a national bank. Treasury Secretary Alexander Hamilton strongly supported the idea. Secretary of State Thomas Jefferson and Attorney General Edmund Randolph both opposed the plan. Based on the written arguments received, Washington sided with Hamilton and signed the bill creating the bank.

Clemency Powers

The third power granted to the president is clemency, or the power to grant pardons and reprieves. In practice these powers are defined as follows:

- A *reprieve* is the postponing of punishment, such as delaying the execution of a prisoner sentenced to death.
- A *pardon* is forgiveness of a crime and the associated penalty.
- *Commutation* is a form of a pardon that changes a convict's punishment to one that is less severe without forgiving the crime itself, such as reducing a convicted murderer's sentence from death to life imprisonment.
- *Amnesty* is another form of a pardon; it is issued to a group rather than a specifically named individual.

The president's clemency power has two restrictions. First, the president can only pardon offenses that are committed against the United States (the president has no ability to pardon those convicted of state crimes). Second, the president cannot pardon those convicted of impeachment.

The clemency power is often used and is at times controversial. In 1794, President Washington pardoned the Whiskey Rebellion's leaders. On his first day in office in 1977, President Jimmy Carter pardoned all Vietnam "draft dodgers." Put differently, he granted amnesty to those who avoided serving in the Vietnam War either by fleeing the country or by not registering for the draft. President Bill Clinton created an uproar by issuing 140 pardons on his last day in office in 2001. Among those receiving pardons were Clinton's former business partner, his half-brother, and a fugitive named Marc Rich. Rich's pardon caused the biggest kerfuffle because of the circumstances surrounding it. Rich fled the United States in 1984 after being charged with 51 counts of tax fraud for not paying $48 million in taxes. Just prior to receiving the pardon, Rich's ex-wife donated substantial amounts of money to the Clinton Presidential Library and to Mrs. Clinton's Senate campaign. In 2005, President George W. Bush controversially commuted the sentence of I. Lewis "Scooter" Libby for his conviction of perjury and obstruction of justice. The hubbub stemmed from the fact that Libby served as a high-ranking official in President Bush's administration, and his criminal conviction resulted from his work there. The commutation only applied to

Libby's 30-month prison term while leaving in place the remainder of Libby's sentence including 2 years' supervised release and a $250,000 fine.[204]

President Barack Obama commuted 1,715 sentences, more than any other in the nation's history. It was also more than the previous 12 presidents combined. This included commuting sentences for 330 persons on President Obama's final full-day in office. Conversely, President Obama pardoned 212 persons, fewer than any modern president except George H.W. Bush and George W. Bush who granted 74 and 189 pardons, respectively.[205]

Clause 2: <u>Treaty-Making and Appointment Powers</u>

He shall have Power, by and with the Advice and Consent of the Senate, to make Treaties, provided two thirds of the Senators present concur; and he shall nominate, and by and with the Advice and Consent of the Senate, shall appoint Ambassadors, other public Ministers and Consuls, Judges of the supreme Court, and all other Officers of the United States, whose Appointments are not herein otherwise provided for, and which shall be established by Law: but the Congress may by Law vest the Appointment of such inferior Officers, as they think proper, in the President alone, in the Courts of Law, or in the Heads of Departments.

The two principal powers granted to the president in this clause make it known as both the "Treaty Clause" and the "Appointments Clause." And it is sometimes called the "Advice and Consent Clause" since the president's power in obligating the United States to treaties and in making appointments is subject to the Senate's advice and consent.

Treaties

The president has the power to negotiate and sign treaties with foreign nations. Before the treaties can become binding on the United States, however, they must be presented to and approved by the Senate. The House has no part in approving treaties.

Approval requires two-thirds of a Senate quorum voting in favor of the treaty. The Senate can accept the treaty unconditionally or approve it with conditions. These conditions may be either amendments or reservations to the agreement. If approved with amendments, the president must submit the amended treaty to the other nation for its approval of the Senate's amendments. If accepted by that nation, then the treaty becomes law in the United States. If the Senate approves with reservations, then the reservations limit the United States's obligations under the treaty without affecting the other nation's treaty obligations. The most recent high-profile treaty approved by the United States under this clause is the New Strategic Arms Reduction Treaty (New START) in December 2010. The treaty limits the number of operational nuclear missile launchers each country may have to 700 and permits deployment of up to 1,550 countable warheads. New START also allows each country 18 inspections per year on the other's territory to verify limits.[206] During its first 200 years, the Senate approved more than 1,500 treaties while rejecting only 21.[207]

The president may always refuse to accept the Senate's changes to a treaty. If he or she rejects the changes, the treaty does not become law. Similarly, the Senate may reject the treaty and return it to the president, or it may prevent the treaty from becoming effective by withholding its approval. In 1919, the Senate rejected the Treaty of Versailles, one of the peace treaties at the end of World War I, because President Woodrow Wilson would not accept the Senate's amendments and reservations and renegotiate the treaty to accommodate conditions. President Clinton signed the Kyoto Protocol in 1997 but never submitted it to the Senate for approval because of the Senate's guaranteed rejection.

This clause is unclear as to how a treaty may be terminated. Consequently, treaty termination has taken various forms. These include: the president terminating a treaty after both the House and Senate passed a law repealing it, the president terminating a treaty based on a Senate resolution alone, the president terminating a treaty and the Senate later approving the termination, and the president terminating a treaty alone.[208] In 1978, President Carter terminated the defense treaty with the Republic of China (Taiwan) without Congressional consent. And in 2002 President George W. Bush withdrew the United States from the Anti-Ballistic Missile ("ABM") Treaty, but he did so according to the treaty's terms.[209]

Since World War II, presidents have increasingly skirted the Treaty Clause's two-thirds requirement by entering into "congressional-executive agreements" with foreign nations rather than treaties.[210] In these situations, the president negotiates an agreement with a foreign nation. The negotiated agreement is then presented as regular legislation to Congress who then only needs to pass the agreement by a majority in both houses. Perhaps the most notorious of these is the North American Free Trade Agreement ("NAFTA") between the United States, Canada, and Mexico. Presented as legislation rather than a treaty in 1993, NAFTA passed the Senate 61-38, five votes short of the two-thirds necessary for a treaty. Having passed 234-200 in the House, NAFTA became law in 1994 after President Clinton signed the legislation.[211]

In some instances, presidents have sought to bypass the legislative branch altogether, claiming that the agreements are purely "executive agreements." President Obama exemplified this approach during his final years in office. Prominent examples include an agreement he reached in 2015 with Iran and other countries regarding Iran's nuclear program, and the Paris Climate Agreement that President Obama signed in 2016.[212] Regarding the latter, the Obama administration openly and consistently referred to the accord as an "executive agreement" rather than a treaty to justify its refusal to seek Congressional approval.[213] Other nations acknowledged their complicity and intentional effort to label the agreement something other than a treaty as well so that it would not be submitted to Congress.[214]

President Obama was far from the first president to claim that an international agreement was strictly an "executive agreement" that could bypass Congress altogether. President George W. Bush made similar arguments in 2008 concerning a long-term agreement with Iraq regarding U.S. troops being stationed in that country.[215]

<u>Appointments</u>

The president appoints principal executive branch officers like ambassadors and Cabinet secretaries. The total number of these executive branch appointments, when including undersecretaries, deputy secretaries, and assistant secretaries in each of the departments, can total over 1,000 individuals.[216] Further, the president appoints members of the judicial branch including Supreme Court justices and federal appellate and district judges. All of these nominations are subject to the Senate's advice and consent. In practice, this means that the nominations must be approved by at least a majority of the Senate.

The Senate's advice on an appointment can come either before or after an individual's nomination for a position. For example, when an opening occurred on the Supreme Court early in President Clinton's presidency, Senator Orrin Hatch of Utah, the ranking minority member on the Senate Judiciary committee at the time, suggested that Clinton appoint Ruth Bader Ginsburg or Stephen Breyer to the position because neither would receive as much opposition as Clinton's preferred choices.[217] Clinton heeded the advice and nominated Ginsburg for the post. The Senate confirmed her 96-3. When a second spot opened one year later, Clinton again recalled the advice and nominated Breyer. The Senate confirmed him by a vote of 87-9. Most of the time, however, the Senate's advice comes after the nomination during confirmation hearings.

Confirmation hearings for Cabinet Secretaries and Supreme Court nominees are perhaps the most prominent examples of the advice and consent process. In modern practice, several senators question the president's nominee in confirmation hearings lasting multiple days. The reason for the hearings is to present the nominee to the Senate, which then allows each senator the opportunity to make an informed decision to approve or reject the nominee. Recent Supreme Court confirmation proceedings, however, suggest that senators have not taken the Advice and Consent Clause too seriously. In 2017, for instance, Senator Jeff Flake of Arizona asked Supreme Court nominee Neil Gorsuch, "Would you rather fight 100 duck-sized horses or one horse-sized duck?"[218] Senator Al Franken of Minnesota asked Supreme Court nominee Sonia Sotomayor during her confirmation hearings in 2009 what case the fictional television attorney Perry Mason had lost. During Elena Kagan's confirmation hearings in 2010, Senator Amy Klobuchar of Minnesota asked Kagan about Kagan's affinity for the characters in the vampire movie "Twilight."[219]

In 2016, the Senate refused to hold confirmation hearings for Merrick Garland, President Obama's choice to fill a Supreme Court vacancy caused earlier that year by Justice Antonin Scalia's death. By not holding hearings or bringing the nomination up for a floor vote, the Senate effectively did not consent to Mr. Garland's nomination. Out of 161 nominations received between 1789 and 2016, the Senate had confirmed 124 of them. It rejected 11 nominees outright in roll-call votes, while the remaining 26 nominees, due to strong opposition, were tabled, postponed, never voted on by the Senate, or withdrawn by the president.[220]

The president may also withdraw a nomination if he or she believes that the Senate will not confirm the nominee. In 1993, President Clinton withdrew his first nominee for Attorney General, Zoe Baird, because of Senate opposition.[221] A nominee may also withdraw him or herself from consideration. Harriet Miers, President George W. Bush's choice for a Supreme Court vacancy in 2005, withdrew her nomination after facing strong criticism. Andy Puzder, President Trump's first nominee to head the Department of Labor, withdrew himself from consideration the day before his confirmation hearing in 2017. Tom Daschle, Judd Gregg, and Bill Richardson, three of President Obama's first nominees for Cabinet positions in 2008, withdrew themselves from consideration before being confirmed by the Senate.

Finally, the last part of the "Appointments Clause" requires some attention. It permits Congress to vest the appointment of "inferior officers" in the president alone, in the courts, or in the heads of the executive departments. The "inferior officers" refers to the approximately one million federal employees beyond those requiring Senate confirmation. Almost all of these are appointed by executive department heads (*i.e.,* Cabinet secretaries). The president does directly appoint some of them, including those who oversee particular policies or initiatives such as the White House Office of Faith-Based and Neighborhood Partnerships or the Office of National Aids Policy. These directors who oversee specific policies or initiatives are popularly known as "czars."

Some think that appointing czars violates the Constitution. Yet this clause specifically permits these appointments. The last phrase states that "Congress may by law vest the appointment of such inferior officers, as they think proper, in the president alone." The unconfirmed "czars" can be among these "inferior officers." Because Congress increasingly allows these appointments without approval, presidents increasingly make them.[222] In his first term in office, President Obama had over 30 czars not receiving Senate confirmation,[223] a number that remained consistent through his second term.

A 2013 report by the Government Accountability Office identified 321 presidentially appointed positions in the federal government that do not require Senate approval.[224] Over half of these positions required Senate approval until August 2012 when President Obama signed the Presidential Appointment Efficiency and Streamlining Act. That act eliminated the need for Senate confirmation for 163 presidential nominations.[225]

Clause 3: <u>Power to Fill Vacancies</u>

The President shall have Power to fill up all Vacancies that may happen during the Recess of the Senate, by granting Commissions which shall expire at the End of their next Session.

Here, the president has power to act alone and fill officer and judicial vacancies without Senate approval at any time the Senate is out of session. These are called "recess appointments." They are only temporary and expire at the end of the Senate's next session; the positions become vacant again at that point. In practice, this means that the appointments must be approved by the Senate by the end of the next calendar year.

Many presidents have exercised this power. In December 2010, President Obama nominated Robert Ford to serve as ambassador to Syria during a Senate recess. Ford's appointment was set to expire at the end of the Senate's next session the following December, but the Senate unanimously confirmed his appointment in October 2011.[226] Similarly, President George W. Bush appointed John Bolton to be the United States ambassador to the United Nations during a Senate recess in August 2005. The Senate failed to confirm Bolton when it came back in session, so Bolton's appointment ended at the close of the Senate's session in December 2006. All in all, President George W. Bush made 171 recess appointments.[227] President Bill Clinton made almost 140.[228] President Barack Obama made 28 through his two terms.[229]

Section 3—<u>Presidential Powers and Duties to Congress</u>

He shall from time to time give to the Congress Information on the State of the Union, and recommend to their Consideration such Measures as he shall judge necessary and expedient; he may, on extraordinary Occasions, convene both Houses, or either of them, and in Case of Disagreement between them, with Respect to the Time of Adjournment, he may adjourn them to such Time as he shall think proper; he shall receive Ambassadors and other public Ministers; he shall take Care that the Laws be faithfully executed, and shall Commission all the Officers of the United States.

For clarity, this section will be explained phrase by phrase.

He shall from time to time give to the Congress Information on the State of the Union, and recommend to their Consideration such Measures as he shall judge necessary and expedient;

Two of the president's duties to Congress are found here. First, the president must provide Congress with information on the "State of the Union" (the nation's condition). Second, the president has the responsibility to recommend perceived necessary legislation to Congress.

105

Presidents traditionally tie the two responsibilities together in an annual "State of the Union" address. President Washington began the practice of personally addressing a joint session of the House and Senate in 1790. In 1801, President Jefferson chose instead to send written reports to Congress rather than personally appear before it. Jefferson's custom continued for the next 112 years until President Woodrow Wilson revived Washington's practice of personal delivery. The only requirement is that the president provides Congress with information. Oral or written delivery fulfills the Constitutional obligation. Since 1934, the president almost always gives a personal address at the United States Capitol in late January.

The State of the Union is not the only time that the president provides Congress with information or appeals to it to pass legislation. The president regularly provides reports on economic, defense, and foreign relations matters.

> *[the President] may, on extraordinary Occasions, convene both Houses, or either of them, and in Case of Disagreement between them, with Respect to the Time of Adjournment, he may adjourn them to such Time as he shall think proper;*

The president is given the power to call either chamber of Congress or both of them into session during extraordinary circumstances. Presidents have exercised this power 27 times.[230] The last occurrence was in July 1948 when President Harry Truman called a special two-week session to address domestic legislation.

While presidents have summoned Congress into session for "extraordinary occasions," they have never exercised the power found in the second part of this phrase to adjourn Congress.

> *[the President] shall receive Ambassadors and other public Ministers;*

This phrase sets out the president's diplomatic responsibilities. It gives the president significant foreign-policy powers.

106

The president's powers come from the fact that he or she is the *sole* party permitted under the Constitution to receive ambassadors. This means, in practice, that the president determines diplomatic relations with a foreign country. The president grants or revokes diplomatic recognition by receiving or refusing to welcome a country's ambassador. Congress does not do so.

Acting under this power, President Woodrow Wilson refused to recognize countries because of ideological differences. ("Recognize" meaning to formally acknowledge the government in control of a country.) He first refused to recognize the Mexican government led by Victoriano Huerta in 1913 because Huerta had come to power through a violent military coup.[231] Wilson refused to recognize the Bolshevik regime in Russia, which came to power through violence and revolution in 1917[232] and later became the Soviet Union.

Other presidents have similarly acted alone in recognizing countries by receiving their ambassadors. For instance, President Franklin Roosevelt recognized the Soviet Union in 1933 through an agreement to exchange ambassadors.[233] President Harry Truman unilaterally recognized Israel in 1948. Most recently, the United States recognized South Sudan as an independent state when President Obama declared: "I am proud to declare that the United States formally recognizes the Republic of South Sudan as a sovereign and independent state upon this day, July 9, 2011."[234] In 2015, President Obama re-established ties with Cuba after more than 50 years of no formal diplomatic relations between the countries.

Separate but related to the issue of recognizing countries, presidents can also determine diplomatic relations by recalling ambassadors. In 2005, for example, President George W. Bush recalled the U.S. ambassador to Syria following that country's alleged involvement in the assassination of Lebanon's Prime Minister. President Obama then mended ties to Syria in 2010 by sending a new ambassador to the country (through a recess appointment). The United States still recognized the Syrian regime as being that country's government between 2005 and 2010; it simply had strained ties during that period.

> *[the President] shall take Care that the Laws be*
> *faithfully executed, and shall Commission all the*
> *Officers of the United States.*

This final phrase contains the most important of the president's responsibilities—to faithfully execute the nation's laws. This responsibility is the reason why the president's branch of government is the *executive* branch. He or she *executes* (enforces) the laws created by Congress and signed by the president, either the current president or a predecessor.

The president enforces the law through fifteen executive departments, each one headed by an appointed member of the president's Cabinet. (These appointed members and their departments are the same ones discussed in Article II, section 2.) The department heads report directly to the president and meet with him or her during Cabinet meetings. The executive departments and the years they were created are as follows (in order of creation):

1. Department of State, 1789 (originally named the "Department of Foreign Affairs")
2. Department of Treasury, 1789
3. Department of the Interior, 1849
4. Department of Agriculture, 1862
5. Department of Justice, 1870 (headed by the Attorney General, a position created in 1789, but which had no department until 1870)
6. Department of Commerce, 1903
7. Department of Labor, 1913
8. Department of Defense, 1947 (the department is a successor to the Department of War, one of the original executive departments created in 1789)
9. Department of Health and Human Services, 1953 (this department was originally called the "Department of Health, Education, and Welfare" in 1953, but renamed the Department of Health and Human Services in 1979 when the education functions were transferred to the newly created Department of Education)
10. Department of Housing and Urban Development, 1965
11. Department of Transportation, 1966
12. Department of Energy, 1977

13. Department of Education, 1979
14. Department of Veterans Affairs, 1988
15. Department of Homeland Security, 2002 (differs from the Department of Defense in that it oversees national defense of United States territory, whereas the Department of Defense focuses on executing laws regarding military actions abroad)

One of the more familiar ways in which federal laws are executed is through the Department of Justice's prosecuting those accused of violating federal laws. United States Attorneys are members of the Department of Justice who are appointed by the president. They act as federal prosecutors and so investigate and press charges against individuals alleged to have violated federal laws. Similarly, these attorneys are responsible for defending federal laws from lawsuits by individuals and organizations regarding a law's validity.

While there should be little question regarding the president's responsibilities to faithfully execute the laws, controversy arose over the issue in early 2011 when President Obama ordered the Department of Justice to no longer defend challenges to the Defense of Marriage Act, a law passed by Congress and signed by President Clinton in 1996. President Obama's decision ran counter to the presidential duty outlined here to execute laws passed by Congress. But he was not the only president to behave in this manner. In 2005, the Department of Justice under President George W. Bush refused to defend a law prohibiting the display of marijuana policy reform ads in public transit systems.[235] And in 1979, the Department of Justice under President Jimmy Carter failed to defend a law requiring membership in the NRA to purchase surplus Army rifles.[236]

Finally, this phrase gives the president the responsibility to commission (officially appoint) "all the Officers of the United States." This includes both military officers and Foreign Service officers who serve in United States diplomatic missions abroad.

Section 4—Impeachment

**The President, Vice President and all
Civil Officers of the United States, shall
be removed from Office on Impeachment
for, and Conviction of, Treason, Bribery,
or other high Crimes and Misdemeanors.**

Impeachment is first addressed in Article I, section 2,
where the House is given authority to impeach an official (*i.e.*,
brings charges against him or her). Article I, section 3 dictates
that the Senate tries and convicts or acquits the official. This
section sets out the basis by which the House may impeach
and the Senate may convict and involuntarily remove any
federal official—but more particularly the president—from
office. The clause also sets out the basis for impeachment and
those officials who are subject to it.

Basis for Impeachment
The House can only impeach for treason, bribery, or
other high crimes and misdemeanors. But what exactly does
this mean?
Treason is defined in Article III, section 3 of the
Constitution as waging war against the United States or giving
aid and comfort to its enemies. Bribery, while not defined in
the Constitution, had an understood definition among the
Framers of offering something of value to influence an official
in carrying out his or her duties. The phrase "high crimes and
misdemeanors" is generally undefined. Debates during the
Constitutional Convention and in the ratifying conventions
that followed gave differing definitions. Some argued that the
phrase meant only serious criminal behavior. Others, including
James Madison, countered that it included acts done in office
that were incompetent or improper but not criminal in
nature.[237] In practice, the definition is left to the House.
During the impeachment of President Andrew Johnson in
1868, for example, Representative Benjamin Butler of
Massachusetts said:

> [A]n impeachable high crime or misdemeanor
> is one in its nature or consequences subversive

110

of some fundamental or essential principle of
government or highly prejudicial to the public
interest, and this may consist of a violation of
the Constitution, of law, of an official oath, or
of duty, by an act committed or omitted, or,
without violating a positive law, by the abuse
of discretionary powers from improper
motives or for an improper purpose.[238]

In 1970, during debates on impeaching Supreme Court Justice
William Douglas, then-Representative Gerald Ford observed,
"an impeachable offense is whatever a majority of the House
of Representatives considers to be at a given moment in
history."[239] The debate continues.

There is often confusion about President Bill Clinton's
impeachment in 1998. Many erroneously believe that the
House impeached Clinton for his marital infidelity, with that
misconduct being labeled a "high crime." In reality, Clinton's
charges were for perjury and obstruction of justice—actual
crimes. He lied under oath about his relationship with a White
House intern. (The questioning under oath related to an
ongoing sexual harassment lawsuit against him.) The House
impeached Clinton for this behavior, but the Senate did not
remove him from office.

Officials subject to impeachment

The president and vice president may be impeached. So
too may other "civil officers." "Civil officers" means members
of the Cabinet, judges, and others who are appointed to their
position.[240]

Impeachment is not common. The House has impeached
only 19 federal officers in history. This number includes two
presidents (Andrew Johnson and Bill Clinton), one cabinet
member, one senator (although senators aren't technically
subject to impeachment because they are not civil officers),
one Supreme Court justice, and fourteen federal judges. The
most recent impeachment occurred in March 2010 when the
House unanimously impeached federal district court judge
Thomas Porteous.

President Richard Nixon is one official who was close to
impeachment but who was never actually impeached. In July

1974, the House Judiciary Committee voted to impeach him for his role in the Watergate scandal. But President Nixon resigned before the full House voted, so the House dropped the issue.

ARTICLE III—The Judicial Branch

Article III creates the judiciary, the federal government's third and final branch. It states that there is one supreme court with limited jurisdiction. It also guarantees trial by jury for all criminal trials, defines treason, and provides limits on the punishment of treason.

Section 1—Judicial Power, Courts, and Judicial Tenure and Salary

The judicial Power of the United States shall be vested in one supreme Court, and in such inferior Courts as the Congress may from time to time ordain and establish. The Judges, both of the supreme and inferior Courts, shall hold their Offices during good Behavior, and shall, at stated Times, receive for their Services a Compensation, which shall not be diminished during their Continuance in Office.

Article III, section 1 vests power just like the first sections in Articles I and II. This section vests the judicial power in the Supreme Court and in the lower courts that Congress may create. Interestingly, the Supreme Court is the only court actually required by the Constitution. This section also sets out the tenure for the judges of these courts and prohibits Congress from decreasing their salary while they serve as judges.

Judicial power
The term "judicial power" means the power to resolve actual legal controversies ("cases") between parties by giving a final, binding decision.[241]

112

Courts

The Constitution creates only one court, the Supreme Court, and vests it with judicial power. It also gives Congress the right to create additional, inferior courts but does not require Congress to do so.

The Supreme Court – This section does not say how big the Supreme Court has to be (although Article I, section 3, clause 6 states that it must have a "Chief Justice" who presides over impeachment trials of the president). Nor does it say what procedure the court must follow.

So who or what determines how many justices are on the Court? Congress decides. The first Congress, with the Judiciary Act of 1789, set the number of Supreme Court justices at six, one chief justice and five associate justices. In 1801, Congress reduced this number to five but increased it back to six the following year. Congress later expanded the court to seven justices in 1807, nine in 1837, and ultimately ten in 1864. It reduced the number to seven in 1866 before fixing the number of justices on the Supreme Court at nine in 1869.[242]

In 1937, President Franklin Roosevelt planned to expand the court to as many as 15 justices. Roosevelt's proposed legislation, pejoratively known as his "court-packing plan," would have added one justice to the court for every justice over the age of 70, with the maximum number being 15. He made this proposal to secure a majority of justices on the court who would support his "New Deal" proposals, which had consistently been on the losing end of court battles. After Roosevelt announced his plan, and in the face of enormous political pressure, Justice Owen Roberts changed positions and began upholding Roosevelt's programs. With a majority of the court now supporting his programs, Roosevelt dropped his controversial proposal so that the number of justices remained at nine. Roberts's change then became known as "the switch in time that saved nine."[243]

Inferior Courts – Acting under the power to create inferior courts, Congress created federal trial courts and appellate courts around the nation. The trial courts are known as "district" courts. Most cases begin in these courts, and juries only exist here. The appellate courts are generally referred to as "circuit" courts. The term comes from the time when judges would ride their horses in a circuit between different towns to hear cases. These circuit courts are intermediate courts between the district courts and the Supreme Court. They hear appeals from the district courts. Multiple district courts are found within each circuit.

There are twelve regional judicial circuits across the country today. Each has a court of appeals. The First Circuit is the smallest, with only 6 judges to serve a circuit population of 14 million.[244] The Ninth Circuit is the largest, having 29 judges to serve a population of over 60 million, more than twice the population of any other circuit. Since it is so large, the Ninth Circuit hears more cases than the other circuits; it thus has a greater chance of being overturned by the Supreme Court on appeal. And it often is, earning the moniker the "Notorious Ninth" because it is the most overturned Circuit of them all. Finally, there is a nationwide circuit court, known as the Court of Appeals for the Federal Circuit, which hears appeals from across the nation in specialized cases such as those dealing with patent laws.

Geographic Boundaries of the United States Courts of Appeals and United States District Courts

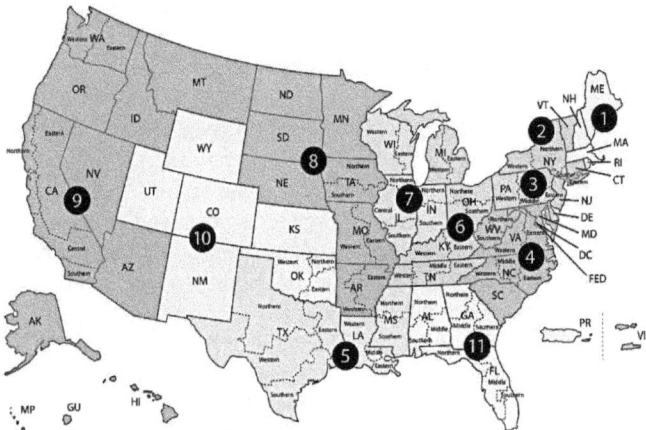

Source: http://www.uscourts.gov/uscourts/images/CircuitMap.pdf

There are 94 judicial districts created under this section. The 50 states are covered by 89 district courts. Some states, like Wyoming, form a single judicial district. Others, such as New York, are made up of multiple judicial districts. In fact, New York City alone has two judicial districts. Additionally, five other "federal district courts" exist. One covers the District of Columbia. Four cover the territories of Guam, the Northern Mariana Islands, Puerto Rico, and the Virgin Islands. The courts in the District of Columbia and Puerto Rico are, by law, considered the same as the federal courts located in the 50 states even though both areas are considered United States territories. The district courts covering Guam, the Northern Mariana Islands, and the Virgin Islands, however, are really territorial courts created under Article IV; so this section's requirements regarding judicial tenure and salary do not apply to the judges serving in those three district courts.

Judicial Tenure and Salary

A stark distinction is made between judges' tenure and the tenure of representatives, senators, and the president. While representatives, senators, and the president have fixed terms of office—two, six, and four years, respectively—this section states that judges shall hold office "during good behavior." It does not set out a fixed term. This means that judges of the courts created under this section hold office for *life* upon good behavior. But a judge does not have to serve until death. He or she can resign at any time, like Justice John Paul Stevens did in 2010. Or Congress can impeach and remove the judge for bad behavior.

The final part of this section preserves judicial independence by prohibiting Congress from decreasing judicial salaries during the judge's service. Were it otherwise, Congress could reduce a judge's salary to zero if it did not like the way that he or she ruled on a case. As of 2017, the annual salary for Supreme Court justices is $251,800 ($263,300 for the Chief Justice), $217,600 for circuit court judges, and $205,100 for district court judges.[245] These salaries were 15% more than they were in 2013, more than double the amounts in 1990, and more than triple the salary levels of 1980.

This section resolved one of the 27 grievances set out in the Declaration of Independence, specifically that the king had "made judges dependent on [the king's] will alone, for the tenure of their offices, and the amount and payment of their salaries."

Finally, as a side note, "justice" is the title given to judges on the Supreme Court while "judge" is the title given to those in the Circuit and District Courts. Attorneys who appear before any of these courts refer to the judge or justice as "Your Honor."

Section 2—Judicial Power, Jurisdiction and Jury Trials

Clause 1: Jurisdiction of Federal Courts

The judicial Power shall extend to all Cases, in Law and Equity, arising under this Constitution, the Laws of the United States, and Treaties made, or which shall be made, under their Authority;—to all Cases affecting Ambassadors, other public ministers and Consuls;—to all Cases of admiralty and maritime Jurisdiction;— to Controversies to which the United States shall be a Party;—to Controversies between two or more States;—[between a State and Citizens of another State;]—between Citizens of different States;—between Citizens of the same State claiming Lands under Grants of different States, [and between a State, or the Citizens thereof, and foreign States, Citizens or Subjects.]

This clause is the longest in Article III and it sets out the federal courts' jurisdiction. "Jurisdiction" is a court's legal authority to hear a case. Without jurisdiction, a court cannot exercise judicial power.

Section 2, clause 1 limits federal court jurisdiction by subject matter, and permits a federal court to hear a case in the following instances:

- Cases "arising under" (based on) the Constitution, federal laws, and treaties. This is generally referred to as "federal question jurisdiction," meaning that the case involves a question of federal law. These federal

116

laws can be those passed by Congress or treaties approved by the Senate.

- <u>Cases affecting ambassadors, public ministers, and consuls.</u> This refers to foreign diplomatic corps serving in the United States, not United States ambassadors, ministers, or consuls serving abroad.[246] So if a foreign ambassador injures someone in a car accident and the injured person wishes to sue for damages, then the person must sue the ambassador in a federal court.

- <u>Admiralty and maritime cases.</u> Although undefined in the Constitution, maritime and admiralty had particular meanings when the Framers drafted the Constitution. English law considered "admiralty" to be local regulations of fishing, harbors, shipping, and so on. "Maritime" meant cases arising on the open ocean. The two were seen as being connected in America rather than separate as they were in England. That is, admiralty and maritime jurisdiction covered (1) cases involving acts committed on the open ocean as well as water that is navigable to the ocean by 10-ton or larger vessels, and (2) cases relating to contracts or other transactions related to shipping on the sea or in navigable waters.[247] The first Congress made this view clear, and it has since remained unchanged.[248] Because federal jurisdiction covers acts on the open ocean, persons finding sunken ships will go to federal court to have the found property declared as theirs. This happened when the wreckage of the Titanic was found in the mid-1980s. RMS Titanic, Inc., the company salvaging artifacts from the ship, sought to have a court declare them as the artifacts' owners.[249]

- <u>Cases in which the United States is a party.</u> This occurs most often in criminal cases where the United States is pressing charges against a person or entity for violating federal law. One example is the federal prosecution in 2004 of merchandising mogul Martha

Stewart for violating federal securities laws. Another example is the federal prosecution in 2015 of Dzhokhar Tsarnaev, one of the Boston Marathon bombers, for breaching federal criminal laws. The United States is also a party in civil cases. (Sovereign immunity prevents the United States from being sued without its permission.) The United States can sue any individual, state, or entity. When it does, the dispute occurs in federal court. This is why the Department of Justice sued four health insurance companies (Anthem, Cigna, Aetna, and Humana) in federal court in 2016 to block Anthem's planned purchase of Cigna and Aetna's purchase of Humana based on perceived antitrust violations.

- Cases between states. States can sue each other. Giving the federal courts jurisdiction to decide these cases was a way to prevent bias against one state by the court of another. A high-profile lawsuit between states occurred in the late 1990s when New Jersey sued New York to have Ellis Island declared as part of New Jersey.[250] An 1834 compact between the two states declared Ellis Island to be part of New York; the submerged area surrounding it was considered part of New Jersey. Over time, the federal government, which owned the land, expanded the island by over 24 acres using landfill to help accommodate the large number of immigrants passing through the island. Once the island was no longer used for immigration, each state asserted that the island was part of its territory. The United States Supreme Court ruled that the once-submerged land was part of New Jersey, and that only the portion of the island above water at the time of the 1834 compact was part of New York.[251]

- Cases between citizens of different states. This jurisdictional grant is supposed to prevent bias by state courts in favor of their own citizens. It puts the two parties in a neutral setting and with a judge who is arguably not susceptible to local prejudice. Today,

118

this "diversity jurisdiction" permits lawsuits to proceed in federal courts if the case involves more than $75,000 and the parties live in different states.

- <u>Cases involving citizens of one state claiming land grants from a different state.</u> This is more of historical significance today. Its inclusion came amidst boundary disputes that affected 10 states at the time of the Constitutional Convention. The disputes involved land being claimed by persons living in a particular state on the basis that they received or purchased the land from a different state. For instance, a party received a land grant from New Hampshire in the 1700s. Later, after Vermont was carved out of New Hampshire, Vermont made a conflicting land grant. The parties filed suit in a federal court because of this clause.[252] The resolution of boundary disputes, the adoption of the Northwest Ordinance of 1787, and states moving away from land grants all resulted in this clause becoming more or less obsolete.[253]

- <u>Cases brought by one state or its citizens against citizens of a foreign state; by foreign states against American citizens; and by American citizens against citizens of a foreign state.</u> The Eleventh Amendment modified the bracketed language to essentially prohibit suits against a state in federal court by its own citizens, citizens of a different state, and by foreign citizens or governments.

Finally, the judicial power and jurisdiction just discussed applies to cases in law and equity. "Law" refers to common law, or law that developed over time through the courts in England and the colonies. It applies when one party sues another for an injury that has already occurred. "Equity" applies when a party seeks to prevent an injury. Equity developed alongside the common law in separate courts; its purpose was to apply principles of fairness and justice that might otherwise be lost by strictly applying the written law.

119

Clause 2: <u>Federal Courts' Original and Appellate Jurisdiction</u>

In all Cases affecting Ambassadors, other public Ministers and Consuls, and those in which a State shall be Party, the supreme Court shall have original Jurisdiction. In all the other Cases before mentioned, the supreme Court shall have appellate Jurisdiction, both as to Law and Fact, with such Exceptions, and under such Regulations as the Congress shall make.

The first sentence contains the basis for the Supreme Court's original jurisdiction. "Original jurisdiction" means the court where the cases are first heard. So the Supreme Court is the first to hear cases concerning ambassadors and other foreign officials, and cases between two or more states. In the case between New Jersey and New York about Ellis Island just discussed, the Supreme Court was the first and only court to hear the case. The Supreme Court acted as a trial court in that instance since this clause gave it original jurisdiction. Congress cannot change the Court's original jurisdiction.

The Supreme Court has appellate jurisdiction for the other cases that federal courts may hear, meaning that the case begins at a lower court but can be reviewed by the Supreme Court after an appeal. Unlike with original jurisdiction, Congress can limit the Supreme Court's ability to hear cases in which the court has appellate jurisdiction. For example, Congress passed a law requiring suits between citizens of different states to have over $75,000 in dispute, otherwise the case must begin in state court.[254] Congress once made it so that certain cases had mandatory appeals to the Supreme Court. The court had no choice; it had to hear and decide those cases. The Judiciary Act of 1925 changed that law so that there were far fewer mandatory appeals.[255] Now the court has greater discretion to decide cases. It decides those that it must by law, as well as those that it feels important. Approximately 7,500 petitions are made to the Court each year, but the Court hears argument in only 80 of them, or just about 1% of all appeals.[256]

Today, the Court's rules require that at least four of the nine justices choose to hear a case before the case can go to the Supreme Court.

Clause 3: <u>Trial by Jury</u>

The Trial of all Crimes, except in Cases of Impeachment, shall be by Jury; and such Trial shall be held in the State where the said Crimes shall have been committed; but when not committed within any State, the Trial shall be at such Place or Places as the Congress may by Law have directed.

This clause mandates a trial by jury for persons charged with federal crimes. This means that a group of ordinary citizens, not a judge, determines whether the accused is guilty or innocent. A defendant may waive this right, however.

The jury trial must occur in the state where the crime was committed. This rule alleviates the burden on witnesses of having to travel elsewhere to testify and incur the expense in doing so.

Finally, impeached persons are not tried by a jury since, as seen in Article I, the Senate is the designated body to decide those cases and, in a sense, serves as an elected jury.

Section 3—<u>Treason</u>

Clause 1: <u>Treason Defined</u>

Treason against the United States, shall consist only in levying War against them, or in adhering to their Enemies, giving them Aid and Comfort. No Person shall be convicted of Treason unless on the Testimony of two Witnesses to the same overt Act, or on Confession in open Court.

Treason is the only crime defined by the Constitution. It can be any of the following:

- Making war against the United States;

- Adhering to (following or being loyal to) America's enemies; or
- Providing America's enemies with aid and comfort

This clause also sets out the burden required for conviction of treason. The accused must either confess to treason in court or two witnesses must testify that the accused committed the same act. A person cannot be tried or convicted for treason by simply thinking about or planning to commit treasonous activities.

Few people have been charged with treason since the Constitution's ratification. Fewer still have been convicted. Among the first charged and convicted were two members of the 1794 Whiskey Rebellion. President Washington subsequently exercised the clemency power to pardon them. Thomas Jefferson accused his former vice president Aaron Burr of treason and issued a warrant for his arrest in 1807. Burr was tried and acquitted.[257] Others have been charged with treason in the years since. Officials charged leaders of the Confederate States with treason following the Civil War, but President Andrew Johnson exercised the pardon power and granted many of them amnesty.[258] Mildred Gillars, known as "Axis Sally," was convicted of treason in 1949 for working as an English-language broadcaster in Germany during World War II. She received a 10 to 30 year sentence and served 12 years before being paroled in 1961.[259] Iva D'Aquino, another World War II-era English language broadcaster known as "Tokyo Rose," was also convicted of treason in 1949 for working in Japan during the war. She served six years of a 10-year sentence before being released for good behavior. President Gerald Ford subsequently pardoned Mrs. D'Aquino in 1977 after a journalist's investigation revealed that the two key witnesses against her had lied under oath.[260] The most recent person accused of treason was Adam Gadahn in 2006 for serving as a spokesman for al-Qaeda and threatening attacks on the United States.[261]

Because treason is so strictly defined, the burden for proving it so high, and because Congress cannot alter treason's limited definition, Congress has created other criminal laws for acts against the United States. These include activities like espionage and conspiracy against the government. One example is the Espionage Act of 1917.[262] That law has been amended multiple times, but essentially makes it a crime to disclose classified information, or other information about national defense, to persons "not entitled to receive it."[263] The disclosure must be done with knowledge or reason to believe that information could be used to injure the United States or be "to the advantage of any foreign nation"[264] Death is one of the penalties called for by the statute. Julius and Ethel Rosenberg were convicted under this act in 1951 for passing secrets of the atomic bomb to the Soviet Union. They were executed in 1953.

In June 2013, federal prosecutors charged Edward Snowden with violating the Espionage Act for his disclosing scores of documents about government surveillance programs.[265] (Snowden fled the United States and sought refuge in Russia to avoid prosecution.) In July 2013, a military court-martial convicted Army Private First Class Bradley Manning on six counts of violating the Espionage Act for his publicly disclosing hundreds of thousands of military and diplomatic documents.[266]

Clause 2: <u>Punishment for Treason</u>

The Congress shall have Power to declare the Punishment of Treason, but no Attainder of Treason shall work Corruption of Blood, or Forfeiture except during the Life of the Person attainted.

While the previous clause limits treason's definition, this clause limits the possible punishment for those convicted of the crime. Congress can choose the penalty for treason – including death – subject to a limitation set out in this clause.

The prohibition imposed here is that the punishment for treason cannot include "attainder" resulting in "corruption of blood." Attainder is where a person convicted of a crime forfeits his or her property.[267] "Corruption of blood" is a consequence of attainder and is that the convicted person cannot inherit property from an ancestor, keep the property he or she had, or transfer any property to his or her heirs because his or her blood is "tainted" by the crime committed.[268] The

Constitution prohibits this multi-generation method of punishment. And it limited attainders to the criminal's own lifetime. So Congress can make laws prohibiting a traitor from inheriting property from an ancestor; they just can't prevent the property from being passed from the ancestor to the traitor's descendants after his or her death.

Punishment for treason has varied. Martin James Monti received a 25-years sentence for working as a Nazi propaganda broadcaster in Germany during World War II.[269] Robert Henry Best was sentenced to life imprisonment for the same crime.[270] Herbert John Burgman received a 6 to 20 year sentence for making Nazi broadcasts.[271] Tomoya Kawakita, an American-born, dual Japanese/ United States citizen, lost his U.S. citizenship and was sentenced to death in 1948 for having tortured American prisoners of war in Japan during World War II. (President Eisenhower commuted his sentence to life imprisonment in 1953; President Kennedy pardoned Kawakita in 1963 on condition that Kawakita be deported to Japan and never return to the United States.)[272] Kawakita was the last person convicted of treason.[273]

ARTICLE IV—States' Relations and Rights

While Articles I through III concerned the federal government, Article IV focuses on the states. It establishes a basic framework for states' relations with one another, with citizens, and with the federal government.

Section 1—Full Faith and Credit

Full Faith and Credit shall be given in each State to the public Acts, Records, and judicial Proceedings of every other State. And the Congress may by general Laws prescribe the Manner in which such Acts, Records and Proceedings shall be proved, and the Effect thereof.

This section is only one clause in length and is often referred to as the "Full Faith and Credit Clause." It requires each state to recognize and respect every other state's official acts, records, or court proceedings. This is what giving "full faith and credit" means. The clause also gives Congress the power to determine what effect the acts, records, and proceedings of one state will have in another state. So Congress by law, and not the Constitution, determines the effect of these proceedings.

In practice this section prevents people from escaping the law by simply moving from one state to another. For example, a court in Florida orders John Smith to pay alimony to Jane Doe. John Smith does not want to and so he moves to Nevada. Rather than having to follow John Smith to Nevada and file a new case against him there, Jane Doe can instead show the Florida court's order to the courts in Nevada, and the Nevada courts will recognize and enforce the order just as if a Nevada court had issued it.

This clause is the basis for lawful marriages contracted in one state being valid in another. Thus, a man and woman who marry in Minnesota can move to Mississippi and still be considered married. At the same time, Congress acted under this clause to permit states to limit the recognition they give to marriages performed in another state. In 1996, Congress passed, and President Clinton signed, the Defense of Marriage Act.[274] The Act allowed states to not recognize same-sex unions as marriages, even if the unions were considered marriages in other states, so long as their own state law did not recognize same-sex unions as marriages.[275] Congress could pass the law because of this section granting it power, "by general Laws," to determine the effect that one state's acts, records, and proceedings have in another state.

Section 2—States' Obligations

Clause 1: Privileges and Immunities Clause

The Citizens of each State shall be entitled to all Privileges and Immunities of Citizens in the several States.

This clause prevents a state from discriminating against out-of-state citizens in favor of its own citizens. Consequently, a person may live in Connecticut but own and operate a business in New York and file his or her taxes there. This clause permits persons to travel freely between states and pay the same price for goods and services in one state as that state's own citizens do.

There are some instances where states seem to discriminate against non-citizens but do not violate this clause. One example is the tuition charges for public universities. Tuition laws distinguish citizens within a state based on the *duration of residency* rather than between citizens and non-citizens. A person could move to a state and immediately become a citizen of the new state. But until the person lives in that state for a certain amount of time, he or she is charged a higher tuition. This explains why state colleges and universities can charge more tuition for out-of-state residents than for their own state residents. Another example is voting requirements. Citizens from out of state must meet the same voting requirements as the citizens of the state that they enter. Laws regarding voting in elections generally have a residency requirement attached to them (one must live in the state and register to vote at least 30 days before an election, for example). Here too the law discriminates among citizens based on the duration of residence, rather than between citizens and non-citizens, and so it does not violate this clause.

An interesting example of this occurrence is Robert Kennedy's election to the United States Senate from New York, discussed earlier in Article I, section 3. Mr. Kennedy had been serving as the United States Attorney General and lived in Washington, D.C. Only in August of 1964 did he decide to run for the Senate. He then moved to New York to establish his "residence" there (as required by Article I, section 3).[276] But since he did not live in New York long enough to meet the state's residency requirement for elections, he was not able to vote in the election.[277]

Clause 2: <u>Fugitive Extradition</u>

A Person charged in any State with Treason, Felony, or other Crime, who shall flee from Justice, and be found in another State, shall on Demand of the executive Authority of the State

**from which he fled, be delivered up, to be
removed to the State having Jurisdiction of the
Crime.**

This "Extradition Clause" serves as the basis for
interstate rendition (or "extradition" as it is commonly
known). Extradition is that if a person commits a crime in one
state and then goes to another, the second state "surrenders"
(sends back) the fugitive to the state in which he or she
committed the crime. A person can be extradited only after the
governor of the state where the fugitive committed the crime
requests the fugitive's return. Just like Article IV, section 1,
this clause prevents a person from escaping the law by moving
to another state.

Extradition occurs on a regular basis even though many
might not be aware of it. An extradition that drew national
attention occurred in 2016 when Louisiana sent real estate heir
Robert Durst to California to stand trial for murder. Durst had
been the focus of a documentary regarding the disappearance
of his first wife and the mysterious killing of one of his female
friends 15 years earlier. During his final interview, Durst took
a restroom break with a microphone still attached and
recording. He then said in the restroom what appeared to be a
confession to having killed his friend in California. Authorities
in California subsequently filed charges against Durst and
requested his extradition.

The *interstate* extradition referred to here is very
different from *international* extradition in which the United
States requests fugitives from or surrenders them to foreign
countries. International extradition occurs only after the
countries sign a treaty setting up the process.

Clause 3: Fugitives from Labor

**[No Person held to Service or Labour in one
State, under the Laws thereof, escaping into
another, shall, in Consequence of any Law or
Regulation therein, be discharged from such
Service or Labour, but shall be delivered up on
Claim of the Party to whom such Service or
Labour may be due.]**

127

This clause also deals with extradition. Here, it concerns slaves who may have escaped from a state permitting slavery into one that prohibited it. The clause gave slaveholders the right to demand the return of fugitive slaves even from states where the escaping slave was considered free. But the clause did not provide the way for slave extradition to happen. That process occurred only after Congress passed the Fugitive Slave Act of 1793. That Act—not the Constitution—made it a crime to protect escaped slaves or to interfere with their capture.

The Thirteenth Amendment made this clause obsolete by abolishing slavery and involuntary servitude.

Again, the Constitution does not use the term "slave" or "slavery." The Framers did this to avoid institutionalizing or sanctioning the practice.[278] The term "Fugitive Slave Clause" developed long after the Convention.

Section 3—Admission of New States and Power Over Federal Property

Clause 1: Rules for Admission of New States

New States may be admitted by the Congress into this Union; but no new State shall be formed or erected within the Jurisdiction of any other State; nor any State be formed by the Junction of two or more States, or Parts of States, without the Consent of the Legislatures of the States concerned as well as of the Congress.

Here, Congress is given the power to set conditions for the admission of new states. This power has two limitations: (1) state legislatures must consent if part of their land is being used to form a state, and (2) Congress must consent to using part of the state as well. Thirty-seven states (all states but the 13 original colonies) have come into existence by Congress acting under this clause. The conditions for newly admitted states have varied from state to state. For instance, Alaska was given twenty-five years to select lands for state ownership (all land belonged to the federal government prior to statehood).[279]

Hawaii, Texas, and Vermont were independent countries before joining the Union as opposed to being federal territories like the other new states. They had to give up their sovereignty over their lands and, for Hawaii and Texas, their coastal water. Further, Texas, unlike any other state, had as part of its admission to the Union the ability to split into as many as five states.[280] If Texas were to invoke this privilege, the Texas state legislature would have to agree to the division since this clause prohibits a state being formed from another state without the original state's consent.

There are five instances in American history where new states were formed from other states. These include: Kentucky (from Virginia) in 1792; Tennessee (from North Carolina) in 1796; Maine (from Massachusetts) in 1820; and West Virginia (from Virginia) in 1863. All of the original states granted permission. West Virginia's creation occurred during the Civil War after Virginia's state legislature in Richmond had rebelled and joined the Confederacy. A separate body claiming to be the legitimate state legislature of Virginia consented to West Virginia's creation. Congress recognized the body as Virginia's legitimate state government and then admitted West Virginia on condition that it include in its constitution a provision for the gradual abolition of slavery (Virginia was a slave-holding state).[281]

For a time, Congress acted under this clause to ensure that a new "free state" (one that prohibited slavery) was admitted to the Union with every new state that permitted slavery. The purpose was to keep the Senate balanced between slaveholding and non-slaveholding states rather than tip the balance in favor of states permitting slavery. This explains the nearly paired admissions of Indiana in 1816 as a free state with Mississippi in 1817 as a state permitting slavery, Maine in 1820 as a free state with Missouri in 1821 as a state permitting slavery, and Arkansas in 1836 as a state permitting slavery with Michigan in 1837 as a free state.

Clause 2: <u>Federal Property Clause</u>

The Congress shall have Power to dispose of and make all needful Rules and Regulations respecting the Territory or other Property

belonging to the United States; and nothing in this Constitution shall be so construed as to Prejudice any Claims of the United States, or of any particular State.

Congress has complete control over land belonging to the federal government, wherever that land may be. Today, nearly 30% of the total land within the United States is owned and controlled by the federal government![282] Most of the federally owned land is located in the Western United States. For example, the federal government owns over 81% of Nevada, 66.5% of Utah, 61% of Alaska, and 47% of California.[283] By comparison, federal land holdings in Connecticut, Iowa, Kansas, New York, and Rhode Island are all less than 1% of the total land in each of those states.[284]

Because Congress controls so much land in some states, Congressional regulation under this clause sometimes results in significant tensions between states with large amounts of federal lands and the federal government. The citizens in states with significant federal land holdings argue that most members of Congress and their constituents do not have to deal with the Congressional regulations and so do not understand the issues associated with the land. A prominent example centers on the creation of the Grand Staircase-Escalante National Monument in southern Utah in 1996. The monument's immense size (almost 2 million acres, or an area double the size of Rhode Island) outraged locals who lost the opportunity to see their average annual wage and salary earnings nearly double through the mining industry because new federal regulations inhibited resource extraction.[285]

Congress also has the power to govern territories belonging to the United States. Today, this includes Puerto Rico, Guam, American Samoa, and the U.S. Virgin Islands. Congress acted under this clause to annex these territories. Congress granted Cuba and the Philippines independence after the United States had gained these territories following the Spanish-American War.

Perhaps one of the most remarkable and popular Congressional actions under this clause was the creation of Yellowstone National Park in 1872. The park was the first of its kind anywhere in the world. Since then, Congress exercised the authority given here to create 58 additional parks across 27 states and two territories. These range from well-known parks like the Grand Canyon in Arizona and Great Smoky Mountains in North Carolina and Tennessee to others like Lake Clark in Alaska and Congaree in South Carolina. The newest is Pinnacles National Park in California, which Congress created in January 2013.

Section 4—Obligations of the United States to the States

Clause 1: Guarantee of a Republican Form of Government

The United States shall guarantee to every State in this Union a Republican Form of Government, and shall protect each of them against Invasion; and on Application of the Legislature, or of the Executive (when the Legislature cannot be convened) against domestic Violence.

This clause makes a guarantee to states of a "republican form of government" without defining what that is. To understand what this clause suggests, think of the pledge of allegiance. We pledge allegiance "to the *republic* for which [the flag] stands." In other words, the federal government is a republic, one in which the power rests with the people but is exercised by elected officials who are responsible to the people. So the federal government is a "republican" form of government. This clause then entitles states to the same form of representative government, effectively prohibiting monarchies, aristocracies, dictatorships, or other non-representative forms of government.

A second obligation given the federal government is protecting the states from invasion. So if one state is attacked or otherwise invaded, the federal government has to respond and defend it.

The third obligation towards the states found here is protection against domestic violence. A good example of this occurred in 1992 when California governor Pete Wilson requested federal assistance to quell the Los Angeles riots. In response, President George H.W. Bush ordered 4,000 active duty soldiers and Marines from Fort Ord and Camp Pendleton to patrol the streets of Los Angeles to stop the violence and restore order.

ARTICLE V—<u>Amendment of the Constitution</u>

Article V concerns the Constitution itself. It sets out the method for amending (modifying) the Constitution. The inclusion of this provision highlights the Framers' recognition that times and circumstances would change and require that aspects of the Constitution be altered to fit those changes. This article thus signifies the genius of the document – that it was meant to endure over time and be peacefully changed without revolutions or otherwise abandoning the Constitution and its form of government. Further, the process preserves the rights of all citizens by requiring not only a super-majority of Congress to pass the amendments, but a super-super majority of the states to approve the amendments as well. So rather than being a "living" document, the Constitution is an unfinished document that the people can continually modify.

The Congress, whenever two thirds of both Houses shall deem it necessary, shall propose Amendments to this Constitution, or, on the Application of the Legislatures of two thirds of the several States, shall call a Convention for proposing Amendments, which, in either Case, shall be valid to all Intents and Purposes, as Part of this Constitution, when ratified by the Legislatures of three fourths of the several States, or by Conventions in three fourths thereof, as the one or the other Mode of Ratification may be proposed by the Congress; [Provided that no Amendment which may be made prior to the Year One thousand eight hundred and eight shall in any Manner affect the first and fourth Clauses in the Ninth Section of the first Article;] and that no State, without its Consent, shall be deprived of its equal Suffrage in the Senate.

One of the shortest articles in the Constitution, Article V creates a simple procedure for amending the Constitution: proposal and ratification. There are two avenues for proposing amendments, and there are two methods for ratification. These are each explained below. Finally, this article prohibits certain amendments.

The focus here is on the amendment process itself as laid out in this article. Each of the amendments to the Constitution resulting from this process will be addressed later.

Proposal

The first approach for proposing amendments is by two-thirds of both the House of Representatives and the Senate voting in favor of an amendment. Unless an amendment achieves this threshold vote, it is not considered a "proposed" amendment that may then be ratified.

The second method is when Congress calls a national convention at the request of two-thirds of the states. No amendment has ever been proposed in this manner, although states have tried but fallen short of the number required. For example, Congress would have been forced to call a convention for an amendment concerning a constitutional limitation on income tax rates if only two more states had petitioned Congress to do so.[286] And it would have had to call a convention for the direct election of senators if only one more state had petitioned Congress on the issue.[287] (Congress made this latter issue moot by finally proposing an amendment for the direct election of senators that became the Seventeenth Amendment when ratified by the states.)

Members of Congress have introduced countless Constitutional amendments over the past two hundred years. Some estimates place this figure near 12,000 throughout U.S. history.[288] Yet, Congress has "proposed" these amendments by the required two-thirds vote only 33 times.

Ratification

The ratification process takes one of two forms. It is either done by approval of the state legislatures or by a convention in each state. Congress decides which of the two ratification methods will be used. To date, all amendments except the 21st (repealing prohibition) have been sent to the legislatures for approval. Congress required the Twenty-first Amendment to be ratified by state conventions.

State legislatures ratify or reject the proposed amendments by a vote just as they would with a regular piece of state legislation. State conventions, on the other hand, bypass state legislatures. The concept is that the general population elects delegates to the state convention, and the delegates then vote on the proposed amendment. So the general population elects persons other than their state legislators to vote on an issue.

The president is entirely absent from the amendment process. Nothing is included in this Article about approval from the president. Other than possibly prompting some members of Congress to vote for an amendment, the president's support is meaningless since an amendment requires a two-thirds vote in each legislative chamber (a veto-proof majority) and then a three-fourths majority of the states. So while President George W. Bush's support for the Federal Marriage Amendment may have helped him win votes in his 2004 reelection campaign, his support had no bearing on the desired amendment going forward.

Of the 33 amendments officially proposed by Congress, only 27 have been ratified. Four of these six are still pending before the states, meaning that they could still be ratified. The other two can no longer be passed by the states because the time for their ratification expired by each of the amendment's terms (*i.e.* the amendments required ratification within a specific time frame that has come and gone). Those four that are still pending and could be ratified include:

1. Congressional Apportionment Amendment – mandating one representative in the House for every 50,000 people (proposed in 1789)
2. Titles of Nobility Amendment – revoking the citizenship of anyone accepting a foreign title of nobility (proposed in 1810)
3. Corwin Amendment – forbidding subsequent amendments to the Constitution that would permit Congress to "abolish or interfere" with the states' "domestic institutions . . . including that of persons

held to labor or service" (*i.e.*, slavery) (proposed in 1861 to prevent Southern secession)
4. Child Labor Amendment – granting Congress power to regulate labor for persons under age 18 (proposed in 1926)

The two proposed amendments that have expired by their specific terms are the Equal Rights Amendment and the D.C. Voting Rights Amendment. The former expired in 1979 after 35 of the 38 required states ratified it; the latter expired in 1985 after receiving only sixteen ratifications.

Prohibited Amendments

The Framers made three prohibitions to the amendment process. Two are obsolete and one prohibition remains.

The first prohibition prevented an amendment affecting the trans-Atlantic slave trade before 1808 (the earliest date specified Article I, section 9, clause 1 for terminating the practice). The second concerned direct taxes under Article I, section 9, clause 4. That clause guaranteed direct taxes being applied according to the 3/5 compromise. These two prohibitions ensured that the earlier compromises regarding slavery could not be undone before 1808; thus assuaging Southern fears that the Northern states would immediately act to alter the practice once the new Constitution was in effect.

The final amendment prohibition relates to equal representation in the Senate. It prevents any amendment that affects a state having the same number of senators as all other states unless the affected state accepts such a proposal. So the Constitution itself prohibits a super majority of states from undoing the Great Compromise (equal representation in the Senate; proportional representation in the House). Consider what could happen without this prohibition: three-fourths of the states could agree to decrease the number of senators from one particular state. Or three fourths of the states could band together to increase the number of senators from their states, but not do the same for the remaining one-fourth. This ban keeps such scenarios from occurring; states must always have equal numbers of senators unless they consent to unequal representation.

ARTICLE VI—<u>Supremacy of the Constitution</u>

To recap the Constitution to this point, Articles I through III create the federal government, Article IV makes guarantees to the states, and Article V concerns the method for amending the Constitution. Here, Article VI has clauses relating to the federal Constitution's preeminence, the assumption of debts incurred during the American Revolution and under the Articles of Confederation, and a prohibition of religious tests for public office.

Clause 1: <u>Validity of Prior Debts and Engagements</u>

All Debts contracted and Engagements entered into, before the Adoption of this Constitution, shall be as valid against the United States under this Constitution, as under the Confederation.

America's national government had borrowed millions of dollars from foreign governments and private financiers to fight the Revolutionary War. While operating under the Articles of Confederation, the nation promised to pay these debts under the 1783 Treaty of Paris that ended the conflict with Britain. As simple as it is, the Framers inserted this clause to reassure creditors that the United States would not use the new government to avoid paying old debts. Doing so bolstered the country's credit and made it easier for the nation to borrow money in the future.

This clause refers to debt incurred *prior to* the Constitution's adoption. The current national debt results from Congress's power in Article I, section 8, to borrow money on the nation's credit.

Clause 2: <u>The Supremacy Clause</u>

The Constitution, and the Laws of the United States which shall be made in Pursuance thereof; and all Treaties made, or which shall be made, under the Authority of the United States, shall be the supreme Law of the Land; and the Judges in every State shall be bound thereby,

136

**any Thing in the Constitution or Laws of any
State to the Contrary notwithstanding.**

This "Supremacy Clause" makes the Constitution the
supreme (highest) law in the United States. The clause also
makes it so that laws passed by Congress, as well as treaties
entered into by the United States and approved by the Senate,
preempt (or "trump") state laws and constitutions.

It is incorrect to think that this supremacy gives the
federal government unlimited power to legislate. The federal
government has only the powers given to it by the
Constitution. So it is only when the federal government acts
on those enumerated powers that the federal law preempts
conflicting state laws. Think of this division by the following
diagram:

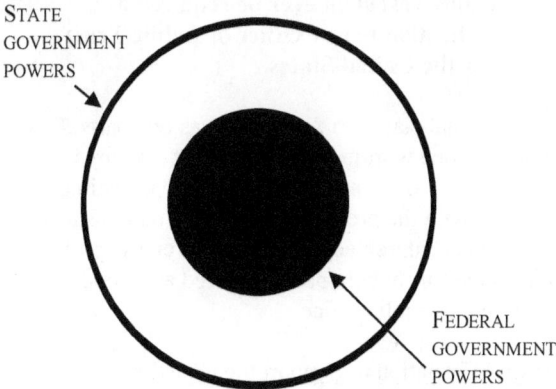

STATE
GOVERNMENT
POWERS

FEDERAL
GOVERNMENT
POWERS

The larger circle represents all possible areas in which a
government could legislate, and here signifies the powers
given by the people to their state governments. The smaller,
darker circle represents the powers expressly granted to the
federal government in the Constitution. The federal
government cannot make laws in areas outside of the dark
circle. Since the state government powers overlap with some
federal government powers, a state government could legislate
in some areas covered by the smaller circle (the federal
government). But when the federal government chooses to
legislate under its powers, its laws trump any conflicting state
laws in the same area because of this clause. And remember

137

that Article I, section 10, prohibits states from passing some laws regardless of whether the federal government has chosen to legislate or not.

Finally, this clause requires state court judges to enforce the Constitution and national laws over state laws and state constitutions when there is a conflict between them.

Clause 3: <u>Oath of Office and No Religious Test</u>

The Senators and Representatives before mentioned, and the Members of the several State Legislatures, and all executive and judicial Officers, both of the United States and of the several States, shall be bound by Oath or Affirmation, to support this Constitution; but no religious Test shall ever be required as a Qualification to any Office or public Trust under the United States.

This final clause in Article VI has two parts. First, it requires anyone working in government – at any level – to take an oath or affirmation to support the Constitution. Combined with the previous clause, this part ensures Constitutional supremacy. Second, this clause prohibits any religious tests from being administered as a condition to serving in any public office.

<u>Oath or Affirmation to Support the Constitution</u>
All members of the legislative, executive, and judicial branches in both federal and state governments must take an oath of allegiance to the Constitution. This includes not only elected officials like senators, representatives, governors, and state legislators, but also all federal and state civil servants (employees) and attorneys admitted to practice before state and federal courts.

Unlike the presidential oath discussed in Article II, the oath to be taken under this clause is not set out in the Constitution. The First Congress followed up on this Constitutional requirement in 1789 through the "Oath Act," the first act ever passed by the new national government. The Oath Act provided a simple, fourteen-word oath: "I do

138

solemnly swear (or affirm) that I will support the Constitution of the United States."[289] But the Civil War prompted Congress to rework the oath in 1862 to be more robust.[290] After various modifications in the ensuing years, Congress in 1884 adopted the oath used today:

> I, [name], do solemnly swear (or affirm) that I will support and defend the Constitution of the United States against all enemies, foreign and domestic; that I will bear true faith and allegiance to the same; that I take this obligation freely, without any mental reservation or purpose of evasion; and that I will well and faithfully discharge the duties of the office on which I am about to enter. So help me God.[291]

Federal legislative officials, civil servants in the executive branch, and military officers all take this particular oath. The vice president also takes this oath (the office of the vice president falls under Article I, the legislative branch). So do members of the judicial branch. Federal judges also take a second oath:

> I, [name], do solemnly swear (or affirm) that I will administer justice without respect to persons, and do equal right to the poor and to the rich, and that I will faithfully and impartially discharge and perform all the duties incumbent upon me as [office] under the Constitution and laws of the United States. So help me God.[292]

The reason the Constitution permits persons to either swear or affirm their allegiance to the Constitution is because certain religious groups, such as Quakers and Mennonites, oppose swearing oaths. (Quakers do not swear oaths based on their understanding of the Bible's injunction in Matthew 5:34 to "swear not at all.") So this language gives everyone the ability to participate in the national government without violating their religious convictions by swearing an oath. Further, this language on oaths relates to the second part of this clause prohibiting religious tests.

Prohibition on Religious Tests

This "No Religious Test Clause" prohibits religious tests for public servants. Yet it does not define the term "religious test." The Framers nonetheless understood its meaning based on their own experience with England and with what occurred in many American states at the Founding.

In 1672, the British Parliament enacted the Test Act. The act required all persons holding public office to receive the sacrament according to the Church of England's rites within three months of taking office and also to take an oath declaring a belief against transubstantiation in Holy Communion. (Transubstantiation is the religious doctrine that sacramental bread and wine literally turn into Jesus Christ's body and blood.) The act had the effect of excluding Catholics and non-Anglicans from public office.[293] In America, religious tests were also rampant at the Founding with roughly 10 of the 13 states having them. For example, New York required public officials to disavow allegiance to a foreign prince (*i.e,* the Pope) in civil and ecclesiastical matters, thereby excluding Catholics from office. Five states—Delaware, Maryland, Massachusetts, North Carolina, and Pennsylvania—had constitutional provisions requiring public officials to swear a belief in Christianity.[294] And Georgia, New Hampshire, New Jersey, and South Carolina specifically prohibited non-Protestants from holding office.[295] In essence, these laws and state constitutional provisions acted as a "test" for persons wishing to hold public office because they mandated that the individual subscribe to certain beliefs. Those who did not hold those beliefs were ineligible to serve. This clause changed that.

ARTICLE VII—Ratification of the Constitution

This final article, only one sentence in length, provides the process by which the Constitution took effect.

> **The Ratification of the Conventions of nine States, shall be sufficient for the Establishment of this Constitution between the States so ratifying the Same.**

This provision departed from the Articles of Confederation's requirement of unanimous consent by all 13 states and required instead approval from only nine of the thirteen for the new government to be established. Note that it required state conventions for ratification rather than approval by Congress under the Articles or even by the existing state legislatures. Doing so ensured that the Constitution's authority came from the people by way of representatives that they elected specifically to approve or reject the charter.

Despite the Constitutional Convention's success, ratification was not guaranteed. Debates raged throughout the union, with several articulate and prominent citizens advocating for and against the new Constitution. Those favoring ratification, such as James Madison and Alexander Hamilton, were known as "Federalists"; those opposing ratification, like Patrick Henry and New York Governor George Clinton, were "Antifederalists". Beginning in October 1787, Madison, Hamilton, and John Jay responded to Antifederalist criticism by writing a series of newspaper essays in favor of the new Constitution. These essays were later compiled into a two-volume work called *The Federalist Papers.* The arguments favoring ratification prevailed.

Delaware became the first state to approve the Constitution, ratifying it on December 7, 1787, less than three months after the Convention. Pennsylvania, New Jersey, Georgia, and Connecticut soon followed. Massachusetts initially opposed the Constitution because it did not guarantee protection of basic rights such as freedom of religion and speech, and it also failed to reserve undelegated powers to the states. Statesmen in Virginia and New York shared the sentiment. Because of the impasse, the Constitution's proponents soon agreed to immediately propose amendments providing these safeguards if Massachusetts and other states would ratify the document. Massachusetts agreed to this compromise and ratified the document in February 1788, with Maryland and South Carolina ratifying it shortly thereafter. New Hampshire became the ninth ratification on June 21, 1788. Under the terms of this Article, the new government became effective after this event, and it was determined that the new government would begin March 4, 1789. Virginia's and New York's ratifications followed shortly after New Hampshire's.

Because of the earlier compromise on ratification, the first Congress adopted 12 amendments to the Constitution in September 1789 and sent them to the states. The states then adopted 10 of the 12; these 10 adopted amendments are known as the "Bill of Rights." North Carolina then ratified the Constitution in November of that same year (1789). Rhode Island, which had rejected the Constitution in a popular referendum in 1788, became the last of the thirteen original colonies to join the United States when it ratified the document in May 1790.

At the end of the Constitution, just below the text of Article VII, delegates to the Constitutional Convention signed the document. They noted immediately before their signatures that the proposed Constitution was done "by the unanimous consent of the states," suggesting that the Convention was done in accordance with the Articles of Confederation, which required unanimity. The delegates, representing their states, unanimously consented to the proposal that each state could "opt out" of the Articles of Confederation to join a new union with an entirely new form of government. Article VII makes clear that that new form of government would be binding only on those states who had opted out of the Articles of Confederation and agreed to the new union; those states who had not done so would remain bound by the Articles of Confederation. So it was that the new government under the Constitution first became operative without two of the states having joined.

done in Convention by the Unanimous Consent of the States present the Seventeenth Day of September in the Year of our Lord one thousand seven hundred and Eighty seven and of the Independence of the United States of America the Twelfth In witness whereof We have hereunto subscribed our Names,

George Washington – President and deputy from Virginia

Attest: William Jackson Secretary

Delaware	New Hampshire
George Read	John Langdon
Gunning Bedford, Jr.	Nicholas Gilman
John Dickinson	
Richard Bassett	Massachusetts
Jacob Broom	Nathaniel Gorham
	Rufus King
Maryland	
James McHenry	Connecticut
Daniel of St. Thomas Jenifer	William Samuel Johnson
Daniel Carroll	Roger Sherman
Virginia	New York
John Blair	Alexander Hamilton
James Madison, Jr.	
	New Jersey
North Carolina	William Livingston
William Blount	David Brearley
Richard Dobbs Spaight	William Paterson
Hugh Williamson	Jonathan Dayton
South Carolina	Pennsylvania
John Rutledge	Benjamin Franklin
Charles Cotesworth Pinckney	Thomas Mifflin
Charles Pinckney	Robert Morris
Pierce Butler	George Clymer
	Thomas FitzSimons
Georgia	Jared Ingersoll
William Few	James Wilson
Abraham Baldwin	Gouverneur Morris

Notably absent from the signatures are any delegates from Rhode Island. The state completely boycotted the Constitutional Convention by refusing to send any delegate.

Article V shows that amendment to the Constitution is a natural and expected occurrence. Twenty-seven amendments have been made to the Constitution since its ratification. The first 10 of these, known as the Bill of Rights, are perhaps the Constitution's most celebrated and well known features.

The Bill of Rights is so named because the amendments protect a number of personal freedoms, limit the government's power in judicial and other proceedings, and make clear that powers not granted to the federal government are reserved to the states and the people. These 10 amendments were added all at once in 1791, just four years after the Constitution's creation. In some way, they can be considered part of the original Constitution because of their rapid proposal and ratification so soon after the new government began to operate, as well as the circumstances that prompted their creation as discussed in Article VII.

Several of the larger states would not ratify the Constitution because they did not feel that it secured an individual citizen's rights. In fact, George Mason, who helped draft the Constitution as a delegate from Virginia, refused to sign the finished Constitution because it did not contain a declaration of rights similar to the Virginia Declaration of Rights he authored in 1776. Larger states like Massachusetts, Virginia, and New York agreed to ratify the Constitution only after the Constitution's advocates promised to amend the Constitution to guarantee individual rights.

True to the promise made by Federalists during the Constitution's ratification debates, Congress passed 12 proposed amendments in September 1789 and submitted them to the states for ratification. The preamble to the proposed amendments stated:

Congress of the United States
begun and held at the City of New-York, on
Wednesday the fourth of March, one thousand
seven hundred and eighty nine.

144

THE Conventions of a number of the States, having at the time of their adopting the Constitution, expressed a desire, in order to prevent misconstruction or abuse of its powers, that further declaratory and restrictive clauses should be added: And as extending the ground of public confidence in the Government, will best ensure the beneficent ends of its institution.

RESOLVED by the Senate and House of Representatives of the United States of America, in Congress assembled, two thirds of both Houses concurring, that the following Articles be proposed to the Legislatures of the several States, as amendments to the Constitution of the United States, all, or any of which Articles, when ratified by three fourths of the said Legislatures, to be valid to all intents and purposes, as part of the said Constitution; viz.

ARTICLES in addition to, and Amendment of the Constitution of the United States of America, proposed by Congress, and ratified by the Legislatures of the several States, pursuant to the fifth Article of the original Constitution.

The required three-fourths of the states ratified 10 of the 12 by December 1791. The ratified "Bill of Rights" became part of the Constitution at that time and is discussed below, amendment by amendment. The two proposed but unratified amendments concerned the number of constituents required for each representative and limits on Congressional compensation.

AMENDMENT I—<u>Religious and Political Freedom</u>

Congress shall make no law respecting an establishment of religion, or prohibiting the free exercise thereof; or abridging the freedom of speech, or of the press; or the right of the people

145

**peaceably to assemble, and to petition the
Government for a redress of grievances.**

This single amendment concerns five fundamental
freedoms: freedom of religion, freedom of speech, freedom of
the press, freedom of assembly, and freedom to petition the
government. Consequently, this single sentence, or rather parts
of it, are known as the "Establishment Clause," the "Free
Exercise Clause," and the "Free Speech Clause."

<u>Freedom of Religion</u>

> *Congress shall make no law respecting an
> establishment of religion, or prohibiting the free
> exercise thereof;*

The first part of this phrase is known as the
"Establishment Clause" because of the words "establishment
of religion." What might be an otherwise straightforward
phrase has become a flashpoint for contention and has led to
two predominant interpretations.

Some take this clause to merely prevent the federal
government from establishing a national religion or otherwise
preferring one religion over another. Supporters of this
interpretation, often called "accomodationists," point to
actions taken by the Framers recognizing religion and making
it a part of public life. An example is what occurred the day
after the House of Representatives voted to adopt the Bill of
Rights – including this clause – in the fall of 1789. That day,
Representative Elias Boudinot of New Jersey introduced a
resolution requesting President George Washington to issue a
"Thanksgiving Day" proclamation because Boudinot "could
not think of letting the session pass over without offering an
opportunity to all the citizens of the United States of joining
with one voice, in returning to Almighty God their sincere
thanks for the many blessings he had poured down upon
them."[296] President Washington subsequently made the
proclamation and so began the tradition of a Thanksgiving
Day proclamation by almost every president since.

Others believe, however, that the clause requires a strict
separation of government from religious affairs. These

"separationists" use this clause to advocate for either a general absence of religion in the public sphere or for the complete prohibition of government recognition of religion, believing that recognizing religion would "establish" it. For support, many separationists cite President Thomas Jefferson's January 1, 1802, letter to the Danbury Baptist Association of Connecticut in which he stated that the clause built "a wall of separation between church and State."[297] President Jefferson's letter came in response to a complaint the Association made concerning the lack of full religious liberty Baptists enjoyed in the state of Connecticut; the state legislature had levied a tax that forced Baptists to subsidize and provide monetary support to Congregationalists.[298] The Association had previously waged a campaign to rescind the tax, and its letter to Jefferson could have been part of that campaign.[299]

The accommodationist view largely prevailed from the Founding through the end of World War II.[300] Indeed, Jefferson's "wall of separation" phrase appeared in only one Supreme Court opinion during that time (in 1878).[301] But in 1947, a divided Supreme Court resurrected Jefferson's "wall of separation" phrase in one of its decisions and effectively propelled a more "separationist" view among courts and elected officials alike. Any government support or preference for religion was seen as violating this clause. The view soon ascended to dominance; it served as the impetus to drive religious displays such as crèches from public property and prayer from public schools in the 1980s and 1990s through today.

The second part of the first amendment's guarantee of religious freedom, the "Free Exercise Clause," also has two major interpretations. One interpretation is that Congress can pass laws effectively hindering religious activity so long as the purpose behind those laws is not to target a particular religious practice. The other view is that Congress may not limit or burden religious activity unless the government has a "compelling interest" in doing so. Both interpretations are based on the premise that Congress can interfere with religious practices, not with religious beliefs. The latter interpretation was dominant from the Founding until 1990 when the Supreme Court adopted the former view. Congress responded in 1993 by passing the Religious Freedom Restoration Act.[302]

The act's purpose was to require the government to show a compelling interest when interfering with religious free exercise.[303]

Freedoms of Speech and Press

abridging the freedom of speech, or of the press;

This "Free Speech Clause" ensures that persons can express themselves free from government restraint. Prior to the American Revolution, the British government actively curbed this freedom. Colonists who spoke openly against the British government could be imprisoned for doing so.[304] The Free Speech Clause ensured that the federal government could not do the same. Citizens would be able to freely speak their mind.

The freedoms of speech and press have never been absolute, either before or after the Free Speech Clause's adoption. Certain forms of speech are considered unprotected by this clause due to the harm they cause, including: lying in court (perjury), defamation (false oral or written statements), threats, blackmail, bribery, obscenity, child pornography, and speech containing copyrighted material. Such speech may be punishable by the injured party (in cases of defamation or copyright infringement) or the government (perjury, blackmail, etc.).

Freedom of Assembly

or the right of the people peaceably to assemble,

Often overlooked, the freedom of assembly directly relates to the prior freedoms protected by this amendment— freedom of religion and freedom of speech. Freedom of assembly permits members of religious groups to congregate for worship services. It also permits people to organize together to speak out against government policies or to otherwise lawfully advocate their ideals.

This freedom's guarantee permitted women's suffragists to organize conventions and parades promoting their cause. It did the same for Martin Luther King, Jr.'s marches during the

148

Civil Rights Movement. The "Occupy Wall Street" movement similarly relied on this guarantee to congregate in public parks in 2011 and 2012. ("Occupy Wall Street" is the name given to a movement protesting various issues, including perceived corporate influence on politicians and government, corruption, and social and economic inequality.) This guarantee likewise permitted organized protests to Donald Trump's election that occurred in late 2016 and early 2017.

Freedom of assembly also permits persons to organize and advocate ideas considered unpopular or repugnant. For example, this freedom prevented Skokie, Illinois, a town that was home to many Holocaust survivors, from prohibiting a march through town by the American Nazi Party in the 1970s. And in 1992, it allowed the Ku Klux Klan to hold a rally in Denver, Colorado, on the Martin Luther King, Jr. holiday.

This freedom is not absolute. The Constitution mandates that Congress cannot interfere with *peaceful* assemblies. Persons who assemble and act out with violence, such as rioters, forfeit this freedom.

Freedom to Petition the Government

> *and to petition the Government for a redress of grievances.*

This freedom often goes unnoticed, but its inclusion is grounded in the Framers' experience. Before the Revolution, British law allowed American colonists to petition the monarch. But King George III and his government ignored the colonists' petitions that protested government actions affecting colonists' rights. In fact, the British government's failure to address these petitions was one of the reasons given in the Declaration of Independence to justify independence:

> In every stage of these Oppressions We have Petitioned for Redress in the most humble terms: Our repeated Petitions have been answered only by repeated injury. A Prince whose character is thus marked by every act which may define a Tyrant, is unfit to be the ruler of a free people.

149

Guaranteeing this freedom ensures that citizens are able to communicate with those who run their government. Citizens may petition all branches of government—legislative, executive, and judicial. But those in government do not have to respond to citizens' petitions.

Common petition methods include picketing, telephone and email campaigns, public demonstrations, signing ballot initiatives, filing lawsuits, and hiring lobbyists (agents to represent one's interests). The general public frequently views lobbyists negatively because many lobbyists are highly paid professionals who often secure large campaign contributions for elected officials. This sometimes suggests that officials favor professional lobbyists' interests in return for additional campaign contributions. (Any person petitioning government can be considered a "lobbyist;" some lobbyists are volunteers.) Because of concerns that lobbyists use money and favors to improperly influence elected officials, the federal government regulates lobbying activity. Paid lobbyists must register with each chamber of Congress and regularly report their lobbying activity. According to the Center for Responsive Politics, there were roughly 11,100 registered federal lobbyists in 2016, down from a high of nearly 15,000 in 2007.[305]

Finally, there are numerous organizations that petition the government for specific issues or interests. The National Rifle Association petitions for legislation favoring gun ownership. The American-Israel Public Affairs Committee petitions for strong U.S.-Israel ties. Mothers Against Drunk Driving petitions for strict laws against alcohol use and driving. And the AARP petitions for legislation benefitting persons age 50 and over. These are just a few of the more prominent lobbying organizations among the scores actively petitioning the federal government.

AMENDMENT II—<u>Right to Keep and Bear Arms</u>

A well regulated Militia, being necessary to the security of a free State, the right of the people to keep and bear Arms, shall not be infringed.

This amendment's unusual phrasing gives rise to various interpretations of its meaning. One view holds that this amendment secures the right to own and use firearms only to members of a state militia. This interpretation derives from the amendment's initial words ("a well regulated militia . . ."). Another interpretation is that the amendment secures each citizen's right to own and use firearms, regardless of militia participation. This view rests on the belief that a militia is made up of ordinary citizens who have an inherent to right bear arms in self-defense as well as to deter government tyranny. After all, proponents of this view argue, the Framers participated in a war against a tyrannical British government and had used their own weapons in doing so. The latter interpretation is one generally followed by courts.[306]

AMENDMENT III—Quartering of Soldiers

No Soldier shall, in time of peace be quartered in any house, without the consent of the Owner, nor in time of war, but in a manner to be prescribed by law.

This amendment may seem oddly placed in the Bill of Rights because of its subject matter—soldiers living in private homes. Immediately before the Revolutionary War, the British government passed the Quartering Act of 1774. The act authorized British soldiers to be stationed or lodged in private citizens' homes without the owners' consent. Scores of soldiers did so, much to the owners' and colonists' chagrin. In fact, the quartering troops among the colonists was one of the grievances cited in the Declaration of Independence.

So this amendment is an understandable response to those actions. It prohibits such invasions of privacy during peacetime. During times of war, however, soldiers may be quartered in private residences if Congress passes a law for that purpose, and only according to the terms of that law.

AMENDMENT IV—Unreasonable Search and Seizure

The right of the people to be secure in their persons, houses, papers, and effects, against unreasonable searches and seizures, shall not be violated, and no warrants shall issue, but upon

151

**probable cause, supported by oath or
affirmation, and particularly describing the
place to be searched, and the persons or things
to be seized.**

The Fourth Amendment protects persons and their
property against government intrusion. In particular, it
prohibits "unreasonable" searches and seizures of persons and
property. A "seizure" of a person occurs when he or she is not
free to leave a location. A "seizure" of property occurs when
there is interference with the owner's right to use or control
the property.

This amendment also requires particularized warrants.
Requiring particularized warrants differed from the general
warrants (known as "writs of assistance") the British
government imposed on the colonists following the Excise
Tax of 1754. Writs of assistance permitted British authorities
to detain and question colonists or enter their homes and
conduct extensive searches in hopes of finding some legal
violation without having previously had any evidence of
wrongdoing.

This amendment was intended to prevent the new
government from repeating the same injustice. It requires law
enforcement officials wanting to search a person's private
property to first have probable cause, meaning enough
evidence to suggest that the search will reveal criminal activity
or contraband but less evidence than needed for a conviction.
So the officials must present specific evidence to a judge
under oath or affirmation (*i.e.,* the official could be punished
for providing false information in support of the warrant). If
the judge determines that probable cause exists, then he or she
must issue a warrant specifically identifying the place to be
searched and the evidence that is expected to be found and
seized at that location.

Some interpret the amendment's requirement of
particularized warrants to mean that a search or seizure is
unreasonable if done without a warrant. Others believe that
warrants are separate from the amendment's search and
seizure restrictions. They contend that searches and seizures
must simply be "reasonable" and a warrant is not always
required for these activities (the amendment prohibits only

unreasonable searches). Either way, there is support for both interpretations as the judicial officer hearing the matter decides whether a search or seizure is unreasonable on a case-by-case basis.

This amendment's protection against unreasonable searches and seizures sharply came into focus in 2013 after Edward Snowden revealed the federal government's massive intelligence gathering operations. Snowden revealed that the National Security Agency was gathering and searching through millions of private citizens' internet and phone records on a daily basis.

AMENDMENT V—Criminal Proceedings Protections, Due Process, and Just Compensation

No person shall be held to answer for a capital, or otherwise infamous crime, unless on a presentment or indictment of a grand jury, except in cases arising in the land or naval forces, or in the militia, when in actual service in time of war or public danger; nor shall any person be subject for the same offense to be twice put in jeopardy of life or limb; nor shall be compelled in any criminal case to be a witness against himself, nor be deprived of life, liberty, or property, without due process of law; nor shall private property be taken for public use, without just compensation.

The Fifth Amendment, the longest of the Bill of Rights, contains five separate clauses. Four clauses concern rights associated with the accused in criminal proceedings; the fifth concerns government taking of private property.

The Grand Jury Clause

No person shall be held to answer for a capital, or otherwise infamous crime, unless on a presentment or indictment of a grand jury, except in cases arising in the land or naval forces, or in the militia, when in actual service in time of war or public danger;

The "Grand Jury Clause" requires the government to use grand juries in cases of crimes that are considered "capital" (where death is a penalty) or "infamous" (where imprisonment is a penalty). A "grand jury" is a group of 16-23 citizens randomly selected by a court to analyze evidence related to a crime and to determine if there is sufficient evidence ("probable cause") for the government to formally prosecute a person suspected of having committed the crime. If a majority of the grand jury determines that there is enough evidence to prosecute (unanimity is not required like it is for a trial jury), the grand jury issues either a "presentment" or "indictment" against the individual. The distinction is simply that a "presentment" is where the grand jury collects the evidence itself (*i.e.,* calls witnesses to testify before it), while an "indictment" is where the grand jury considers evidence submitted by the prosecuting officer. If the grand jury believes that there is insufficient evidence for the case to go to trial, it issues a "no bill."

The grand jury does not determine the person's guilt or innocence; that is left to a trial jury. In 2011 a federal grand jury indicted one-time Democratic vice presidential nominee John Edwards on charges of violating campaign finance laws, conspiracy, and false statements in connection with his use of campaign contributions to cover up an extramarital affair. The case then went to trial in 2012. The trial jury found Edwards not guilty on one of the charges and was unable to come to an agreement on the remaining charges, resulting in a "hung jury" for those charges.

This clause excludes military personnel from the protection of grand juries. Members of the militia also lose grand jury protection when they are in actual military service. There, they are subject to military court-martial.

Finally, the grand jury system has its roots in British common law. The practice of convening a grand jury occurred before colonization and was used to prevent improper prosecution by the government. Today, this clause ensures that the right exists for the same reasons.

The Double Jeopardy Clause

> *nor shall any person be subject for the same offense*
> *to be twice put in jeopardy of life or limb;*

These twenty words making up the "Double Jeopardy Clause" guarantee that a person cannot be prosecuted twice for the same alleged crime. This means that a second prosecution cannot occur after either a conviction or an acquittal (being declared not guilty). The clause also ensures that a person will not receive multiple punishments for the same offense. Multiple prosecutions or punishments for the same offense are called "double jeopardy."

"Jeopardy" here refers to the threat to life or liberty a person faces for being convicted of a crime. An individual is in jeopardy once the jury is empaneled (if the case is tried by a jury), or when the first witness is sworn (in cases tried by a judge without a jury).

Double jeopardy protection has been part of Western civilization since before the Roman Empire, and it was technically a principle of the British common law. Yet the British government narrowly applied the principle, and it was subject to abuse by the monarchy. Its inclusion here ensures protection of individual rights and clearly prohibits the government from repeatedly prosecuting an individual until a jury reaches the government's desired verdict. This means that the government cannot appeal an acquittal. But if there is a "hung jury" like there was in the John Edwards case discussed above, the person can be prosecuted again because he or she has not been convicted or acquitted.

The amendment's language suggests that the protection applies only to prosecutions affecting "life or limb." In practice, however, courts apply this protection to all crimes.

Finally, this clause does not prevent two separate trials against the same individual for the same act *if* that act violates *both* state *and* federal laws. Both the state and federal governments, as separate sovereigns, could prosecute the accused in their respective courts. The Elizabeth Smart kidnapping case provides a good example of this concept. In 2002, Brian David Mitchell kidnapped Elizabeth Smart from her home in Salt Lake City, Utah. He was apprehended the next year and faced criminal kidnapping charges from the state of Utah. A state court judge ruled that Mitchell was incompetent to stand trial and ordered him to be detained at a mental hospital. Federal prosecutors also pressed kidnapping charges against Mitchell because he had transported Elizabeth across state lines after abducting her. A federal judge ruled that Mitchell was competent to stand trial and the case proceeded. A trial jury then convicted Mitchell of the federal kidnapping charge in May 2011.

The Self-Incrimination Clause

> *[N]or shall any person . . . be compelled in any criminal case to be a witness against himself,*

When you hear of someone "pleading the Fifth," they are referring to this clause. It prevents a person from being forced to testify against him or herself in any proceeding where the testimony is legally required. So in a court proceeding or Congressional hearing, for example, a person may refuse to answer a question if doing so could result in future criminal prosecution or reveal additional evidence against him or her in a current proceeding. This means if a suspect in a criminal prosecution for robbing a bank was asked "Did you conspire with others to rob the bank?" he could refuse to answer because answering "yes" would subject him to charges of conspiracy and express his guilt; he would be a witness against himself. Answering "no" and denying he conspired with others could expose the suspect to perjury charges if there was evidence that he did in fact conspire to rob the bank. At the same time, if the government gave the witness immunity from prosecution for testifying against the other conspirators, then the witness would be required to testify since he or she could no longer criminally incriminate him or herself.

The protection against self-incrimination applies to all statements that may be made in a criminal investigation and not just in court. That is why you hear police inform those they arrest: "You have the right to remain silent."

Some high profile examples of persons "pleading the Fifth" include:

- Dozens of individuals brought to testify before the House Un-American Activities Committee in the 1950s when asked about their involvement with the Communist Party USA
- Lieutenant Colonel Oliver North in a 1986 Congressional hearing concerning the Iran-Contra scandal
- Detective Mark Fuhrman of the Los Angeles Police Department during the 1995 O.J. Simpson murder trial when evidence appeared contradicting his earlier testimony on behalf of the prosecution
- Solyndra Corporation executives in an October 2011 Congressional hearing when asked about a government loan made to the company
- Internal Revenue Service official Lois Lerner in May 2013 and March 2014 Congressional hearings when asked about the IRS targeting conservative groups for tax exempt status leading up to the 2012 elections
- Bryan Pagliano, a former State Department employee who set up and serviced a private email server for Hillary Clinton while she was Secretary of State, during a Congressional hearing on the issue in 2016
- Former National Security Advisor Michael Flynn in response to a 2017 Congressional subpoena seeking documents regarding his contacts with Russia

The Due Process Clause

[N]or shall any person . . . be deprived of life, liberty, or property, without due process of law;

"Due process" is a concept dating back to the Magna Carta and it requires the government to act fairly towards its citizens by following the law and providing fair procedures.

The federal government must apply due process before depriving a person of life, liberty, or property. The result is that government officials cannot change the rules depending

157

on their preferences. For instance, a Treasury employee could not withhold Jane Smith's income tax refund check (Jane Smith's property) simply because the Treasury employee knew Jane Smith and did not like her.

The Takings Clause

nor shall private property be taken for public use, without just compensation.

This final Fifth Amendment clause simultaneously ensures the federal government's ability to take private property for public use and the property owner's right to be compensated for the loss. The government's ability to take the property is known as "eminent domain."

An everyday example of the federal government exercising this power is the Interstate Highway System. The federal government built thousands of miles of the Interstate after acquiring private property for that purpose by exercising eminent domain.[307] Because of this clause, all of the property owners affected by the government takings received "just compensation." Just compensation is the fair market value of the property (*i.e.,* what the property owner would have received had he or she sold the property to a private party).

AMENDMENT VI—Rights of the Criminally Accused

In all criminal prosecutions, the accused shall enjoy the right to a speedy and public trial, by an impartial jury of the State and district wherein the crime shall have been committed, which district shall have been previously ascertained by law, and to be informed of the nature and cause of the accusation; to be confronted with the witnesses against him; to have compulsory process for obtaining witnesses in his favor, and to have the Assistance of Counsel for his defense.

Like the Fifth Amendment, the Sixth Amendment concerns the criminal justice system. It enumerates specific protections for everyone accused of a crime:

1. Right to a speedy trial
2. Right to a public trial
3. Right to an impartial jury in the district where the accused allegedly committed the crime
4. Right to be informed of the charges against him or her
5. Right to confront and question (cross-examine) the witness against him or her
6. Right to compel witnesses to testify in his or her favor
7. Right to an attorney to assist in his or her defense

Some of these protections came from the British system as inherited by the colonies and adapted by the states. Some were direct responses to the abuses colonists faced under the British monarchy and that the Framers identified in the Declaration of Independence. Two of the grievances identified in the Declaration were depriving citizens of jury trials and "transporting [colonists] beyond seas to be tried for pretended offenses . . ." (*i.e.*, not trying the colonists in the area where they allegedly committed the crime).

The Sixth Amendment's guarantee of a trial by jury is the second time the Constitution guarantees this right. Article III, section 2 also provides for trials by jury in the state where the crime was committed. The Sixth Amendment adds to Article III's guarantee by narrowing the area of the trial to be in the district (local area) where the crime was committed and including the mandate that the jury be "impartial."

The guarantee of an impartial jury can sometimes result in the case being moved from the district where the crime occurred since a fair and impartial jury may not be possible due to publicity about the crime and/or the defendant(s). An example of this is the case of Timothy McVeigh, one of the Oklahoma City bombers. In 1995, McVeigh detonated a bomb in front of the Alfred P. Murrah Federal Building in Oklahoma City that killed 168 people, injured almost 700 more, and damaged or destroyed over 300 buildings. Because of the widespread publicity in the case, and the perceived prejudice of the populace due to the crime's severe impact on the community, the presiding judge ordered that the trial be moved to Denver, Colorado, where the jury would be seen as less partial.

This amendment's protection of the right to confront witnesses is known as the "Confrontation Clause." Confronting the witness means that the accused is able to both see the witness face to face and ask him or her questions in court (known as cross-examining the witness). The accused person's attorney will generally cross examine the witness rather than the accused asking the questions him or herself.

Finally, accused persons can waive all but one of these rights if they desire. (A person cannot waive the right to be informed of the charges against him or her.) This often happens when persons plead guilty before trial. The guilty plea waives all of the rights relating to trial and confronting and securing witnesses. Bernard Madoff famously waived these rights in 2009 when he pled guilty to 11 federal felonies two days after being charged. The felonies all related to Madoff's Ponzi scheme, the largest in U.S. history. Madoff's younger brother Peter also waived these rights by pleading guilty in 2012 to federal charges of conspiracy and falsifying records.

AMENDMENT VII—<u>Trial by Jury in Civil Cases</u>

> **In Suits at common law, where the value in controversy shall exceed twenty dollars, the right of trial by jury shall be preserved, and no fact tried by a jury, shall be otherwise re-examined in any Court of the United States, than according to the rules of the common law.**

To understand this amendment, one must first understand its subject matter. "Suits at common law" refers to civil lawsuits, which are non-criminal cases between private parties. "Common law" means laws based on "precedent" (past judicial decisions) rather than "statutes" (legislative enactments). It includes claims such as fraud, breach of contract, slander, and trespass. The common law referred to here is the law in place when the states adopted this amendment, meaning the law that the States had inherited from Britain and modified during the colonial period. Finally, "trial by jury" means a trial in which a judge presides over a jury of 12 persons. The jury answers questions of fact (did John Doe commit fraud against Jane Smith?). The judge answers questions of law (is the fraudulent letter allegedly written by Mr. Doe admissible in evidence?).

This amendment ensures that civil cases valued over $20 will go to a jury. Adjusted for inflation, $20 in 1789 when the amendment was written would be worth around $521 in 2017. The amendment's adoption of common law rules also ensures that a jury's decision on the facts cannot be reversed by another court, including the Supreme Court. Common law rules permitted facts to be reconsidered only by another jury in a new trial, not by appellate judges. This distinction of the jury determining the facts and the judge deciding the law preserved the common law distinction of the judge and the jury's responsibilities.

The right to a jury trial protected by this amendment only applies to cases in federal courts and not state courts. In addition, it applies only to civil cases and not to lawsuits based on a statute, maritime law, or equity. Equity cases are where a person seeks an order directing a party to act or refrain from acting rather than asking for money damages. A lawsuit seeking a restraining order is a good example of equity.

AMENDMENT VIII—Bail and Punishment

Excessive bail shall not be required, nor excessive fines imposed, nor cruel and unusual punishments inflicted.

The Eighth Amendment is the shortest of the Bill of Rights. It has three monikers: the "Excessive Bail Clause," the "Excessive Fines Clause," and the "Cruel and Unusual Punishment Clause." Like the Fifth and Sixth Amendments, it addresses the criminal justice system.

This amendment's text derives from the English Bill of Rights of 1689, which provided "that excessive bail ought not to be required, nor excessive fines imposed, nor cruel and unusual punishments inflicted." Virginia had adopted this provision in the Virginia Declaration of Rights of 1776, and the Virginia convention that ratified the Constitution in 1788 recommended that it be added to the Constitution. When drafting the proposed amendment, James Madison changed "ought" to "shall."

Excessive Bail Clause

Bail is an amount of money an accused person pays the court so that he or she may be released from jail until trial. Its purpose is to ensure that the accused returns for future court hearings and ultimately trial. If the accused appears at these proceedings, he or she will receive the bail money back when the case is over. If the accused fails to appear, then he or she forfeits the bail money.

This clause has never been understood to guarantee the right to bail. At the time the British Parliament adopted the English Bill of Rights in 1689, laws concerning bail dated back almost four hundred years. Those laws set out the offenses for which one could receive bail and those offenses where bail was forbidden. In America, various laws likewise permitted bail for some crimes but not others. Examples include the Northwest Ordinance in 1787 and the Judiciary Act of 1789, both of which permitted bail except in instances where the accused was charged with a capital crime (a crime punishable by death). Further, the same Congress that passed the Judiciary Act drafted and passed the Eighth Amendment, suggesting that the protection against excessive bail was a safeguard for those instances where bail was permitted rather than a guarantee to bail in all cases.

Today, if an accused believes that the bail is excessive, he or she may appeal the bail amount to a higher court or ask the court setting bail to lower the amount. The highest bail ever set in the United States by a federal court was $100 million in Raj Rajaratnam's insider trading case in 2009.[308]

Excessive Fine Clause

A fine is the government's ability to demand money as punishment for a crime. A fine may be in addition to, or in the place of, imprisonment. This amendment limits the government's ability to impose fines by entirely prohibiting those that are "excessive."

An excessive fine might be one requiring $10,000 to be paid for failing to declare in customs one item worth only $100. Ultimately, courts decide whether a fine is excessive. Perhaps the most familiar instance of when one might face a federal fine relates to copyright laws. Notices at the beginning of DVDs contain an FBI anti-piracy warning stating that a person may face a fine up to $250,000 and/or imprisonment for violating copyright laws. Illegally downloading music is another example. An excessive fine in that context could be a $250,000 fine for illegally downloading one song and not sharing it with anybody.

Cruel and Unusual Punishment Clause

This clause guarantees that criminal convicts will not be subjected to cruel and unusual punishment. The Constitution does not define "cruel and unusual." Even so, common sense provides some guidance on this issue.

For example, an "unusual" punishment could be one that is excessive in comparison to the crime, such as a 20-year prison sentence for shoplifting a 50-cent candy bar. A "cruel" punishment could be cutting off one's hand for theft, a practice common in some countries of the world today.

Finally, capital punishment (the death penalty) is not considered cruel and unusual under the Constitution. In fact, the Constitution expects capital punishment to occur. The Fifth Amendment makes this clear in its discussion of "capital crimes" and its guarantee that one shall not be deprived of "life" without due process of law. But the method of execution could be prohibited as being cruel and unusual. For instance, death by elephant stomping (as was practiced in India) could be cruel because of the tortuous method of death. So too could be death by stoning or dissection. Today, execution methods used in the United States include death by firing squad, electrocution (the electric chair), lethal gas or injections, and hanging. At the federal level, capital punishment is rare. The most recent federal execution occurred in March 2003 when officials executed Louis Jones, Jr. by lethal injection at a federal prison in Terre Haute, Indiana. The federal government executed two others in June 2001, including

Timothy McVeigh, one of the Oklahoma City bombers. Before McVeigh, the most recent federal execution was Victor Feguer in March 1963 in Fort Madison, Iowa. Two of the most notorious executions occurred in 1953 when the federal government executed Julius and Ethel Rosenberg by electrocution after their conviction for espionage.

AMENDMENT IX—<u>Rights Retained by the People</u>

The enumeration in the Constitution, of certain rights, shall not be construed to deny or disparage others retained by the people.

This amendment enshrines the basic philosophy underlying the American Constitution—that the *people* have certain natural rights, the citizens granted some of their rights to the government through the Constitution, and then they enacted the Bill of Rights to protect the rights they retained from government infringement.

This philosophy ran contrary to the government systems in Europe where the monarch was the sovereign and the people were his or her subjects. In other words, the monarch held all rights and granted some of them to the people. The Framers repudiated this view and set up the new government based on the philosophy described above – a philosophy made famous by the British philosopher John Locke. It is also the philosophy embodied in the Declaration of Independence, which declares that men and women are "endowed by their Creator with certain unalienable Rights" and that the people create governments "to secure [protect] these rights."

In essence, the Ninth Amendment establishes that listing some rights in the Constitution and in the previous amendments does not limit or eliminate the natural rights retained by the people. Rights do not come from the Constitution; they come from the people.

AMENDMENT X—<u>Powers Reserved to the States or People</u>

The powers not delegated to the United States by the Constitution, nor prohibited by it to the

164

States, are reserved to the States respectively, or to the people.

The Tenth Amendment reiterates the concept of federalism, *i.e.,* that the federal government only has the powers granted to it by the Constitution. All other governmental powers, except those prohibited by Article I, section 10, remain with the states or, more particularly, to the people of the states. This means that the states have the power to make laws concerning such things as marriage, adoption, education, and the legal age for obtaining a driver's license—all areas not covered by the federal Constitution. So it is that a person can first obtain a driver's license at age 14 in South Dakota but must wait until age 16 in Kentucky.[309] And it explains why Mississippi is able to require persons to be 21 to marry without parental consent, Nebraska requires them to be 19, and the remaining 48 states set the age at 18.[310]

This amendment also ensures that a state's power may be limited by the people in it, with the people being the ultimate source of authority as suggested in the Ninth Amendment. For example, the citizens of a state could deny their state power to take certain actions, such as imposing a personal income tax, by means of the state's constitution.

The remaining seventeen amendments were added here and there over the next 200 years. The 11th and 12th Amendments were added by 1804. The states ratified the 13th through 15th Amendments between 1865 and 1870, shortly after the Civil War, which is why these three are generally known as the "Civil War Amendments." Four additional amendments were ratified between 1913 and 1920, two more followed in 1933, and another four were added between 1951 and 1971. Finally, the 27th Amendment became effective in 1992. These amendments concern issues related to the presidency, voting, prohibition of alcohol, or they otherwise modify the law set forth in the Constitution.

AMENDMENT XI—Restricting Judicial Power for Suits Against States

Passed by Congress March 4, 1794. Ratified February 7, 1795.

> **The Judicial power of the United States shall not be construed to extend to any suit in law or equity, commenced or prosecuted against one of the United States by Citizens of another State, or by Citizens or Subjects of any Foreign State.**

The Eleventh Amendment is the first amendment to actually modify language used in the original Constitution; it modified Article III, section 2's grant of judicial power to federal courts. The amendment was in direct response to a Supreme Court decision involving a lawsuit against one of the states where the states felt that the federal courts infringed on their sovereignty.

The case prompting this amendment was *Chisholm v. Georgia*, where Alexander Chisholm sued the state of Georgia on behalf of Robert Farquhar to recover debts Georgia owed to Farquhar's estate. Farquhar was a South Carolina merchant who sold supplies to Georgia during the Revolutionary War.

166

Farquhar died before being paid, and his will appointed Chisholm to settle his affairs. Relying on Article III, section 2, which gave federal courts power to decide cases "between a State and Citizens of another State," Chisholm sued Georgia in federal court in 1792. Claiming sovereign immunity (*i.e.*, the concept of a government not being able to be sued without its consent), Georgia refused to participate in the case. In 1793, the Supreme Court ruled in favor of Farquhar's estate.

The decision set off a brouhaha among the states who saw their sovereignty being infringed. In response to *Chisholm*, the Senate and House proposed this amendment in March 1794. The necessary three-fourths of the states ratified the amendment less than one year later, in February 1795, to ensure that the states would not face similar lawsuits in the future.

The net effect of this amendment is that the states, like the federal government, enjoy sovereign immunity in federal courts and cannot be sued without their consent.

AMENDMENT XII—Modifying the Electoral College Process

Passed by Congress December 9, 1803. Ratified June 15, 1804.

> The Electors shall meet in their respective states and vote by ballot for President and Vice-President, one of whom, at least, shall not be an inhabitant of the same state with themselves; they shall name in their ballots the person voted for as President, and in distinct ballots the person voted for as Vice-President, and they shall make distinct lists of all persons voted for as President, and of all persons voted for as Vice-President, and of the number of votes for each, which lists they shall sign and certify, and transmit sealed to the seat of the government of the United States, directed to the President of the Senate; -- the President of the Senate shall, in the presence of the Senate and House of Representatives, open all the certificates and the

votes shall then be counted; -- The person having the greatest number of votes for President, shall be the President, if such number be a majority of the whole number of Electors appointed; and if no person have such majority, then from the persons having the highest numbers not exceeding three on the list of those voted for as President, the House of Representatives shall choose immediately, by ballot, the President. But in choosing the President, the votes shall be taken by states, the representation from each state having one vote; a quorum for this purpose shall consist of a member or members from two-thirds of the states, and a majority of all the states shall be necessary to a choice. [And if the House of Representatives shall not choose a President whenever the right of choice shall devolve upon them, before the fourth day of March next following, then the Vice-President shall act as President, as in case of the death or other constitutional disability of the President. --] The person having the greatest number of votes as Vice-President, shall be the Vice-President, if such number be a majority of the whole number of Electors appointed, and if no person have a majority, then from the two highest numbers on the list, the Senate shall choose the Vice-President; a quorum for the purpose shall consist of two-thirds of the whole number of Senators, and a majority of the whole number shall be necessary to a choice. But no person constitutionally ineligible to the office of President shall be eligible to that of Vice-President of the United States.

The Twelfth Amendment resulted from challenges occurring in the 1796 and 1800 elections that the Framers had not envisioned. It modified the process for electing the president and vice president originally set out in Article II, section 3.

As written, Article II specified that Electors were to vote for two persons for president, with no distinction made between president and vice president. The person receiving the most Electoral votes became president; the person coming in second became vice president. In the event of a tie, the House of Representatives voted as states rather than individually to determine the winner. A majority of the states was needed to win. The process worked well for the 1788 and 1792 presidential elections when the nation unanimously elected George Washington as president and when no political parties existed.

By the 1796 presidential election, however, political parties existed in the young country. And the two persons receiving the most Electoral votes that year, John Adams and Thomas Jefferson, were from opposing parties. Because Adams received the most Electoral votes, he became president. Finishing second, Jefferson became vice president. Over the next four years, Jefferson used his position as vice president (and so president of the Senate) to attack Adams and his policies rather than working effectively with Adams.

Seeking to avoid the problem of the 1796 election, Jefferson's and Adams's political parties each nominated two candidates for the 1800 presidential election. The Democratic-Republican Party nominated Jefferson and Aaron Burr, with Jefferson intended to be the candidate for president and Burr for vice president. The Federalist Party nominated Adams for president and Charles Pinckney for the vice-presidency. Yet under the electoral system from Article II, the electors simply cast two votes for president without designating who the Elector wanted as president. Both Jefferson and Burr received 73 electoral votes, which threw the election into the House of Representatives. The House cast repeated ballots but could not select a winner until after Alexander Hamilton convinced members of his party (the Federalist Party) to select Jefferson over Burr. This occurred on the thirty-sixth ballot! (Aaron Burr ended up killing Hamilton in a duel in 1804.)

Because of the problems associated with the 1796 and 1800 elections, legislators swiftly moved to modify the Constitution's process for electing the president and vice president. This amendment resulted from that effort.

The Twelfth Amendment made the following changes to the Electoral process:

- Electors must designate their votes for president and vice president, separately
- At least one of the persons an elector votes for cannot be from the same state as the Elector (*i.e.*, an Elector from Iowa could not vote for both presidential and vice presidential candidates from Iowa)
- If no presidential candidate obtains a majority of the Electors, the House of Representatives chooses the president from the three highest Electoral vote earners rather than the five highest as the Constitution originally prescribed (although the amendment left in place the original formula of the House voting as states rather than by individual representatives in the case of a tie)
- If no vice-presidential candidate obtains a majority of the Electors, the Senate chooses the vice president from the two candidates with the highest number of Electors by a simple majority vote
- It extends the Constitution's eligibility requirements for the president (natural-born citizen, at least 35 years of age, resided in the United States for 14 years) to the vice president

Besides the 1800 Election, the only other election to be decided by the House of Representatives was the 1824 Election when none of the five main candidates achieved an Electoral majority. That year, the House of Representatives selected John Quincy Adams (John Adams's son) as president even though he originally finished second in electoral votes to Andrew Jackson. The Senate similarly chose the vice president under this amendment only once, in 1836, when it selected Richard Johnson.

In recent times, this amendment played a small role in the 2000 presidential election. That year, both presidential candidate George W. Bush and vice presidential candidate Dick Cheney lived in and voted in Texas. Bush was the state's governor, and Cheney had moved to the state a few years before for employment reasons. Mindful of this amendment's prohibition of Electors voting for two inhabitants from their state, Cheney changed his voter registration to Wyoming, a state he had previously represented in Congress and where he owned a vacation home, four months before the election.

This amendment briefly found its way into the spotlight during the 2012 presidential election. Polls in late October suggested that Republican challenger Mitt Romney and President Barack Obama could end up in an electoral tie, thus throwing the election to the House of Representatives for president and the Senate for vice president. Because Republicans controlled the House and Democrats controlled the Senate, pundits speculated that if an Electoral tie were to occur, Romney would be selected president by the House and Joseph Biden, President Obama's running mate, would be selected vice president, thus giving America the first president and vice president from different parties since Adams and Jefferson following the 1796 election. But it didn't happen.

Finally, the Twentieth Amendment superseded the bracketed language when it became part of the Constitution in 1933.

AMENDMENT XIII—Abolishing Slavery

Passed by Congress January 31, 1865. Ratified December 6, 1865.

Section 1—Ending Slavery

> **Neither slavery nor involuntary servitude, except as a punishment for crime whereof the party shall have been duly convicted, shall exist within the United States, or any place subject to their jurisdiction.**

Short and to the point, the Thirteenth Amendment prohibits slavery in all areas subject to the federal government's control. It came sixty-one years after the Twelfth Amendment, and 58 years after Congress acted to prohibit importing slaves into the country. This amendment also contains the first instance of the word "slavery" in the Constitution.

The amendment effectively repealed portions of Article I, section 9, concerning slave importation and Article IV, section 2, about returning fugitive slaves.

Some misunderstand this amendment's import and believe that President Abraham Lincoln's "Emancipation Proclamation" ended slavery in the United States. Not so. Issued in 1863, the Proclamation declared the freedom of slaves in ten Confederate states rebelling against the United States. It had no impact in states loyal to the Union where slavery was legal (Missouri, Kentucky, Maryland, and Delaware), nor did it affect Tennessee, a state that had once been part of the Confederacy but had come under Union control in 1862. The Proclamation ordered the Union military to treat slaves in Confederate territory as free; it was a temporary measure based on the president's war powers and would have expired at the end of the war. Further, the Proclamation did not outlaw slavery. Slavery remained legal in Delaware and Kentucky until the Thirteenth Amendment officially became part of the Constitution in December 1865. (Both Delaware and Kentucky had rejected the amendment in February 1865.) So this amendment, not the Emancipation Proclamation, is the reason slavery no longer exists in the United States. President Lincoln recognized this reality, which is why he vigorously promoted this amendment. (The 2012 film "Lincoln" dramatized Lincoln's push for the Thirteenth Amendment.)

Even though all states are not required to ratify a Constitutional amendment for it to become effective, many states will show their support for an amendment by ratifying it even after the amendment is officially part of the Constitution. For the Thirteenth Amendment, Mississippi became the last state to ratify the amendment; it officially did so only in 2013! Mississippi had voted to ratify the amendment in 1995, 20 years after Kentucky did the same. Due to a clerical error, however, the state never notified the United States Archivist of its ratification.

As discussed in Article V, the president's signature is not required for Congress to propose an amendment to the states. President Lincoln nevertheless signed the Thirteenth Amendment, the first amendment to be signed by a president.

Section 2—<u>Granting Congress Enforcement Power</u>

Congress shall have power to enforce this article by appropriate legislation.

Section 2 plainly grants the federal government power to enforce the amendment when doing so may interfere with a state's internal matters. This differed from previous amendments where the federal government lacked this ability.

Congress acted under this power in 1867 to pass the Peonage Act. "Peonage" is involuntary servitude where a debtor pays his or her creditor through labor. It was a common system in former Spanish colonies, and was prevalent in New Mexico following the Civil War. The 1867 Peonage Act stated:

> The holding of any person to service or labor under the system known as peonage is abolished and forever prohibited in the territory of New Mexico, or in any other territory or state of the United States; and all acts, laws, … made to establish, maintain, or enforce, directly or indirectly, the voluntary or involuntary service or labour of any persons as peons, in liquidation of any debt or obligation, or otherwise, are declared null and void.

This statute's current version does not directly mention New Mexico or any other state.[311]

Involuntary servitude is not entirely prohibited. Prisoners can be forced to labor as part of their sentences. This explains the occurrence of "chain gangs" cleaning highways and parks and performing other forced labor.

AMENDMENT XIV—<u>Civil and Political Rights</u>

Passed by Congress June 13, 1866. Ratified July 9, 1868.

The Fourteenth Amendment, the second of the three "Civil War Amendments" passed in the five years following the Civil War, is the Constitution's longest amendment. It contains five sections dealing with various civil and political rights.

Section 1—Citizenship Rights

All persons born or naturalized in the United States, and subject to the jurisdiction thereof, are citizens of the United States and of the State wherein they reside. No State shall make or enforce any law which shall abridge the privileges or immunities of citizens of the United States; nor shall any State deprive any person of life, liberty, or property, without due process of law; nor deny to any person within its jurisdiction the equal protection of the laws.

Section 1's four clauses concern rights associated with United States citizenship. And they prohibit the states from taking actions that infringe the rights of United States citizens.

The Citizenship Clause

All persons born or naturalized in the United States, and subject to the jurisdiction thereof, are citizens of the United States and of the State wherein they reside.

The Constitution defines United States citizenship for the first time in this clause. Essentially, a person is a United States citizen if he or she is naturalized or born in the United States and "subject to the jurisdiction thereof." Persons born in the United States but who are not subject to the United States's jurisdiction include children of foreign diplomats and children or members of Indian tribes subject to tribal laws. So a child born in New York to a Moroccan diplomat to the United Nations would not be a United States citizen, while a child born to Ukrainian parents studying at a university in the United States would be a United States citizen. (The Ukrainian parents are subject to the United States government's legal and political control.)

174

A child born to American parents in a foreign country is also a United States citizen, but that is the result of legislation rather than this amendment. The reason is that Congress has power over citizenship (as discussed in Article I), and Congress has provided for children born to American parents to have United States citizenship regardless of where the child is born.

This amendment did not apply to American Indians living on reservations because they were governed by tribal law. Congress granted citizenship to American Indians only in 1924.

This clause also grants *state* citizenship to persons based on their residence; a person enjoys state citizenship and its accompanying rights simply by living within a state's borders. State citizenship has practical consequences. For example, Alaska citizens receive money annually from the Alaska Permanent Fund Corporation, a state-owned corporation that pays dividends from the oil-lease revenue the state receives for leases on public lands. Another example is tuition for state-owned colleges and universities.

Finally, this clause repudiated the Supreme Court's 1857 decision in *Dred Scott v. Sandford* where the Court declared that black persons were not and could not become citizens. This clause's most practical and immediate effect was to secure citizenship for all former slaves and their children. Congress had passed a law granting citizenship to these persons through the Civil Rights Act of 1866, but Congress chose to also pursue a Constitutional amendment so that a future Congress could not change the law by a simple majority vote.[312] (President Andrew Johnson had vetoed the law granting citizenship to former slaves, but two-thirds majorities in both the House and Senate overturned his veto.)

The Privileges or Immunities Clause

> *No State shall make or enforce any law which shall abridge the privileges or immunities of citizens of the United States;*

Not to be confused with the Privileges *and* Immunities Clause from Article IV, section 2, this Privileges <u>or</u>

Immunities clause prohibits states from reducing the full privileges of *United States* citizenship from any of their residents. It does not prohibit states from restricting or altering the privileges and immunities of *state* citizenship.

Privileges and immunities associated with United States citizenship include rights to:

1. Protection while traveling abroad
2. Move freely from state to state
3. Petition Congress
4. Access writs of habeas corpus
5. Vote in federal elections
6. Enter public lands
7. Protection while in federal custody
8. Inform United States authorities of federal law violations
9. Conduct interstate commerce
10. Exercise rights secured by treaty[313]

Essentially, the privileges and immunities protected here are those related to powers granted the federal government.

The limited number of national privileges and immunities shows that most civil and political privileges derive from state citizenship. This is consistent with the basic philosophy underlying the Constitution and as confirmed by the Ninth Amendment.

The Due Process Clause

[N]or shall any State deprive any person of life, liberty, or property, without due process of law;

This clause repeats the Fifth Amendment's due process protection but now applies it to the states. Consequently, state governments must act fairly towards their citizens by following the law and providing fair procedures before depriving a person of life, liberty, or property.

The Equal Protection Clause

[N]or deny to any person within its jurisdiction the
equal protection of the laws.

This clause guarantees all persons—not just citizens—
equal protection of the laws. It requires *laws* to treat everyone
equally, not for everyone to be equal politically, economically,
socially, or otherwise. Still, some assert that the clause
requires government to make all persons equal, including their
respective advantages and disadvantages. Such a philosophy
ignores the clause's words mandating "equal protection *of the*
laws" and not "equality." (The adoption of the Fifteenth and
Nineteenth Amendments and their guarantee of the right to
vote to all men and women, for example, are instances of
political equality that had to occur outside of this clause.)

The clause's primary purpose was to protect the rights of
former slaves.[314] Following the Civil War, many former
Confederate states enacted "Black Codes" that severely
restricted former slaves' rights. These laws treated blacks
different from whites in several ways, including: restricting
blacks' right to own property; prohibiting blacks from serving
on juries or testifying in court; and providing for stricter
punishments for blacks than whites for the same criminal
offenses. This amendment eliminated the Black Codes. "Jim
Crow" laws, different from the Black Codes, reintroduced
discrimination after the Reconstruction period ended in the
late 1870s. They too violated the Equal Protection Clause. But
courts nevertheless permitted them until the 1950s.

Finally, this clause applies only to government actions. It
does not affect actions by private individuals.

Section 2—Congressional Apportionment

Representatives shall be apportioned among the
several States according to their respective
numbers, counting the whole number of persons
in each State, excluding Indians not taxed. But
when the right to vote at any election for the
choice of electors for President and Vice-
President of the United States, Representatives

177

**in Congress, the Executive and Judicial officers
of a State, or the members of the Legislature
thereof, is denied to any of the male inhabitants
of such State, being twenty-one years of age, and
citizens of the United States, or in any way
abridged, except for participation in rebellion,
or other crime, the basis of representation
therein shall be reduced in the proportion which
the number of such male citizens shall bear to
the whole number of male citizens twenty-one
years of age in such State.**

This section's first sentence eliminated the "three-fifths clause" found in Article I, section 2. That clause counted a slave as three-fifths of a person for purposes of taxes and representation in Congress. As discussed earlier in Article I, section 2, counting a slave as three fifths of a whole person was a compromise between the Northern and Southern states. It was not intended as a slight to these persons. Southern states had wanted to count slaves for purposes of representation (thereby giving Southern states more representation in Congress even though the slaves could not vote), but not count them for purposes of taxation (which was apportioned according to a state's entire population). Counting five slaves as three persons for both apportionment and taxes thus induced the Southern states to move forward in adopting the new Constitution. Since the Thirteenth Amendment had eliminated slavery, the three-fifths compromise was moot. There was no reason for it to continue.

The rest of this section provides that if a state denies any male age 21 or over the right to vote, then that state's representation in Congress will be reduced by basing the apportionment of representatives only on males aged 21 and over rather than *all* persons within a state. The purpose was to encourage (but not force) Southern states to provide voting rights to former slaves, particularly since the first part of this section made it so that former slaves increased the South's representation in Congress. But Congress never acted on this section. The Fifteenth Amendment made this section mostly redundant because it granted former male slaves the right to vote. (The Twenty-sixth Amendment changed the voting age to 18.)

Finally, this section explicitly permits a state to abridge a person's right to vote as punishment for a crime. And most states do. As of 2017, 48 states imposed various voting restrictions on those convicted of a crime.[315] Eleven of those states ban ex-convicts from voting even after they complete their prison sentences and probation or parole. Only Maine and Vermont do not restrict convicts or ex-convicts' right to vote, meaning that persons may still vote in those states even while incarcerated.

Section 3—<u>Disqualifying Those Who Fight Against the United States from Public Office</u>

No person shall be a Senator or Representative in Congress, or elector of President and Vice-President, or hold any office, civil or military, under the United States, or under any State, who, having previously taken an oath, as a member of Congress, or as an officer of the United States, or as a member of any State legislature, or as an executive or judicial officer of any State, to support the Constitution of the United States, shall have engaged in insurrection or rebellion against the same, or given aid or comfort to the enemies thereof. But Congress may by a vote of two-thirds of each House, remove such disability.

Sometimes referred to as the "Disqualification Clause," section 3 bans persons from serving in any state or federal position, either elected or appointed, if they have taken an oath to support the Constitution and then fight against the United States or give aid or comfort to its enemies. The section also limits the effect of the president's pardon power in that it gives Congress alone the power to lift this ban.

As with the other sections in this amendment, Congress wrote and adopted section 3 as a means to deal with the Civil War's aftermath.

This clause immediately affected Confederate officials (many of whom had previously served in state and federal offices that required an oath to protect the Constitution) following the Fourteenth Amendment's ratification in July 1868. These persons could not serve in state or federal offices without Congressional approval. This restriction remained in effect even though President Andrew Johnson, after this amendment's adoption, issued a "full pardon" and amnesty to everyone who fought against the United States during the Civil War.

Congress lifted the ban for certain individuals by name in 1869.[316] In 1872, Congress lifted the ban from all persons except senators and representatives from the Thirty-sixth and Thirty-seventh Congresses (1859-1863), and also former civil, military, and judicial officers of the federal government.[317] Congress removed the ban entirely in 1898.[318]

Although generally thought of as being of historical interest only, this section is still in effect. It would apply to anyone who takes an oath to support the Constitution (a military officer, a legislative official, etc.) and then rebels against the United States or gives aid or comfort to its enemies.

Section 4—Validating United States Public Debt; Invalidating Confederate Debt

The validity of the public debt of the United States, authorized by law, including debts incurred for payment of pensions and bounties for services in suppressing insurrection or rebellion, shall not be questioned. But neither the United States nor any State shall assume or pay any debt or obligation incurred in aid of insurrection or rebellion against the United States, or any claim for the loss or emancipation of any slave; but all such debts, obligations and claims shall be held illegal and void.

Section 4 makes a clean distinction concerning the repayment of the debt incurred during the Civil War. First, it commits the United States to pay the Union's debt—without

180

question. Second, it prohibits the United States federal government and all state governments from paying debt incurred by the Confederacy or by any state to fund the war against the United States. Third, it prohibited the federal and state governments from paying former slave owners for the loss of slaves. This prohibition applied to all former slave states, whether or not they had been part of the rebellion.

As with section 3, this section is still in effect even though it was written to address the Civil War. This section most recently came to the spotlight in 2013 when politicians like California Representative Nancy Pelosi and Nevada Senator Harry Reid recommended that President Barack Obama invoke this section to increase the national debt limit without Congressional consent.[319] President Obama did not do so; his press secretary had previously stated that the Fourteenth Amendment did not give the president the power to unilaterally increase the national debt.[320]

Section 5—Granting Enforcement Power

The Congress shall have the power to enforce, by appropriate legislation, the provisions of this article.

Section 5 explicitly grants the federal government power to enforce each of the Fourteenth Amendment's four previous sections. Some of the laws Congress passed soon after this amendment's ratification include: the Enforcement Act of 1870; the Ku Klux Klan Act in 1871; and the Civil Rights Act of 1875.

A provision of the Ku Klux Klan Act that is still in effect today permits persons to sue for money damages when government officials violate the persons' civil rights.[321] Persons alleging police brutality or false arrest regularly file claims under this law. In 2012, members of the Occupy Wall Street movement used the law to sue the NYPD for alleged civil rights violations related to the NYPD's crackdown on the Occupy protestors.[322]

AMENDMENT XV—Suffrage Based on Race, Color, or Previous Servitude

Passed by Congress February 26, 1869. Ratified February 3, 1870.

Section 1—Suffrage Not Denied Based on Race

The right of citizens of the United States to vote shall not be denied or abridged by the United States or by any State on account of race, color, or previous condition of servitude.

The final of the three Civil War amendments, the Fifteenth Amendment was intended to grant suffrage (the right to vote) to former slaves. Yet it does not explicitly give blacks or any other persons of color the right to vote. Instead, the amendment prohibits the federal and state governments from depriving citizens of the right to vote because of their race, color, or previous status as slaves.

Because this amendment did not affirmatively grant the right to vote, many Southern states attempted to get around the prohibition of race-based criterion in voting laws by enacting laws that did not overtly use race as the basis for denying blacks the right to vote. These laws included poll taxes, literacy tests, "whites-only" primary elections, and "grandfather clauses." Grandfather clauses were laws that only let men register and vote if their grandfathers could vote in 1867, before the federal government pushed for the right to vote to be granted to freed slaves. Such actions largely disenfranchised Southern blacks and poor whites for decades.

Section 2—Power of Enforcement

Congress shall have power to enforce this article by appropriate legislation.

As with the other Civil War amendments, this section grants Congress power to enforce the amendment's provisions. Its inclusion is similar to what the Constitution's Framers did with the Necessary and Proper Clause in Article I, section 8, where Congress is given power to make laws that are necessary and proper to carry out the responsibilities delegated to it in the Constitution.

Because of the disenfranchisement problems noted above, Congress acted under this section to pass the Voting Rights Act of 1965. That act prohibits literacy tests on a nationwide basis. It also gives the federal government oversight over elections in areas of the country that Congress believes have the greatest potential for race-based discrimination. Jurisdictions subject to federal oversight were forbidden to implement any change in voting laws until the United States Attorney General or the United States District Court for the District of Columbia determined that the change did not have a discriminatory purpose and would not have a discriminatory effect. All or portions of 16 states are subject to this oversight known as "preclearance." Congress renewed and amended the act in 1970, 1975, 1982, and 2006.

In 2012, U.S. Attorney General Eric Holder challenged voter identification laws in Texas and South Carolina, two states subject to preclearance. He argued that persons of color would not be able to secure a government-issued photo id to comply with the voter identification laws, and so alleged that the laws limited a person's ability to vote because of his or her race (thus violating this amendment).[323] A federal court agreed with the Attorney General and blocked the Texas law from taking effect.[324] The same court came to the opposite conclusion concerning South Carolina's law, but prevented the law from taking effect until after the 2012 election.[325] In 2013, the Supreme Court held that for preclearance to continue under the Voting Rights Act, Congress would need to devise a new formula to determine which areas of the country would be subject to federal oversight rather than relying on 50-year-old data.[326]

AMENDMENT XVI—Income Tax

Passed by Congress July 2, 1909. Ratified February 3, 1913.

The Congress shall have power to lay and collect taxes on incomes, from whatever source derived, without apportionment among the several

183

States, and without regard to any census or enumeration.

Congress proposed the Sixteenth Amendment, like the Eleventh Amendment before it, in response to a Supreme Court decision. The case, *Pollock v. Farmer's Loan & Trust Co.* (1895), held that an income tax was a "direct tax" and so violated Article I, sections 2 and 9. Those sections mandate that direct taxes be apportioned among the states based on each state's population (*i.e.*, a state with 5% of the population would be required to pay 5% of the nation's tax, no matter the total income in the state). This amendment changed that requirement.

The federal government first imposed an income tax during the Civil War to pay war expenses. The tax expired in 1872. Twenty-two years later, the federal government again enacted an income tax. That law is the one the Supreme Court negated in *Pollock*. Undeterred, income tax proponents moved to amend the Constitution. Congress proposed the amendment in 1909; the states ratified it in 1913.

This amendment has been a flash point for debate since its adoption 100 years ago. Some of the debate centers on the propriety of taxing a person's income, while much of the quarrel concerns how the income tax law is written and applied. For example, politicians and citizens alike argue about the percentage of the population that pays no income tax and whether that is fair. An average of 40% of Americans pays no income tax in any given year.[327] (The number changes from year to year according to the most recent tax laws passed by Congress.) In 2009, that number rose to 51%. In 2011, an estimated 46% of the population paid no income tax. That number declined to an estimated 43% in 2013[328] before growing again to 45% in 2015.[329] The high numbers of persons not paying income tax cause many who pay the taxes to complain of unfair treatment; they argue that those not paying income tax disproportionately receive more public benefits. Similarly, some who pay no income tax contend that those who pay the tax have more than enough money to spare and so should pay their "fair share." The net result is that the two sides aggressively court candidates to represent their views, thus perpetuating the debate.

AMENDMENT XVII—Direct Election of Senators

Passed by Congress May 13, 1912. Ratified April 8, 1913.

Section 1—Direct Election

The Senate of the United States shall be composed of two Senators from each State, elected by the people thereof, for six years; and each Senator shall have one vote. The electors in each State shall have the qualifications requisite for electors of the most numerous branch of the State legislatures.

Under Article I, section 3, state legislatures *selected* their senators. This process gave the states a voice within the federal government. A senator theoretically represented the state's interests while a representative represented the people's interests. This amendment altered that process so that the people *elect* the senators just the same as representatives.

Proposals to make this change first surfaced in the mid-1820s.[330] Deadlocks in state legislatures, which resulted in some states not having two senators serving, occurred on an increasing basis beginning in the 1850s. Eight states legislatures (California, Delaware, Montana, Oregon, Pennsylvania, Utah, Washington, and Wyoming) failed to select two senators and had only one senator serving for periods of 10 months to four years.[331] And an impasse in the Delaware legislature resulted in that state sending *no* senators to Washington *for two years!*[332]

Vacancies in the Senate were not the only reason voters increasingly pushed for a change. A series of magazine articles published by *Cosmopolitan* magazine in 1906 added fuel to the fire. Called "The Treason of the Senate," the articles portrayed the Senate as riddled with corruption and painted senators as beholden to special interest "political machines."

In 1907, Oregon changed its laws to permit voters to designate whom they wanted as senator, and the legislature was bound to select the candidate chosen by voters.[333] Others states soon followed suit. The thinking was that giving the power of direct election would eliminate corruption and ensure that senators were concerned with the public interest rather than special interests. By 1911, twenty-nine states nominated senators either by party primaries or general elections. Congress reacted by proposing the Seventeenth Amendment in 1912. The states ratified it less than one year later.

Section 2—<u>Filling Vacancies</u>

> **When vacancies happen in the representation of any State in the Senate, the executive authority of such State shall issue writs of election to fill such vacancies: Provided, That the legislature of any State may empower the executive thereof to make temporary appointments until the people fill the vacancies by election as the legislature may direct.**

This section modifies the process for filling Senate vacancies. The original Constitutional provision permitted state governors to make temporary appointments if a Senate seat became vacant while the state legislature was in recess. The appointment ended once the legislature returned to session and selected a senator. This clause mandates that a governor call for a special election unless the state legislature has given the governor power to make temporary appointments.

Many state legislatures have acted under this clause and continue to grant their governors power to appoint senators until an election is held. Other states reject the idea and require a special election. Still others are ambivalent about this appointment power depending on who holds it. Before 2004, Massachusetts granted its governors the appointment power. But that year, Senator John Kerry of Massachusetts was the Democratic nominee for president. The Democrat-controlled state legislature changed the law to strip the governor of the appointment power and mandated that Senate seats be filled by special election. The purpose was to prevent Governor Mitt Romney, a Republican, from appointing a Republican if Kerry won the White House. Five years later, with the death of

186

Senator Edward Kennedy, and with a Democrat serving as governor, the legislature changed the law again to grant the governor power to appoint a temporary replacement until a special election was held between 145 and 160 days after the vacancy occurred. The appointed senator was under a pledge to not run in the special election. In 2010, at the height of the national debate on the Affordable Care Act ("Obamacare"), Massachusetts voters elected Scott Brown, a Republican, to fill the vacancy created by Kennedy's death. Then in late 2012, when Senator Kerry's seat was to become vacant following his appointment as Secretary of State, Governor Deval Patrick, a Democrat, publicly stated that he would support a return of the law as it stood before 2004.[334]

Governors appointed 194 senators in the first 100 years after the Seventeenth Amendment's adoption.[335] Just over one-third of these senators was subsequently elected, slightly less than one-third lost their election bid, and the rest chose not to run for another term.[336] Fourteen of these appointed senators were women; seven of them were the incumbent senators' widows who agreed to serve until a successor was elected, two were spouses of the governor who appointed them, and one was the daughter of the governor who appointed her.[337] Three of those appointed were men appointed to fill vacancies created by the death of their fathers. Luther Strange became the 195th appointed senator in 2017 when Alabama's governor selected him to fill the seat vacated by Jeff Sessions when Sessions resigned to become the United States Attorney General.

Section 3—Implementation

This amendment shall not be so construed as to affect the election or term of any Senator chosen before it becomes valid as part of the Constitution.

This section ensured that all of the senators serving in the Senate when this amendment was ratified would be able to finish out their terms of office. They would face direct election only upon the expiration of their terms. (Not all senators are elected at once. Article I, section 3 provides that one third of the Senate stands for reelection every two years.) So it is that the Senate was entirely comprised of directly elected senators only in 1919, six years after the Seventeenth Amendment's ratification.

Those who advocated for direct election as a way to oust corrupt senators may have been disappointed in the results. While some of the 20 "corrupt" senators featured in "The Treason of the Senate" magazine series died or resigned before the Seventeenth Amendment's adoption, every one of the 24 incumbent senators on the ballot in the first direct election, held in 1914, won reelection.[338]

AMENDMENT XVIII—Prohibition

Passed by Congress December 18, 1917. Ratified January 16, 1919. Repealed in 1933 by Amendment XXI.

The Eighteenth Amendment resulted from the determined efforts of a decades-old temperance movement. "Temperance societies" were groups that opposed the sale and consumption of alcohol. Several had formed in various regions across the United States. They pushed to prohibit alcohol and found some success. Maine passed a law prohibiting alcohol in 1851. Kansas did the same in 1880 (although the law was generally not enforced). By 1913, approximately half of the national population lived in areas that had adopted prohibition.

Congress responded to lobbying by the various temperance societies, many of which helped elect candidates who supported prohibition, by passing the Interstate Liquor Act in 1913. The Act prohibited the interstate transportation of alcohol from "wet states," states permitting the manufacture and sale of alcohol, to "dry states," those that prohibited it.

The call for nationwide prohibition increased in 1917 with the United States's entry into World War I. The country needed grain to feed its troops; public opinion also remained opposed to anything associated with Germany (America's enemy in the war), including drinking German-made beer.[339] So it was that Congress passed the Eighteenth Amendment in December 1917, eight months after the United States entered the war. The necessary three-fourths of states ratified the amendment by January 1919.

Section 1—Prohibition of Intoxicating Liquor

[After one year from the ratification of this article the manufacture, sale, or transportation of intoxicating liquors within, the importation thereof into, or the exportation thereof from the United States and all territory subject to the jurisdiction thereof for beverage purposes is hereby prohibited.]

This section prohibited the "manufacture, sale, or transportation" – but not the consumption – of "intoxicating liquors" throughout the United States and its territories. Neither this section nor any other part of the amendment defined "intoxicating liquors." This created a problem when Congress acted under this amendment (as will be seen in the next section). The one-year "grace period" found in this section permitted businesses that manufactured or sold alcohol to wind down their affairs.

Section 2—Enforcement Power

[The Congress and the several States shall have concurrent power to enforce this article by appropriate legislation.]

Congress enacted the "National Prohibition Act" in 1919 as the legislation to enforce this amendment.[340] President Woodrow Wilson vetoed the bill, but both the House and Senate overrode the veto. Also known as the Volstead Act after its sponsor Representative Andrew Volstead, the bill caused immediate controversy.

To begin with, the Act defined "intoxicating liquors" as beverages containing an alcohol concentration greater than 0.5%. This effectively included all wine and beer, perhaps to the great disappointment of prohibition proponents who had intended to ban only hard liquor. (By comparison, today's beer has an average alcohol concentration of 4.65%, and wine averages 11.45%.)[341]

Second, the act contained several exemptions that made it difficult to enforce. These exemptions included permitting

189

liquor for medicinal, sacramental, and industrial purposes. Consequently, a physician could prescribe whiskey for a patient simply because the patient liked to drink it. And persons could make gin in their bathtubs by using industrial alcohol and other materials they were legally able to purchase.

Finally, this section also gave states the right to enforce prohibition.

Section 3—Seven-Year Time Limit

[This article shall be inoperative unless it shall have been ratified as an amendment to the Constitution by the legislatures of the several States, as provided in the Constitution, within seven years from the date of the submission hereof to the States by the Congress.]

This clause differs from those in the previously ratified amendments because it applied a time-limit to ratification. The necessary number of states ratified the amendment within fourteen months, far less than the seven years this clause permitted.

AMENDMENT XIX—Women's Suffrage

Passed by Congress June 4, 1919. Ratified August 18, 1920.

Section 1—Suffrage Not Denied Based on Sex

The right of citizens of the United States to vote shall not be denied or abridged by the United States or by any State on account of sex.

Since suffrage (the right to vote) comes from state law and not the federal Constitution, each state can create their own laws regarding voting. This amendment does not change that. Rather, it prohibits the federal and state governments from depriving citizens from voting because of their sex.

States, with few exceptions, had prohibited women from voting even before the Constitutional Convention in 1787. After New Jersey revoked women's suffrage in 1807, no state

190

permitted women to vote. In 1869, however, the Wyoming Territory gave women the right to vote in all elections. Wyoming kept equal suffrage when it achieved statehood in 1890. Other states followed suit, and 38 states (of 48) granted women at least some voting rights by 1919 (15 gave full voting rights).[342] Montana even elected a woman (Jeannette Rankin) to the U.S. House of Representatives in 1916, four years before this amendment's ratification! This amendment eliminated the need to further pursue women's suffrage on a state-by-state basis.

Section 2—Enforcement Power

Congress shall have power to enforce this article by appropriate legislation.

Congress has never enacted legislation under this section.

AMENDMENT XX—Altering Presidential and Congressional Terms

Passed by Congress March 2, 1932. Ratified January 23, 1933.

Section 1—Beginning of Terms of Office

The terms of the President and the Vice President shall end at noon on the 20th day of January, and the terms of Senators and Representatives at noon on the 3rd day of January, of the years in which such terms would have ended if this article had not been ratified; and the terms of their successors shall then begin.

This clause changed the starting date for the president and vice president's terms. It also changed the start date for new congressional terms. When the nation adopted the Constitution in the late 1700s, communication and travel were slow and difficult. So the Framers provided for a four-month period between November elections and the winners assuming their offices in early March. This allowed the winners to learn of their election, settle their affairs, and make their way to Washington.

Dramatic advances in travel and communication over the next 130 years made a four-month period between elections and inauguration largely unnecessary. Additionally, the extended break between election and inauguration provided a sort of leadership vacuum with the outgoing president at times failing to act and the president-elect being powerless to take action. The most acute example occurred after the 1860 election when several Southern states attempted to secede from the Union. Outgoing President James Buchanan did little to resist these states' taking control of federal property in their territory because he did not believe that Congress had "the power by force of arms to compel a State to remain in the Union" as "no such power ha[d] been delegated to Congress or to any other department of the Federal Government" by the Constitution.[343] President-elect Abraham Lincoln had a different view, stating that "no State upon its own mere motion can lawfully get out of the Union; that resolves and ordinances to that effect are legally void" and making clear his determination to maintain possession of federal property by force, if necessary.[344] The Civil War ensued after Lincoln's election when South Carolina attacked and seized Fort Sumter and Lincoln mobilized states militias to reclaim the property.[345]

Another example occurred after the 1932 election. A series of bank failures came about between the November election and President Franklin Roosevelt's inauguration in March. President Hoover perhaps felt powerless to act since he had just lost the election, and President-elect Roosevelt had no ability to act until taking office. This amendment shortened the period by approximately two months and so reduced the likelihood of such predicaments in the future.

Section 2—Beginning of Congressional Sessions

The Congress shall assemble at least once in every year, and such meeting shall begin at noon

**on the 3d day of January, unless they shall by
law appoint a different day.**

This section modified Article I, section 4, of the
Constitution, which mandated that Congress meet every year
beginning the first Monday of December. That section resulted
in an incoming Congress having to wait over one year between
its election and its first meeting. This amendment made the
wait time between election and the first meeting a matter of
two months.

Section 2 also shortened potential "lame duck" sessions
but did not necessarily eliminate them. (A politician who is
defeated in November but who remains in office until the end
of his or her term is known as a "lame duck.") Lame duck
sessions were typically unproductive with senators and
representatives failing to conduct meaningful legislative
activity during that time. Concurrently, lame duck sessions
pose problems in that defeated members of Congress are able
to vote on legislation without any accountability to voters. A
recent example of this scenario occurred in 2010. The
Democratic Party suffered substantial losses in the November
2010 elections and lost control of the House of
Representatives and its filibuster-proof majority in the Senate.
In response, the party aggressively pushed through a flurry of
legislation during a lame duck session. The measures
included: repealing the military's "Don't Ask, Don't Tell"
policy; ratifying a controversial nuclear arms treaty with
Russia known as New START; and confirming 19 federal
judges. A high-profile lame duck session occurred in 1998
when the House voted to impeach President Clinton for
perjury and obstruction of justice.[346]

Section 3—Presidential Succession

**If, at the time fixed for the beginning of the term
of the President, the President elect shall have
died, the Vice President elect shall become
President. If a President shall not have been
chosen before the time fixed for the beginning of
his term, or if the President elect shall have
failed to qualify, then the Vice President elect**

193

**shall act as President until a President shall have
qualified; and the Congress may by law provide
for the case wherein neither a President elect
nor a Vice President shall have qualified,
declaring who shall then act as President, or the
manner in which one who is to act shall be
selected, and such person shall act accordingly
until a President or Vice President shall have
qualified.**

This section addresses various hypothetical aspects of
presidential succession. In particular, it resolves questions of
what to do if the newly elected president or vice president
cannot assume his or her position.

If the president-elect dies before being inaugurated, this
section mandates that the vice president-elect become
president. If the president-elect fails to qualify for the
presidency (*i.e.*, fails to meet the requirements of Article II,
section 1), then the vice president-elect *acts* as president until
a president has qualified. The same is true if a president has
not been chosen before the beginning of the new term. This
latter scenario could play out if the House of Representatives
became responsible for selecting a president according to the
Twelfth Amendment but failed to choose a president before
January 20th at noon.

If neither the president-elect nor vice president-elect
qualifies for the presidency, then this section gives Congress
authority to select an individual to act as president until a
president or vice president has qualified for the position.
Congress acted under this provision to pass the Presidential
Succession Act of 1947. That law provides that if there is
neither a president nor vice president, then the Speaker of the
House acts as president. If there is no Speaker, or if the
Speaker fails to qualify, then the Senate president *pro tempore*
acts as president. Similarly, if he or she fails to qualify, then
the succession continues among the Cabinet officers in the
order in which their departments were created (*i.e.*, first the
Secretary of State, second the Secretary of the Treasury, third
the Secretary of Defense, etc.). To date, this section has not
been applied.

Section 4—<u>Vacancies</u>

The Congress may by law provide for the case of the death of any of the persons from whom the House of Representatives may choose a President whenever the right of choice shall have devolved upon them, and for the case of the death of any of the persons from whom the Senate may choose a Vice President whenever the right of choice shall have devolved upon them.

This section slightly differs from the last one. It specifically addresses a situation where the House of Representatives must choose a president or the Senate a vice president under the Twelfth Amendment (*i.e.*, no candidate secured a majority of the electoral votes, so the respective chamber of Congress makes the decision). Essentially, it gives Congress power to make a law directing what to do if one of the three candidates put before the House or Senate dies before a vote is taken. Congress has not acted under this section.

Section 5—<u>Effective Date</u>

Sections 1 and 2 shall take effect on the 15th day of October following the ratification of this article.

According to this section's terms, the start date for terms of office and also for convening Congress became effective on October 15, 1933. The 73rd Congress (1933-1935) thus convened its second session on January 3, 1934.

Section 6—<u>Time Limit</u>

This article shall be inoperative unless it shall have been ratified as an amendment to the Constitution by the legislatures of three-fourths of the several States within seven years from the date of its submission.

This provision was easily met with the amendment being ratified in less than one year.

AMENDMENT XXI—Repeal of Prohibition

Passed by Congress February 20, 1933. Ratified December 5, 1933.

Section 1—Repeal of the Eighteenth Amendment

The eighteenth article of amendment to the Constitution of the United States is hereby repealed.

This section repealed the Eighteenth Amendment only thirteen years after its ratification! It ended the "noble experiment" of prohibiting alcohol on a national scale.

Prohibition had succeeded in reducing overall alcohol consumption for a time. But it had also increased crime. Organized crime syndicates flooded the lucrative but now illegal market of alcohol production and distribution. They operated secret bars, known as "speakeasies," and violently clashed with rivals. The dramatic increase in crime soured prohibition advocates who soon pushed for its repeal.

The Eighteenth Amendment is the only amendment to be repealed.

Section 2—Preserving State Jurisdiction over Alcohol

The transportation or importation into any State, Territory, or possession of the United States for delivery or use therein of intoxicating liquors, in violation of the laws thereof, is hereby prohibited.

While the last section eliminated Prohibition on a national level, this section ensures that states are free to pass laws restricting or prohibiting alcohol without interference from the federal government or any other state. In essence, if a state has laws restricting alcohol, then alcohol cannot be transported or imported into that state if doing so violates the state's laws.

Following Prohibition's repeal, several states chose to remain "dry" and forbid the manufacture or sale of alcohol within their borders. Kansas continued statewide prohibition until 1948. Oklahoma did so until 1959. In 1966, Mississippi became the last state to repeal prohibition. Today, some states have delegated control over alcohol to the county or municipality level. So alcohol is prohibited in dozens of cities and counties across the United States. In Texas, for instance, seven counties are completely dry as of 2016. (There were 51 completely dry counties in Texas in 2003, and 53 completely dry counties within the state in 1995.)[347] And there are eight completely dry towns and 39 partially dry towns in New York state.[348]

Seventeen states continue to have a significant role in the sale of alcoholic beverages as of 2016. Known as "alcoholic beverage control states," these states maintain a monopoly over the wholesaling or retailing of alcoholic beverages. North Carolina is one of them. There, alcoholic beverages other than beer and wine must be purchased in liquor stores owned by local alcohol beverage control boards, often known as "ABC Stores."

Finally, despite this amendment's language guaranteeing state sovereignty over alcohol, Congress passed the National Minimum Drinking Age Act in 1984. The act dictated that states who did not legislate 21 years as the minimum age for purchasing and publicly possessing alcohol would lose portions of their annual federal highway apportionment funds. Not wanting to lose federal highway funds, all 50 states adopted 21 years as the minimum age. That is why today there appears to be a "national" minimum drinking age. Congress used a similar process in the 1990s to pressure states into adopting a 0.08 blood alcohol limit for drunk driving or lose 2% or more of their federal highway funds.[349]

Section 3—Seven-Year Time Limit for Ratification by Convention

This article shall be inoperative unless it shall have been ratified as an amendment to the

197

Constitution by conventions in the several States, as provided in the Constitution, within seven years from the date of the submission hereof to the States by the Congress.

This is the first and, to date, only time that an amendment to the Constitution has been ratified by state conventions rather than by the state legislatures. (Article V permits ratification by state conventions or by votes in the state legislatures.) The decision to submit the vote directly to the people permitted a swift repeal because it did not require state legislatures to convene. Ratification occurred less than 10 months after this amendment's proposal when Utah became the 36th state to ratify the amendment (out of the then-existing 48 states).

AMENDMENT XXII—Limiting Presidential Terms

Passed by Congress March 21, 1947. Ratified February 27, 1951.

Section 1—Two Term Limit

No person shall be elected to the office of the President more than twice, and no person who has held the office of President, or acted as President, for more than two years of a term to which some other person was elected President shall be elected to the office of President more than once. But this Article shall not apply to any person holding the office of President when this Article was proposed by Congress, and shall not prevent any person who may be holding the office of President, or acting as President, during the term within which this Article becomes operative from holding the office of President or acting as President during the remainder of such term.

This amendment limits a president's time in office to two terms, or a total of ten years if he or she served part of a previous president's term. So if a person either had acted as or had been president for more than two years of a previous president's term, then he or she could be elected to the presidency only once.

The amendment enshrines a tradition begun by George Washington of a president serving only two terms in office. President Washington voluntarily stepped down at the end of his second term. Presidents Jefferson, Madison, and Monroe (the third through fifth presidents) followed suit, and the practice become a sort of Constitutional tradition.

But not every president accepted this custom. President Ulysses S. Grant, who had served two terms as president from 1869 to 1877, unsuccessfully ran for a third term in 1880. President Theodore Roosevelt sought a third term in 1912 after having served as president from 1901 to 1909. President Franklin Roosevelt sought for, and won, a third term in office in 1940. And he was elected to a fourth term in 1944. This amendment's timing suggests that it was a reaction to President Franklin Roosevelt's actions.

This section's second sentence specifically exempted its application to President Harry Truman who was president when Congress proposed this amendment. President Truman assumed office upon President Franklin Roosevelt's death in 1945, and he served all but three months of President Roosevelt's fourth term. Once President Truman chose not to seek a third term in 1952, this amendment became effective for all future presidents.

Section 2—<u>Seven-Year Time Limit</u>

This article shall be inoperative unless it shall have been ratified as an amendment to the Constitution by the legislatures of three-fourths of the several States within seven years from the date of its submission to the States by the Congress.

States ratified the Twenty-second Amendment in a little less than four years; thus well within this section's seven-year time limit.

AMENDMENT XXIII—Electors for the District of Columbia

Passed by Congress June 16, 1960. Ratified March 29, 1961.

Section 1—Appointing of Electors

The District constituting the seat of Government of the United States shall appoint in such manner as Congress may direct:

A number of electors of President and Vice President equal to the whole number of Senators and Representatives in Congress to which the District would be entitled if it were a State, but in no event more than the least populous State; they shall be in addition to those appointed by the States, but they shall be considered, for the purposes of the election of President and Vice President, to be electors appointed by a State; and they shall meet in the District and perform such duties as provided by the twelfth article of amendment.

The District of Columbia gained presidential electors by this amendment. Article I, section 8 gives Congress power over a federal district that would be the seat of the national government. From that power, Congress created the District of Columbia (later renamed Washington, D.C.). Since the district was not a state, it did not have the right of representation in Congress, and its citizens lacked the ability to vote for president. This amendment resolved the latter issue by granting the district electors. As a compromise to states with small populations, the amendment fixes the number of electors to an amount equal to that of the smallest states rather than the district's population. So the district has three electoral votes.

This amendment only gives District residents the right to vote in presidential elections. Congress thus proposed the District of Columbia Voting Rights Amendment in 1978 to repeal the Twenty-third amendment and instead grant the District full representation in the House and the Senate, full representation in the Electoral College, and full participation in the amendment process. But the amendment would not have made the District into a state. The amendment expired by its terms in 1985 after only 18 of the required 38 states ratified it.

Despite this background, Senator Orrin Hatch of Utah sponsored legislation in 2009 to give Washington, D.C., a voting representative in Congress. (The District has never received Congressional representation under Article I of the Constitution because it is not a state.) Senator Hatch nevertheless stated, "I have studied the constitutional and policy issues in depth and am convinced now as much as ever that the Constitution allows Congress to provide a House seat for the District."[350] Senator Lisa Murkowski of Alaska disagreed and proposed instead a Constitutional amendment that would have achieved the same objective.[351]

Section 2—Power of Enforcement

The Congress shall have power to enforce this article by appropriate legislation.

This section simply grants Congress power to legislate the manner in which the District appoints its Electors. The District has appointed Electors for every presidential election since 1964.

AMENDMENT XXIV—Abolition of Poll Taxes

Passed by Congress August 27, 1962. Ratified January 23, 1964.

Section 1—*Prohibition of Poll Taxes in Federal Elections*

The right of citizens of the United States to vote in any primary or other election for President or Vice President, for electors for President or Vice President, or for Senator or Representative in Congress, shall not be denied or abridged by the United States or any State by reason of failure to pay poll tax or other tax.

This amendment ended the practice of poll taxes for federal elections. A "poll tax" is a tax, usually no more than a few dollars, that a person must pay in order to vote in an election.

Following the Fifteenth Amendment's adoption, several Southern states enacted poll taxes (among other measures) to prevent blacks from voting. The taxes prevented poor whites from voting as well. All eleven former Confederate states adopted poll taxes by 1902. But only five of them still had poll taxes when the nation ratified this amendment: Alabama, Arkansas, Mississippi, Texas, and Virginia.

The amendment is broadly worded to prohibit states from requiring payment of other taxes, such as a property tax, in place of the traditional poll tax.

Some, including former U.S. Attorney General Eric Holder, contend that laws requiring voters to present picture identification violate this amendment.[352] They claim that the cost associated with securing proper identification serves as a form of poll tax that disenfranchises the poor.

Section 2—Power of Enforcement

The Congress shall have power to enforce this article by appropriate legislation.

Congress has not specifically acted under this provision. While the Voting Rights Act of 1965 followed this amendment chronologically, that act was based on the power granted by the Fifteenth Amendment.

AMENDMENT XXV—Changes to Presidential Succession

Passed by Congress July 6, 1965. Ratified February 10, 1967.

Section 1—Presidential Vacancies

In case of the removal of the President from office or of his death or resignation, the Vice President shall become President.

This section formalized the vice president becoming president following the latter's death. The practice had been in place since 1841 when vice president John Tyler proclaimed that he was president following President William Harrison's death. Tyler's claim seemingly related back to Article II, section 6, which provides that the president's powers and duties "shall devolve on the Vice President" upon the president's removal from office, death, resignation, or inability to perform his or her duties. While some referred to Tyler as "Acting President," the nation accepted this succession.[353] The practice occurred seven more times over the next century as presidents died in office. The nation first applied this section in 1974 when President Richard Nixon resigned and Vice President Gerald Ford became President. The following chart shows each of the eight successions in U.S. history:

Year	Vice President Who Became President
1841	John Tyler (succeeded William Henry Harrison)
1850	Millard Fillmore (succeeded Zachary Taylor)
1865	Andrew Johnson (succeeded Abraham Lincoln)
1881	Chester A. Arthur (succeeded James A. Garfield)
1901	Theodore Roosevelt (succeeded William McKinley)
1923	Calvin Coolidge (succeeded Warren G. Harding)
1945	Harry Truman (succeeded Franklin Roosevelt)
1963	Lyndon Johnson (succeeded John F. Kennedy)
1974	Gerald Ford (succeeded Richard Nixon)

Section 2—Filling Vice Presidential Vacancies

Whenever there is a vacancy in the office of the Vice President, the President shall nominate a Vice President who shall take office upon

**confirmation by a majority vote of both Houses
of Congress.**

The president can nominate any person who qualifies for the office to be vice president if there is no vice president for any reason. That person then assumes the office if confirmed by a simple majority of both the House and Senate.

This section resolved an issue that had the Constitution had not provided for—a vacancy in the office of vice president. While the original text of the Constitution provided for the vice president to act as/become president, it made no provision for what to do if the office of vice president became vacant. So a vacancy could be filled only upon the next election. Prior to this amendment's proposal and ratification, the office of vice president had been vacant sixteen different times (seven deaths, one resignation, and eight succeeding to the presidency) for a total of 37 years—roughly 21% of the time to that point since the Founding!

Since its passage in 1967, this section has been applied twice. The first occurred in 1973 when Vice President Spiro Agnew resigned amid criminal charges. President Nixon nominated Gerald Ford, who was serving as the House minority leader, to be the vice president. Congress subsequently confirmed Ford.

The second instance occurred ten months after Ford's confirmation when President Nixon resigned amid the Watergate scandal. Ford became president as dictated by the previous section. With the office of vice president again being vacant, President Ford nominated Nelson Rockefeller to serve as vice president. Congress subsequently confirmed Rockefeller's nomination and he became the nation's forty-first vice president.

Section 3—<u>Presidential Disability: Declared by President</u>

**Whenever the President transmits to the
President pro tempore of the Senate and the
Speaker of the House of Representatives his
written declaration that he is unable to
discharge the powers and duties of his office,
and until he transmits to them a written**

> **declaration to the contrary, such powers and
> duties shall be discharged by the Vice President
> as Acting President.**

The president can temporarily transfer power to the vice president who serves as an Acting President. If the president believes that he or she will be unable to discharge the duties of office, then the president will send a letter stating so to both the Speaker of the House and the Senate president pro tempore. Power is then transferred to the vice president until the president again sends a letter to the same persons stating that he or she is again able to act as president.

Two presidents have invoked this section and temporarily transferred power a total of three times. The first occurred in 1985 when President Ronald Reagan transferred power to Vice President George H.W. Bush while Reagan had colon surgery. The second instance happened in 2002 when President George W. Bush transferred power to Vice President Dick Cheney during the time Bush was sedated for a colonoscopy. President Bush invoked this section again in 2007 when he was sedated for another colonoscopy.

This section's genesis was an agreement between President Dwight Eisenhower and Vice President Richard Nixon in the late 1950s. After suffering a heart attack in 1955, President Eisenhower asked Congress to pass a Constitutional amendment concerning a president's inability to discharge presidential duties, including who would make the determination. Congress failed to act; Eisenhower responding by making an agreement with Nixon. Eisenhower wanted to eliminate the Constitutional uncertainty regarding presidential disability and clearly spell out how a vice president takes over for a disabled president. Eisenhower ensured that his agreement with Nixon was public knowledge, in part so that Nixon could not be accused of usurping authority. Eisenhower and Nixon never acted under the agreement despite two instances when they could have: Eisenhower's hospitalization in 1956 and when he suffered a stroke in 1957.[354] President John F. Kennedy and Vice President Lyndon Johnson had a similar agreement.

Section 4—Presidential Disability: Declared by Others

Whenever the Vice President and a majority of either the principal officers of the executive departments or of such other body as Congress may by law provide, transmit to the President pro tempore of the Senate and the Speaker of the House of Representatives their written declaration that the President is unable to discharge the powers and duties of his office, the Vice President shall immediately assume the powers and duties of the office as Acting President.

Thereafter, when the President transmits to the President pro tempore of the Senate and the Speaker of the House of Representatives his written declaration that no inability exists, he shall resume the powers and duties of his office unless the Vice President and a majority of either the principal officers of the executive department or of such other body as Congress may by law provide, transmit within four days to the President pro tempore of the Senate and the Speaker of the House of Representatives their written declaration that the President is unable to discharge the powers and duties of his office. Thereupon Congress shall decide the issue, assembling within forty-eight hours for that purpose if not in session. If the Congress, within twenty-one days after receipt of the latter written declaration, or, if Congress is not in session, within twenty-one days after Congress is required to assemble, determines by two-thirds vote of both Houses that the President is unable to discharge the powers and duties of his office, the Vice President shall continue to discharge the same as Acting President; otherwise, the President shall resume the powers and duties of his office.

While section 3 concerned a president claiming his or her own disability, this section concerns *others* declaring presidential incapacity. It allows the vice president and a majority of the Cabinet to declare the president unable to discharge presidential duties, and so allow the vice president to serve as Acting President. These persons must send a declaration of presidential disability to both the Speaker of the House and the Senate president pro tempore. The president will resume the powers and duties of the presidency only after he or she informs both the Speaker and the president pro tempore that no disability exists.

If the president informs the Speaker and the president pro tempore that no disability exists, the vice president and a majority of the Cabinet may contest the president's assertion and submit a second declaration of the president's inability to fulfill his or her duties. This second declaration forces the matter into Congress. Only if two-thirds of Congress considers the president to be unable to fulfill his or her duties will the vice president continue as Acting President. Otherwise, the president resumes all presidential powers and duties.

Some question whether this section should have been invoked in 1981 following an assassination attempt on President Ronald Reagan. President Reagan underwent emergency surgery to remove the would-be assassin's bullet and so was in no condition to declare the disability himself. He was then in the hospital for two weeks after surgery, was able to work only a few hours per day upon returning from the hospital, and did not preside over a cabinet meeting for almost one month. Even so, neither Vice President Bush nor members of the Cabinet seriously considered using this section. It has never been applied.

AMENDMENT XXVI—Lowering the Voting Age to 18

Passed by Congress March 23, 1971. Ratified July 1, 1971.

Section 1—Suffrage Not Denied Based on Age

The right of citizens of the United States, who are eighteen years of age or older, to vote shall

**not be denied or abridged by the United States
or by any State on account of age.**

The final suffrage (right to vote) amendment, the
Twenty-sixth Amendment, lowered the voting age from 21 to
18 in all elections (federal, state, and local). It came during the
Vietnam War, amid protests that since 18 to 21-year-olds were
being drafted into the military and forced to fight, they should
have the right to vote and so select the leaders who made the
decisions about fighting. Prior to this amendment, only a few
states permitted persons under 21 to vote: Georgia and
Kentucky granted voting rights at 18, Alaska at 19, and
Hawaii at 20.[355]

States responded by ratifying this amendment in less
than four months, record time for a Constitutional amendment.
After a 55% turnout in 1972, the first election in which 18 to
21-year-olds were permitted to vote, turnout among this group
has been relatively low. In 2012, for example, only 38% voted
compared to 45% four years earlier.[356]

Section 2—Enforcement Power

**The Congress shall have power to enforce this
article by appropriate legislation.**

Congress has never enacted legislation under this
section.

AMENDMENT XXVII—Congressional Compensation

*Passed by Congress September 25, 1789. Ratified May 7,
1992.*

**No law, varying the compensation for the
services of the Senators and Representatives,
shall take effect, until an election of
representatives shall have intervened.**

Short and to the point, the Twenty-seventh Amendment
requires any changes to Congressional compensation to occur
only at the beginning of the representatives' next term of

office. In other words, any act by Congress to give its members a raise (or even to decrease their salary) is effective only after the next election for representatives has occurred. This amendment thus prohibits Congress from giving itself an immediate pay raise. It also gives the people a restraint—an election—on their elected representatives.

This amendment is actually the second of the first twelve amendments presented to the states in 1789. (The final ten of these were ratified and are known as the Bill of Rights.) But a sufficient number of states failed to ratify the amendment at that time. In 1982, Gregory Watson, a student at the University of Texas, noted that the amendment could still be ratified. Watson then organized and led a nationwide push to ratify the amendment. Congress significantly helped his effort by voting itself large pay increases throughout the 1980s, with Congressional salaries more than doubling between 1979 and 1991. In 1992, Michigan became the 38th state to ratify the amendment, thus making it part of the Constitution – 202 years after being proposed!

Congress has largely skirted the effects of this amendment through annual "Cost of Living Adjustments" mandated by a law Congress passed shortly before this amendment's ratification. That law mandates annual pay increases, tied to increased living costs resulting from inflation, unless Congress specifically passes legislation declining the annual adjustment. Consequently, Congressional salaries in 2017 stood at $174,000 – nearly a thirty percent increase from the salary set by law in 1991 before this amendment took effect. (Salaries reached that figure in 2009; Congress declined the increases over the next several years.)[357]

For purposes of comparison, the first Congress in 1789 set annual compensation at $6 per day (approx. $1,500 per year).[358] Adjusted for inflation, that amount equaled roughly $39,112 in 2017. With such a small salary, could this perhaps explain the term "public servant?"

> I doubt . . . whether any Convention we can obtain,
> may be able to make a better Constitution. For
> when you assemble a number of men to have the
> advantage of their joint wisdom, you inevitably
> assemble with those men, all their prejudices, their
> passions, their errors of opinion, their local
> interests, and their selfish views. From such an
> Assembly can a perfect production be expected? It
> therefore astonishes me, Sir, to find this system
> approaching so near to perfection as it does . . . .
>   — Benjamin Franklin, to the
>   Constitutional Convention,
>   September 17, 1787[359]

The Constitution isn't perfect. The document's almost
doubling in size—from 4,400 words to approximately 7,591
through 27 amendments—makes that clear. But it's not
supposed to be perfect. The Constitution's preamble says it is
to "form a more perfect union." It does. The form of
government created by the United States Constitution still is
more perfect than any other on earth in protecting natural
rights and preserving freedom.

Indeed, the Constitution is the world's oldest written
national constitution and has been a model for all later
constitutions.[360] None of them have achieved the same lasting
power or success. One reason is that the Constitution creates a
government that exists to protect rights, not to grant them at a
monarch's or a ruling party's whim. Another reason is its
source. Many Framers attributed the Constitution's creation to
a source greater than man. James Madison, writing in
Federalist No. 37, commented: "It is impossible for the man
of pious reflection not to perceive in [the Constitution] a
finger of that Almighty hand which has been so frequently and
signally extended to our relief in the critical stages of the
revolution."

The Constitution is unique. It has withstood over two
centuries of a changing world, vast social and political
movements, and significant population growth. If it is to

endure and fulfill its purpose of preserving "the blessings of liberty to ourselves and our posterity," then it must be maintained in the minds of the people and the leaders they elect. And if it is to be maintained in the minds of the people and their leaders, then all need to study the document for themselves, come to their own conclusions, and then *act* with their knowledge.

Different views on the Constitution's constraints will necessarily result. Yet having different views is not wrong. The Framers certainly did not agree on the Constitution's influence in practice as shown by various examples in this book. Their differing opinions caused the nation's civil and political discourse to center on and relate back to the Constitution. So if the same occurs now, then we are one step closer to achieving Lincoln's goal of having the Constitution and its laws becoming America's political religion.

Form your own opinions based on your knowledge of the Constitution. Encourage others to do the same. Then bring your informed views to the public square and the issues facing society. When this occurs, the discourse will be centered on the Constitution. People will no longer be sidetracked by someone else's interpretation. Actions will be grounded in the Constitution's principles, the most unique and enduring in the world. The Constitution will be our political religion. And our nation will endure as we form a more perfect union.

Term	Definition	Location
Acquittal	Being declared not guilty of a crime	Amend. V
Amnesty	A form of a pardon issued to a group rather than a specifically named individual	Art. II, § 2
Appropriation Bill	Legislation authorizing the government to spend money; required to begin in the House of Representatives	Art. I, § 7
Attainder	An instance in which a person convicted of a crime forfeits his or her property	Art. III, § 3
Bill of Attainder	A law that criminally punishes a named person or group of people without a judicial trial	Art. I, § 9
Blue Slip	A formal rejection notice given by the House to the Senate for appropriations bills that have not begun in the House	Art. I, § 7
Capital Crime	A crime punishable by death	Amend. VIII
Civil Arrest	Physically detaining an individual if there was a civil lawsuit against him or her	Art. I, § 6
Clemency	The ability to reduce punishment imposed on those convicted of crimes by granting pardons and reprieves	Art. II, § 2

Term	Definition	Location
Commutation	A form of a pardon that changes a convict's punishment to one that is less severe without forgiving the crime itself, such as reducing a convicted murderer's sentence from death to life imprisonment	Art. II, § 2
Congress	The national legislature made up of the Senate and House of Representatives	Art. I
Copyright	An exclusive right granted to an author to protect his or her writings	Art. I, § 8
Corruption of Blood	Prohibiting a person convicted of attainder from inheriting property from an ancestor, keep the property he or she had, or transfer any property to his or her heirs because the person's blood "tainted" by the crime committed	Art. III, § 3
Court-Martial	A military court to try members of the armed forces	Art. III, § 3
Diversity Jurisdiction	The federal courts' legal authority to hear and rule on cases between citizens of different states	Art. III, § 2
Double Jeopardy	Prosecuting a person twice for the same crime	Amend. V

Term	Definition	Location
Due Process	A concept requiring the government to act fairly towards its citizens by following the law and providing fair procedures	Amendments V and XIV
Duty of Tonnage	A charge imposed on commercial ships entering, remaining in, or exiting a port	Art. I, § 10
Electoral College	The body that elects the president and vice president	Art. II, § 1
Eminent Domain	The government's ability to take private property for a public use	Amend. V
Emolument	The salary and/or benefits associated with an office of government	Art. I, § 6
Equity	The judicial power permitting courts to apply principles of fairness and justice that might otherwise be lost by strictly applying the written law	Art. III, § 2
Ex Post Facto	A law that is adopted after an act is committed but that applies retroactively	Art. I, § 9
Excise	A tax on the manufacture, consumption, or sale of goods	Art. I, § 8

Term	Definition	Location
Executive	The branch of government responsible for "executing" (carrying out/implementing) the laws passed by Congress	Art. II
Extradition	A process in which if a person commits a crime in one state and then goes to another, the second state "surrenders" (sends back) the fugitive to the state in which he or she committed the crime	Art. IV, § 2
Federal Appellate Courts/Circuit Courts	Intermediate courts between federal district courts and the Supreme Court that the federal judicial power by hearing appeals from the district courts	Art. III, § 1
Federal District Courts	Trial courts exercising the federal judicial power	Art. III, § 1
Filibuster	An act, such as an extended speech or series of speeches, that blocks action by prolonging debate and prohibiting voting on an issue	Art. I, § 5

Term	Definition	Location
Grand Jury	A group of 16-23 citizens randomly selected by a court to analyze evidence related to a crime and to determine if there is sufficient evidence ("probable cause") for the government to formally prosecute a person suspected of having committed the crime	Amend. V
Great Compromise	The proposal put forth by Roger Sherman in the Constitutional Convention that incorporated aspects of both the Virginia and New Jersey plans—proportional representation in the lower house and equal representation in the upper. The compromise also required that all laws generating revenue start in the lower house. Also known as the "Connecticut Compromise" because Roger Sherman was a delegate from Connecticut.	Art. I, § 1

216

Term	Definition	Location
Habeas Corpus/Writ of Habeas Corpus	A Latin phrase meaning "you shall have the body;" a writ of habeas corpus is a legal tool requiring a jailed/imprisoned person to be brought in front of a court or a judge	Art. I, § 9
House of Representatives	One of the legislative branch's two chambers; comprised of 435 representatives from the 50 states who are elected to two-year terms of office	Art. I, § 2
Hung Jury	A jury in a criminal case that cannot agree on a verdict because there are not enough votes to either convict or acquit the accused	Amend. V
Impeachment	The power to formally accuse and bring charges against government officials for wrongdoing	Art. I, § 2; Art. II, § 4
Indictment	A proceeding where the grand jury considers evidence submitted by the prosecuting officer	Amend. V
Infamous Crime	A crime where imprisonment is a penalty	Amend. V
Joint Resolution	Legislation similar to a public bill that may involve multiple issues	Art. I, § 7

Term	Definition	Location
Judicial Power	The power to resolve cases by giving a final, binding decision	Art. III, § 1
Jurisdiction	A court's legal authority to hear a case	Art. III, § 2
Lame Duck	A politician who is defeated in an election but who remains in office until the end of his or her term	Amend. XX
Letter of Marque	A formal document licensing a private citizen to attack and seize goods or citizens of other nations	Art. I, § 8
Original Jurisdiction	The court where cases are first heard	Art. III, § 2
Pardon	An act granting forgiveness of a crime and the associated penalty	Art. II, § 2
Patent	An exclusive right granted to inventors to protect their discoveries	Art. I, § 8
Pocket Veto	A term given to presidential vetoes that occur by the president holding the bill without signing it for 10 days and Congress adjourning during that time	Art. I, § 7
Poll Tax	A tax, usually no more than a few dollars, that a person must pay in order to vote in an election	Amend. XXIV

Term	Definition	Location
Precedent	Past judicial decisions that create law	Amend. VII
Presentment	A proceeding where the grand jury collects the evidence itself (*i.e.*, calls witnesses to testify before it	Amend. V
Private Bill	A type of legislation providing specified benefits to named individuals	Art. I, § 7
Pro Forma	Legislative sessions often lasting less than a minute, with only a few members of a chamber and with no formal business being conducted, that are done "as a matter of formality"	Art. I, § 5
Pro Tempore	A Latin phrase meaning "for the time being" or "temporarily," it refers to the Senate president pro-tempore, the Senate's presiding officer in the vice president's absence	Art. I, § 3
Probable Cause	enough evidence to suggest that the search will reveal criminal activity or contraband but less evidence than needed for a conviction	Amend. IV
Public Bill	A type of legislation providing for general application to the public	Art. I, § 7

Term	Definition	Location
Quorum	A majority of a legislative chamber's members	Art. I, § 5
Reconciliation	A Senate rule that limits debate in the Senate to twenty hours before a vote is taken, and requires only a simple majority to pass, essentially prohibiting a filibuster	Art. I, § 5
Reprieve	A form of clemency postponing of punishment, such as delaying the execution of a prisoner sentenced to death	Art. II, § 2
Saxbe Fix	A procedure decreasing a Cabinet official's salary to its prior level so that a member of Congress who previously voted to raise that official's salary can assume the office without violating the Emoluments Clause	Art. I, § 6
Senate	One of the legislative branch's two chambers; comprised of 100 senators (two from each state) who are elected to six-year terms of office	Art. I, § 3
Simple Majority	A bare majority, such as 51 senators out of the 100	Art. I, § 5

Term	Definition	Location
Sine Dine	Legislative adjournments done without fixing a date for a new meeting at the end of a congressional session, with each chamber adopting a resolution to adjourn	Art. I, § 5
Sovereign Immunity	The concept of a government not being able to be sued without its consent	Art. I, § 11
Statute	Laws passed by legislative enactments	Art. I
Super Majority	A term generally applied to a two-thirds majority	Art. V
Tariff	A tax on exports or imports	Art. I, § 8
Treason	Waging war against the United States or giving aid and comfort to its enemies	Art. III, § 3
Treaty	An agreement between two national governments	Art. I
Veto	A Latin phrase meaning "I forbid," the term applied to the president's rejection of legislation from Congress	Art. I, § 7

THE U.S. CONSTITUTION – AN OVERVIEW

Article I – The Legislative Branch
Section 1: The Federal Congress
Section 2: The House of Representatives
Section 3: The Senate
Section 4: Congressional Elections
Section 5: Congressional Rules and Procedures
Section 6: Congressional Compensation, Privileges and
            Immunities, and Prohibitions
Section 7: The Legislative Process
Section 8: Powers Granted Congress
Section 9: Powers Denied Congress
Section 10: Powers Denied the States

Article II – The Executive Branch
Section 1: The President – Elections and Qualifications
Section 2: Powers of the President
Section 3: Presidential Powers and Duties to Congress
Section 4: Impeachment

Article III – The Judicial Branch
Section 1: Federal Judicial Power, Courts, and Judges
Section 2: Federal Jurisdiction and Jury Trials
Section 3: Treason Defined

Article IV – States' Relations and Rights
Section 1: Full Faith and Credit
Section 2: States' Obligations
Section 3: Admission of New States and Power Over
            Federal Property
Section 4: Obligations of the United States

Article V – Amending the Constitution

Article VI – Constitutional Supremacy

Article VII – Ratification

Amendments I through X – The Bill of Rights

Amendment I:	Freedom of Religion, Speech, Press, Assembly, and Petition
Amendment II:	Right to Keep and Bear Arms
Amendment III:	Quartering of Soldiers
Amendment IV:	Unreasonable Search and Seizure
Amendment V:	Criminal Protections, Due Process, and Just Compensation
Amendment VI:	Rights of the Accused
Amendment VII:	Trial by Jury in Civil Cases
Amendment VIII:	Bail and Punishment
Amendment IX:	Rights Retained by the People
Amendment X:	Powers Reserved to the States or People

Amendments XI through XXVII – Other Amendments

Amendment XI:	Restricting Judicial Power for Suits Against States
Amendment XII:	Modifying the Electoral College Process
Amendment XIII:	Abolishing Slavery
Amendment XIV:	Civil and Political Rights
Amendment XV:	Voting Rights Not Denied Based on Race or Color
Amendment XVI:	Income Tax
Amendment XVII:	Direct Election of Senators
Amendment XVIII:	Prohibition of Alcohol
Amendment XIX:	Voting Rights Not Denied Based on Sex
Amendment XX:	Presidential and Congressional Terms
Amendment XXI:	Repeal of Prohibition
Amendment XXII:	Two-term Limit of President
Amendment XXIII:	Electors for the District of Columbia
Amendment XXIV:	Abolition of Poll Taxes
Amendment XXV:	Presidential Succession
Amendment XXVI:	Voting Rights Not Denied Based on Age
Amendment XXVII:	Congressional Compensation

NOTES

[1] THE COLLECTED WORKS OF ABRAHAM LINCOLN, Vol. I, p. 112 Roy P. Basler, editor. Rutgers University Press, 1953.

[2] First Inaugural Address of Abraham Lincoln, THE AVALON PROJECT, Yale Law School, http://avalon.law.yale.edu/19th_century/lincoln1.asp (last viewed July 27, 2017) (capitalization modernized).

[3] *See Kentucky v. Dennison,* 65 U.S. 66 (1860).

[4] *See Puerto Rico v. Branstad,* 483 U.S. 219 (1987).

[5] *Compare Plessy v. Ferguson,* 163 U.S. 537 (1896), *with Brown v. Board of Education,* 347 U.S. 483 (1954).

[6] Madison Debates, September 17, THE AVALON PROJECT, Yale Law School, http://avalon.law.yale.edu/18th_century/debates_917.asp (last viewed July 6, 2015).

[7] WILLIAM EWART GLADSTONE: LIFE AND PUBLIC SERVICES, ed. Thomas W. Handford (Chicago: The Dominican Co., 1898), p. 323.

[8] The FEDERALIST No. 53.

[9] *Id.*

[10] *Id.*

[11] *Id.*

[12] Ronald Brownstein, *Heartland Heartache,* THE NATIONAL JOURNAL (November 4, 2010), *available at* http://www.nationaljournal.com/columns/political-connections/a-heartland-headache-for-dems-20101104 (last viewed February 23, 2015).

[13] CNN Wire Staff, *Republicans capture control of House,* CNN (November 3, 2010), *available at* http://www.cnn.com/2010/ POLITICS/11/03/election.house/ (last viewed February 23, 2015).

[14] *The 115th Congress By the Numbers,* LEGISTORM, *available at* https://www.legistorm.com/congress_by_numbers/index/by/house/mode/religion .html (last viewed February 10, 2017); Jennifer E. Manning, *Membership of the 115th Congress: A Profile,* Congressional Research Service (March 13, 2017), *available at* https://fas.org/sgp/crs/misc/R44762.pdf (last viewed May 29, 2017).

[15] Lee Davidson, *Chaffetz home a hurdle?* DESERET MORNING NEWS (July 6, 2008), *available at* http://www.deseretnews.com /article/700240960/Chaffetz-home-a-hurdle.html?pg=all (last viewed May 29, 2013).

[16] *Id.*

[17] *Id.*

[18] Jennifer Feehan, *Gillmore family rarely seen at new 'residence' in Tiffin,* TOLEDO BLADE, (Nov. 2, 2006), available at <http://toledoblade.com/apps/pbcs.dll/article?AID=/20061102/NEWS09/611020353/-1/NEWS> (last viewed February 19, 2010).

[19] Javier Panzar, *These California lawmakers don't live in the districts they represent,* THE LOS ANGELES TIMES (Dec. 22, 2015), *available at* <http://www.latimes.com/politics/la-pol-ca-congress-living-outside-district-20151222-html-htmlstory.html> (last viewed January 17, 2017).

[20] Apportionment Data, US Census Bureau http://www.census.gov/2010census/data/apportionment-data-text.php (last viewed July 23, 2013).

[21] Current Vacancies of the 115h Congress, 1st Session, clerk.house.gov, http://clerk.house.gov/member_info/vacancies.aspx (last viewed May 29, 2017).

[22] Edition for Educators—The House By the Numbers, history.house.gov, (November 29, 2016), http://history.house.gov/Blog/Detail/15032440091, (last viewed December 15, 2016).

[23] THE FEDERALIST No. 53.

[24] "Class," *United States Senate Glossary*, https://www.senate.gov/reference/glossary_term/class.htm (last viewed March 9, 2015).

[25] *The 115th Congress By the Numbers*, LEGISTORM, *available at* https://www.legistorm.com/congress_by_numbers/index/by/house/mode/religion.html (last viewed February 10, 2017).

[26] Jennifer E. Manning, *Membership of the 115th Congress: A Profile*, Congressional Research Service (March 13, 2017).

[27] *See Senators Born Outside of the United States*, U.S. SENATE, www.senate.gov (direct cite at http://www.senate.gov/pagelayout/reference/three_column_table/Foreign_born.htm).

[28] *See Shields, James (1806/1810 - 1879)*, Biographical Directory of the United States Congress, http://bioguide.congress.gov/scripts/biodisplay.pl?index=S000362 (last viewed May 29, 2013); *see also Senator for Three States*, http://www.senate.gov/artandhistory/history/minute/Senator_for_three_states.htm (last viewed July 27, 2013).

[29] Adam Nagourney, *In a Kennedy's Legacy, Lessons and Pitfalls For Hillary Clinton; Carpetbagger Issue Has Echoes of '64, But Differences Could Prove Crucial*, THE NEW YORK TIMES (September 10, 2000), *available at* http://www.nytimes.com/2000/09/10/nyregion/kennedy-s-legacy-lessons-pitfalls-for-hillary-clinton-carpetbagger-issue-has.html?pagewanted=all&src=pm (last viewed July 27, 2013).

[30] Stephanie Condon, *Sen. Richard Lugar declared ineligible to vote in home Indiana precinct*, CBS NEWS (March 15, 2012), http://www.cbsnews.com/news/sen-richard-lugar-declared-ineligible-to-vote-in-home-indiana-precinct/ (last viewed March 9, 2015).

[31] Jonathan Martin, *Lacking a House, a Senator Is Renewing His Ties in Kansas*, THE NEW YORK TIMES (February 7, 2014), *available at* https://www.nytimes.com/2014/02/08/us/senator-races-to-show-ties-including-an-address-in-kansas.html (last viewed June 30, 2017).

[32] *Sen. Richard Lugar*, govtrack.us, https://www.govtrack.us/congress/members/richard_lugar/300070 (last viewed March 9, 2015).

[33] *Sen. Orrin Hatch*, govtrack.us, <https://www.govtrack.us/congress/members/orrin_hatch/300052> (last viewed December 14, 2016).

[34] Thomas Jefferson, 2nd Vice President (1797-1801), US Senate, senate.gov, http://www.senate.gov/artandhistory/history/common/generic/VP_Thomas_Jefferson.htm (last viewed July 27, 2013).

[35] *President Pro Tempore*, US Senate, senate.gov, http://www.senate.gov/artandhistory/history/common/briefing/President_Pro_Tempore.htm (last viewed July 27, 2013).

[36] October 2, 2008 Debate Transcript, COMMISSION ON PRESIDENTIAL DEBATES (October 2, 2008) http://www.debates.org/index.php?page=2008-debate-transcript-2 (last viewed March 9, 2015).

[37] *President Pro Tempore*, US Senate, senate.gov, http://www.senate.gov/artand history/history/common/briefing/President_Pro_Tempore.htm (last viewed March 9, 2015).

[38] October 2, 2008 Debate Transcript, COMMISSION ON PRESIDENTIAL DEBATES (October 2, 2008).

[39] Senate Organization Chart for the 113th Congress, http:// www.senate.gov/ pagelayout/senators/a_three_sections_with_teasers/leadership.htm

[40] Monica Davey, *Blagojevich Sentenced to 14 Years in Prison*, THE NEW YORK TIMES (December 7, 2011), *available at* http://www.nytimes.com/2011/12/08/us/blagojevich-expresses-remorse-in-courtroom-speech.html?_r=0 (last viewed May 29, 2013).

[41] Jennifer Steinhauer, *Senate, for Just the 8th Time, Votes to Oust a Federal Judge*, THE NEW YORK TIMES (December 8, 2010), *available at* http://www.nytimes.com/2010/12/09/us/ politics/09judge.html?_r=0 (last viewed July 27, 2013).

[42] 17 Stat. 28.

[43] *See Gallatin, Albert (1761 - 1849)*, Biographical Directory of the United States Congress, http://bioguide.congress.gov/scripts/biodisplay.pl?index=G000020 (last viewed May 30, 2013).

[44] The Senate eventually seated Smoot only after the vote to expel him fell short of the two-thirds majority. *Expulsion and Censure*, United States Senate, *available at* http://www.senate.gov/artandhistory/history/common/briefing/ Expulsion_Censure.htm (last viewed May 30, 2013)

[45] *The Election Case of Frank L. Smith of Illinois (1928)*, http://www.senate.gov/artandhistory/history/common/contested_elections/110Fr ank_Smith.htm (last viewed May 30, 2013)

[46] Lee Davidson, *Chaffetz home a hurdle?* DESERET MORNING NEWS (July 6, 2008).

[47] Christopher M. Davis, *Invoking Cloture in the Senate*, Congressional Research Service (November 25, 2013), *available at* http://www.senate.gov/CRSReports/crs-publish.cfm?pid=%26 *2%3C4QLS%3E%0A (last viewed March 4, 2014).

[48] Robert C. Byrd, *Topic A -- The End of Bipartisanship for Obama's Big Initiatives?*, THE WASHINGTON POST (March 22, 2009), *available at* http://www.washingtonpost.com/wp-dyn/ content/article/2009/03/20/ AR2009032002941.html (last viewed March 4, 2014).

[49] Jack Maskell, *Expulsion, Censure, Reprimand, and Fine: Legislative Discipline in the House of Representatives*, Congressional Research Service (June 27, 2016), available at https://www.fas.org/sgp/crs/misc/RL31382.pdf (last viewed October 5, 2016).

[50] *Expulsion and Censure*, United States Senate, available at http://www.senate.gov/artandhistory/history/common/briefing/Expulsion_Censur e.htm#censure (last viewed December 15, 2016).

[51] Ida A. Brudnick, *Salaries of Members of Congress: Recent Actions and Historical Tables*, Congressional Research Service (February 23, 2016), *available at* https://www.fas.org/sgp/crs/misc/97-1011.pdf (last viewed March 16, 2016).

[52] Stephen Losey, *1 in 6 retired lawmakers get six figure pensions*, THE FEDERAL TIMES (November 5, 2012), *available at* http://www.federaltimes.com/article/20121105/BENEFITS02/311050001/1-6-retired-lawmakers-get-six-figure-pensions (last viewed May 30, 2013).

[53] Katelin P. Isaacs, *Retirement Benefits for Members of Congress*, Congressional Research Service (November 10, 2016), *available at* <https://fas.org/sgp/crs/misc/RL30631.pdf> (last viewed January 20, 2017).

[54] David F. Forte, *Privilege from Arrest*, THE HERITAGE GUIDE TO THE CONSTITUTION, p. 80 (Edwin Meese and David F. Forte, eds.) (2006).

[55] Pete Kasperowicz, *Rep. Luis Gutierrez arrested after protesting ICE headquarters in Chicago*, WASHINGTON EXAMINER (March 13, 2017), available at <http://www.washingtonexaminer.com/rep-luis-gutierrez-arrested-after-protesting-ice-headquarters-in-chicago/article/2617225> (last viewed May 30, 2017).

[56] Julia Preston, *8 Lawmakers Arrested at Immigration Protest*, THE NEW YORK TIMES (October 8, 2013), *available at* http:// www.nytimes.com/2013/10/09/us/8-lawmakers-arrested-at-immigration-protest.html?_r=0 (last viewed March 11, 2015).

[57] Neda Semnani, *Clooneys, Members of Congress Arrested*, ROLL CALL (March 16, 2012), *available at* http://hoh.rollcall.com/clooneys-members-of-congress-arrested/ (last viewed May 30, 2013).

[58] *Wuterich v. Murtha*, 562 F.3d 375 (2009).

[59] Al Kamen, *Hillary Clinton's Fix*, THE WASHINGTON POST (November 19, 2008) *available at* http://voices.washingtonpost .com/44/2008/11/hillary-clintons-fix.html (last viewed May 30, 2013).

[60] Mary Russell, *Robert Byrd Sees Saxbe Job Illegal*, THE WASHINGTON POST (November 20, 1973), A1, *available at* http://media.washingtonpost.com/wp-srv/nation/pdf/saxbeand byrd_112073.pdf (last viewed March 23, 2015).

[61] H.R. 3997, The U.S. Congress Votes Database, THE WASHINGTON POST, http://projects.washingtonpost.com/ congress/110/house/2/votes/674/ (last viewed May 30, 2013).

[62] U.S. Senate Roll Call Votes 110th Congress - 2nd Session, Dodd Amdt. No. 5685, http://www.senate.gov/legislative/LIS/ roll_call_lists/roll_call_vote_cfm.cfm?congress=110&session=2&vote=00212 (last viewed May 30, 2013).

[63] Final Vote Results for Roll Call 681, Emergency Economic Stabilization Act of 2008, www.house.gov, http://clerk.house.gov/evs/2008/roll681.xml.

[64] James V. Saturno, *The Origination Clause of the U.S. Constitution: Interpretation and Enforcement*, Congressional Research Service (March 15, 2011), *available at* http://www .fas.org/sgp/crs/misc/RL31399.pdf (last viewed April 15, 2014).

[65] Gerhard Peters. "Presidential Vetoes." The American Presidency Project. Ed. John T. Woolley and Gerhard Peters. Santa Barbara, CA: University of California. 1999-2013. Available at <http://www.presidency.ucsb.edu/data/vetoes.php> (last viewed January 20, 2017).

[66] Summary of Bills Vetoed: 1789 to Present, United States Senate, *available at* <http://www.senate.gov/reference/Legislation/Vetoes/vetoCounts.htm> (last viewed January 20, 2017).

[67] Richard S. Beth, *Bills and Resolutions: Examples of How Each Kind is Used*, Congressional Research Service (January 27, 1999), *available at* Washington D.C., USA. UNT Digital Library. http://digital.library.unt.edu/ark:/67531/metacrs913/ (last viewed March 23, 2015); *Annexation of Texas. Joint Resolution of the Congress of the United States, March 1, 1845* The Avalon Project, Yale Law School, *available at* http://avalon .law.yale.edu/19th_century/texan01.asp (last viewed March 23, 2015).

[68] This breakdown of powers is not unique and has been applied by others authors. *See, e.g.,* Reva Marx Wadsworth, *American Constitution Made Easy: A Constitution Quiz Bowl Game,* p. 17 (ACME: North Salt Lake City, Utah) (1991).

[69] *See* John Eastman, *The Spending Clause*, THE HERITAGE GUIDE TO THE CONSTITUTION, pp. 93-96 (Edwin Meese and David F. Forte, eds.) (2006).

[70] *See id.*

[71] *See id.*

[72] *See id.*

[73] W. Davis Folsom and Rick Boulware, ENCYCLOPEDIA OF AMERICAN BUSINESS, p. 49 (2009).

[74] Airlines for America, *Government-Imposed Taxes on Air Transportation*, http://airlines.org/data/government-imposed-taxes-on-air-transportation/ (last viewed January 20, 2017).

[75] Major Foreign Holders of Treasury Securities, U.S. Treasury, http://ticdata.treasury.gov/Publish/mfh.txt (last viewed May 29, 2017).

[76] Government Debt Chart: United States 1920-1930 - Federal State Local Data, http://www.usgovernmentdebt.us/spending_ chart_1920_1930USp_13s1li011 mcn_H0f (last viewed March 23, 2015).

[77] Matt Phillips, *The Long Story of U.S. Debt, From 1790 to 2011, in 1 Little Chart*, THE ATLANTIC (November 13, 2012), *available at* http://www.the atlantic.com/business/archive/2012 /11/the-long-story-of-us-debt-from-1790-to-2011-in-1-little-chart/265185/ (last viewed March 23, 2015).

[78] Information for this section taken from Bureau of the Public Debt, http://www.publicdebt.treas.gov/history/history.htm (last viewed August 31, 2010); Historical Tables of Debt Subject to Statutory Limit, Table 7.2, available at http://www.whitehouse.gov/omb/budget/Historicals (last viewed August 31, 2010); and Foreign Holdings of US Debt, *available at* http://www.treas.gov /tic/mfh.txt.

[79] *The Debt to the Penny and Who Holds It*, (January 19, 2017), <https://www.treasurydirect.gov/NP/debt/current> (last visited January 20, 2017).

[80] 127 Stat. 51.

[81] *See* D. Andrew Austin and Mindy R. Levit, *The Debt Limit: History and Recent Increases*, Congressional Research Service (October 28, 2014), *available at* http://www.senate.gov/CRSReports/crs-publish.cfm?pid='0E%2C*P%5C%3F %3D% 23%20%20%20%0A (last viewed March 6, 2014); Damian Paletta, *Suspending Debt Ceiling Is New Norm*, THE WALL STREET JOURNAL (February 11, 2014), *available at* http://blogs .wsj.com/washwire/2014/02/11/suspending-debt-ceiling-is-new-norm/ (last viewed May 7, 2016).

[82] Gabrielle Levy, *U.S. to Hit Debt Ceiling March 16*, U.S. NEWS AND WORLD REPORT (March 9, 2015), *available at* http://www.usnews.com/news/articles/ 2015/03/09/lew-us-will-hit-debt-ceiling-next-week (last viewed March 23, 2015).

[83] *Debt Limit*, U.S. Treasury, treasury.gov, < https://www.treasury.gov/initiatives/Pages/debtlimit.aspx> (last viewed January 21, 2017).

[84] *See Bipartisan Budget Act of 2015*, Pub.L. 114-74, 129 Stat. 584, enacted November 2, 2015.

[85] *See* "H.Res. 683--112th Congress: Expressing the regret of the House of Representatives for the passage of laws that adversely affected the Chinese in the United States, including the Chinese Exclusion Act." www.GovTrack.us. 2012. May 31, 2013 http:// www.govtrack.us/congress/bills/112/hres

[86] 8 U.S.C. § 1422 *et seq.*

[87] 8 U.S.C. § 1424.

[88] Immigration Reform and Control Act (a.k.a. Simpson-Mazzoli Act), Pub.L. 99–603, 100 Stat. 3359, enacted November 6, 1986.

[89] 8 U.S.C. § 1481.

[90] Al Kamen, *Tina Turner formally 'relinquishes' U.S. citizenship*, THE WASHINGTON POST (November 12, 2013), *available at* http://www.washingtonpost.com/blogs/in-the-loop/wp/2013/11/12/tina-turner-formally-relinquishes-u-s-citizenship/ (last viewed March 23, 2015).

[91] Suzanne Wooley, *Americans Renouncing Citizenship at Record High*, BLOOMBERG (February 9, 2017), *available at* https://www.bloomberg.com/news/articles/2017-02-09/americans-renouncing-citizenship-at-record-high (last viewed February 10, 2017); Laura Sanders, *Record Number Gave Up U.S. Citizenship or Long-Term Residency in 2014*, THE WALL STREET JOURNAL (February 10, 2015), *available at* http://www.wsj.com/articles/ record-number-gave-up-u-s-citizenship-or-long-term-residency-1423582726 (last viewed March 23, 2015).

[92] 1 Stat. 246.

[93] *Id.*

[94] 34 Stat. 163.

[95] 1 Stat. 300.

[96] 12 U.S.C. § 251; ch. 6, 38 Stat. 251.

[97] 15 USC 205a *et seq*

[98] 1790 Crimes Act, § 14, 1 Stat. 115.

[99] 1825 Crimes Act, § 17, 4 Stat. 115, 119-20.

[100] 18 U.S.C. § 471.

[101] 18 U.S.C. § 472.

[102] 12 U.S.C. § 418.

[103] Jackie Calmes, *Harriet Tubman Ousts Andrew Jackson in Change for a $20*, THE NEW YORK TIMES (April 20, 2016), available at <https://www.nytimes.com/2016/04/21/us/women-currency-treasury-harriet-tubman.html?_r=0> (last viewed January 21, 2017); *see also* Modern Money, US Treasury, <https://modernmoney.treasury.gov/> (last viewed January 21, 2017).

[104] Ruth Judson and Richard Porter, *Estimating the Volume of Counterfeit U.S. Currency in Circulation Worldwide: Data and Extrapolation*, The Federal Reserve Bank of Chicago (March 1, 2010) p. 32, *available at* <http://www.chicagofed.org/digital_assets/publications/policy_discussion_papers/2010/PDP2010-2.pdf>

[105] Annual Report 2015, U.S. Secret Service, p. 26, *available at* <https://www.secretservice.gov/data/press/reports/USSS_FY2015AR.pdf > (last viewed January 21, 2017).

[106] RECORDS OF THE FEDERAL CONVENTION, [2:615; Madison, 14 Sept.] Volume 3, Article 1, Section 8, Clause 7, Document 1, http://press-pubs.uchicago.edu/founders/documents/a1_8_7s1.html (The University of Chicago Press) (last viewed June 5, 2013).

[107] *The Storied History of the United States Postal Service*, TIME Magazine online http://www.time.com/time/photogallery/0,29307,2085535,00.html#ixzz2awtRwusN (last viewed August 3, 2013).

[108] *Postal Facts*, United States Postal Service, https://about.usps.com/who-we-are/postal-facts/welcome.htm; https://about.usps.com/who-we-are/postal-facts/size-scope.htm (last viewed October 8, 2016).

[109] 17 U.S.C. § 106.

[110] 112 Stat. 2827; Timothy B. Lee, *15 years ago, Congress kept Mickey Mouse out of the public domain. Will they do it again?*, THE WASHINGTON POST (October 25, 2013), *available at* https://www.washingtonpost.com/news/the-switch/wp/2013/10/25/15-years-ago-congress-kept-mickey-mouse-out-of-the-public-domain-will-they-do-it-again/?utm_term=.198d16b14fcc (last viewed July 14, 2017).

[111] *See Lawrence Lessig,* Copyright's First Amendment, 48 UCLA L. REV. 1057, 1061 (2001).

[112] Timothy B. Lee, *15 years ago, Congress kept Mickey Mouse out of the public domain. Will they do it again?*, THE WASHINGTON POST (October 25, 2013).

[113] 35 U.S.C. § 101.

[114] 35 U.S.C. § 171.

[115] 35 U.S.C. § 161. *See also* http://www.uspto.gov/patents/

[116] *U.S. Patent Activity, Calendar Years 1790 to the Present,* USPTO, http://www.uspto.gov/web/offices/ac/ido/oeip/taf/ h_counts.htm (last viewed August 3, 2013).

[117] 35 U.S.C. § 154.

[118] 35 U.S.C. § 173.

[119] *Leahy-Smith America Invents Act*, Public Law 112-29 (September 16, 2011); 125 Stat. 284. (35 U.S.C. § 1); *available at* http://www.uspto.gov/sites/default/files/aia_implementation/ 20110916-pub-l112-29.pdf (last viewed March 24, 2015).

[120] Pub. L. No. 109-366; 120 Stat. 2600.

[121] Caleb Groos, *Wife's Cruise Ship Death: Murder on the High Seas?*, FINDLAW BLOTTER (July 17, 2009), *available at* http://blogs.findlaw.com/blotter/2009/07/wifes-cruise-ship-death-murder-on-the-high-seas.html.

[122] Greg Moran, *Cruise Ship Killer Gets Life Sentence*, U-T SAN DIEGO (December 8, 2011), available at http://www.utsandiego.com/news/2011/Dec/08/cruise-ship-killer-gets-life-sentence/.

[123] The Associated Press, *3 Somalis Convicted In Hijacking That Left 4 Dead* (July 9, 2013); available at http://www.npr.org/templates/story/story.php?storyId=200359557 (last viewed August 3, 2013).

[124] The Associated Press, *3 Somalis Convicted In Hijacking That Left 4 Dead* (July 9, 2013); available at http://www.npr.org/templates/story/story.php?storyId=200359557 (last viewed August 3, 2013).

[125] *See generally* FEDERALIST No. 69.

[126] James Madison, *The Debates in the Federal Convention of 1787: August 17*,The Avalon Project, Yale Law School, *available at* http://avalon.law.yale.edu/18th_century/debates_817.asp (last viewed August 5, 2013).

[127] 7 WORKS OF ALEXANDER HAMILTON, J. Hamilton ed. (New York: 1851), 746–747.

[128] Jennifer K. Elsea and Richard F. Grimmett, *Declarations of War and Authorizations for the Use of Military Force: Historical Background and Legal Implications*, Congressional Research Service (March 17, 2011), *available at* http://www.fas.org/sgp/crs/natsec/RL31133.pdf (last viewed August 5, 2013).

[129] 2 Stat. 129.

[130] Elsea and Grimmett, *Declarations of War and Authorizations for the Use of Military Force: Historical Background and Legal Implications*, Congressional Research Service (March 17, 2011), *supra.*

[131] Tim Merrill, ed. *Nicaragua: A Country Study. Washington*: GPO for the Library of Congress, 1993 ("United States Intervention, 1909-33") *available at* http://countrystudies.us/nicaragua/ (last viewed August 5, 2013).

[132] Barbara Salazar Torreon, *Instances of Use of United States Armed Forces Abroad, 1798-2016*, Congressional Research Service (October 7, 2016), *available at* https://fas.org/sgp/crs/natsec/R42738.pdf (last viewed July 28, 2017).

[133] James Madison, FEDERALIST No. 24.

[134] Press Release, *Department of Defense (DoD) Releases Fiscal Year 2017 President's Budget Proposal*, U.S. Department of Defense (February 9, 2016), *available at http://www.defense.gov/News/News-Releases/News-Release-View/Article/652687/ department-of-defense-dod-releases-fiscal-year-2017-presidents-budget-proposal* (last viewed May 7, 2016).

[135] *Id.; Air Force Military Demographics* (as of March 31, 2016), Air Force Personnel Center, *available at http://www.afpc .af.mil/library/airforcepersonneldemographics.asp* (last viewed May 7, 2016); *The Air Force in Facts and Figures*, 2012 USAF ALMANAC, *available at* http://www.airforcemag.com/Magazine Archive/Magazine%20Documents/2012/May%202012/0512facts_figs.pdf (last viewed August 10, 2013).

[136] *See* FEDERALIST No. 24.

[137] *Mission of the Navy*, U.S. NAVY, *available at* http://www .navy.mil/navydata/organization/org-top.asp (last viewed August 13, 2013).

[138] Michael A. Palmer, *The Navy: The Continental Period, 1775–1890*, Naval History & Heritage Command, United States Navy, *available at* http://www.history.navy.mil/history/history2.htm (last viewed August 10, 2013).

[139] *Status of the Navy*, United States Navy, *available at* http://www.navy.mil/ navydata/nav_legacy.asp?id=146 (last viewed May 7, 2016).

[140] *Our Purpose*, U.S. Marines, *available at* http://www.marines .com/history-heritage/our-purpose (last viewed August 10, 2013).

[141] Press Release, *Department of Defense (DoD) Releases Fiscal Year 2017 President's Budget Proposal*, U.S. Department of Defense (February 9, 2016), available at < https://www.defense.gov/News/News-Releases/News-Release-View/Article/652687/department-of-defense-dod-releases-fiscal-year-2017-presidents-budget-proposal> (last viewed January 21, 2017).

[142] 10 U.S.C. §§ 801–946

[143] 10 U.S.C. § 311.

[144] The law setting forth the ability to call the National Guard into federal service is found at 10 U.S.C. §12406.

[145] Erin Chapman, *The National Guard's Evolving Mission*, The Daily Need (PBS February 25, 2011), *available at* http://www .pbs.org/wnet/need-to-know/the-daily-need/the-national-guards-evolving-mission/7623/ (last viewed March 4, 2014).

[146] *See* 10 U.S.C. §10503

[147] James Madison, FEDERALIST No. 43.

[148] 1 Stat. 130.

[149] Washington D.C. – History and Heritage, Smithsonian.com (November 6, 2007) http://www.smithsonianmag.com/travel/ destination-hunter/north-america/united-states/east/washington-dc/washingtondc-history-heritage.html?c=y&story=fullstory (last viewed August 12, 2013).

[150] *Id.*

[151] 1 Stat. 191.

[152] *Hamilton's Opinion as to the Constitutionality of the Bank of the United States: 1791*, Avalon Project, Yale University, *available at* http://avalon.law.yale.edu/18th_century/bank-ah.asp (last viewed August 12, 2013).

[153] *Id.*

[154] *Jefferson's Opinion as to the Constitutionality of the Bank of the United States: 1791*, Avalon Project, Yale University, *available at* http://avalon.law .yale.edu/18th_century/bank-tj.asp (last viewed August 13, 2013).

[155] *Id.*

[156] *Secret Service History*, www.secretservice.gov, http://www.secretservice.gov /history.shtml

[157] *Habeas Corpus*, Merriam-Webster Dictionary online, http://www.merriam-webster.com/dictionary/habeas%20corpus (last viewed August 14, 2013).

[158] 17 Stat. 951.

[159] 110 Stat. 1214; Public Law 104-132.

[160] Kenneth R. Thomas, *The Proposed "Defund ACORN Act": Is It a "Bill of Attainder?"* Congressional Research Service (September 22, 2009), *available at* http://www.volokh.com/files/ acornattainder.pdf (last viewed March 12, 2014).

[161] *ACORN v. United States*, 618 F.3d 125 (2d Cir. 2010).

[162] Robert Sedler, *Why GOP attack on Planned Parenthood is doomed*, USA TODAY (May 6, 2017), *available at* <https://www.usatoday.com/story/opinion/ 2017/05/06/targeting-planned-parenthood/101287078/> (last viewed May 29, 2017).

[163] *See* David F. Forte, *Export Taxation Clause*, THE HERITAGE GUIDE TO THE CONSTITUTION, p. 161 (Edwin Meese and David F. Forte, eds.) (2006).

[164] United States Government Publishing Office, *Fiscal Year 2017 Historical Tables Budget of the U.S. Government*, (table 1.1) *available at* < https://www.govinfo.gov/content/pkg/BUDGET-2017-TAB/pdf/BUDGET-2017-TAB.pdf > (last viewed January 28, 2017).

[165] Office of Management and Budget, *Fiscal Year 2017 Historical Tables, Budget of the U.S. Government* (Table 1.1), *available at* < https://www.gpo.gov/fdsys/pkg/BUDGET-2017-TAB/pdf/BUDGET-2017-TAB.pdf > (last viewed February 9, 2017).

[166] *Id.*

[167] Brian Faler, *Fannie Mae, Freddie Mac to Be Kept Off Budget, White House Says*, BLOOMBERG NEWS (September 12, 2008), *available at* http://www .bloomberg.com/apps/news?pid=newsarchive&sid=aXJSThdqLsXg (last viewed March 28, 2015).

[168] Mick Mulvaney, *The Republican Budget Is a Deficit Bust*, THE WALL STREET JOURNAL (March 29, 2015), *available at* http://www.wsj.com/articles/mick-mulvaney-the-republican-budget-is-a-deficit-bust-1427662664 (last viewed March 31, 2015); *Funny Money on Iraq*, THE NEW YORK TIMES (May 8, 2006) (editorial), *available at* http://www.nytimes.com/2006/ 05/08/opinion/08iht-ediraq.html (last viewed March 28, 2015); Michael Boyle, *How the US Public was defrauded by the hidden cost of the Iraq war*, THE GUARDIAN (March 11, 2013), *available at* http://www.theguardian.com/commentisfree/2013/ mar/11/us-public-defrauded-hidden-cost-iraq-war (last viewed March 28, 2015).

[169] *Constitution Is Cited as Bar to Pension for Reagan*, THE NEW YORK TIMES (August 29, 1987), *available at* <http://www.nytimes.com/1987/08/29/us/ constitution-is-cited-as-bar-to-pension-for-reagan.html?pagewanted=print> (last viewed January 28, 2017).

[170] Alexander Hamilton, FEDERALIST No. 22.

[171] Public Law 77-670; 56 Stat. 662 (1942)

[172] Peter Grier, *Obama joins 3 other US presidents who have won the Nobel Peace Prize*, THE CHRISTIAN SCIENCE MONITOR (October 9, 2009), *available at* <http://www.csmonitor.com/USA/Politics/The-Vote/2009/1009/obama-joins-3-other-us-presidents-who-have-won-the-nobel-peace-prize> (last viewed January 28, 2017).

[173] Clarence B. Carson, *The Constitution and Paper Money*, FOUNDATION FOR ECONOMIC EDUCATION (July 1, 1983), *available at* http://fee.org/freeman/detail/the-constitution-and-paper-money (last viewed July 6, 2015).

[174] *California Border Protection Stations (BPS): First Line of Defense in Protecting Our Environment and Resources from Invasive Species*, CALIFORNIA DEPARTMENT OF FOOD AND AGRICULTURE, http://www.cdfa.ca.gov/plant/PE/Exterior Exclusion/borders.html (last viewed August 21, 2013).

[175] *Id.*

[176] *Id.*

[177] "Duty of Tonnage" USLEGAL.COM http://definitions.uslegal.com/d/duty-of-tonnage/ (last viewed August 21, 2013).

[178] "Tonnage Duty" THE LAW DICTIONARY, FEATURING BLACK'S LAW DICTIONARY FREE ONLINE LEGAL DICTIONARY 2ND ED. http://thelawdictionary.org/tonnage-duty-2/ (last viewed August 21, 2013).

[179] *Understanding Interstate Compacts*, COUNCIL OF STATE GOVERNMENTS— NATIONAL CENTER FOR INTERSTATE COMPACTS, *available at* http://www.cglg.org/projects/water/CompactEducation/Understanding_ Interstate_Compacts--CSGNCIC.pdf (last viewed August 21, 2013).

[180] 43 U.S.C. § 617l; 42 Stat. 171

[181] WMATA Compact, *available at* http://www.wmata.com/about_metro/ docs/Compact_Annotated_2009_final.pdf (last viewed August 21, 2013).

[182] Public Law 104-321.

[183] *Interstate Compact on Educational Opportunity for Military Children*, AMERICA'S PROMISE ALLIANCE, http://www.americas promise.org/Our-Work/Military-Families/Issues/Interstate-Compact.aspx (last viewed August 21, 2013).

236

[184] *Fact Sheet on the Interstate Compact on Educational Opportunity for Military Children*, AASA, http://www.aasa.org/content.aspx?id=9460 (last viewed August 21, 2013).

[185] *FAQ*, Military Interstate Children's Compact Commission, http://mic3.net/pages/FAQ/faq_indexnew.aspx (last viewed March 31, 2015).

[186] Alexander Hamilton and James Madison, *The Pacificus-Helvidius Debates of 1793-1794: Toward the Completion of the American Founding* (Morton J. Frisch, ed.) p. 13 *available at* The Liberty Fund http://files.libertyfund.org/files/1910/3953_LFeBk.pdf (last viewed August 22, 2013).

[187] *2000 Official Presidential General Election Results*, Federal Election Commission (December 2001), *available at* http:// www.fec.gov/pubrec/2000presgeresults.htm (last viewed August 22, 2013).

[188] *Sick of Hearing About "Swing States"? Blame the Electoral College*, PBS NEWSHOUR EXTRA (October 29, 2012), *available at* http://www.pbs.org/newshour/extra/features/us/july-dec12/electoralcollege_10-29.html (last viewed August 22, 2013).

[189] Statutes at Large, 28th Congress, 2nd Session, p. 721, *available at* http://memory.loc.gov/ll/llsl/005/0700/07590721.tif. Codified at 3 U.S.C. § 1.

[190] 3 U.S.C. § 7.

[191] 1 Stat. 103. http://memory.loc.gov/cgi-bin/ampage?collId=llsl&fileName=001/llsl001.db&recNum=226

[192] Jack Maskell, *Qualifications for President and the "Natural Born" Citizenship Eligibility Requirement*, CONGRESSIONAL RESEARCH SERVICE (November 14, 2011) p. 34, available at http://www.fas.org/sgp/crs/misc/R42097.pdf (last viewed August 23, 2013).

[193] 8 U.S.C. § 1403.

[194] Jack Maskell, *Qualifications for President and the "Natural Born" Citizenship Eligibility Requirement*, CONGRESSIONAL RESEARCH SERVICE (November 14, 2011) p. 34, *available at* http://www.fas.org/sgp/crs/misc/R42097.pdf (last viewed August 23, 2013).

[195] 3 U.S.C. § 102.

[196] *The Congressional Register; or History of Proceedings and Debates of the First House of Representatives of the United States of America* (2nd Ed., Vol. 2), (p. 71).

[197] Adam Chandler, *The Dollar-a-Year Man*, THE ATLANTIC (Nov. 16, 2016), *available at* <http://www.theatlantic.com/politics/archive/2016/11/trump-presidential-salary/507965/> (last viewed January 28, 2017); Lily Rothman, *The History Behind Donald Trump's Refusing a Presidential Salary*, TIME (Nov. 15, 2016), available at <http://time.com/4570858/donald-trump-salary-president-history/> (last viewed January 28, 2017).

[198] Richard Norton Smith and Timothy Walch, *The Ordeal of Herbert Hoover*, PROLOGUE MAGAZINE Vol. 26, No. 2 (Summer 2004); *available at* http://www.archives.gov/publications/ prologue/2004/summer/hoover-1.html (last viewed March 15, 2014); Mary Kenney, *Charitable U.S. Presidents*, timesunion .com (February 21, 2011), http://blog.timesunion.com/payit forward/charitable-u-s-presidents/1688/.

[199] Adam Chandler, *The Dollar-a-Year Man*, THE ATLANTIC (Nov. 16, 2016), *available at* <http://www.theatlantic.com/politics/archive/2016/11/trump-presidential-salary/507965/> (last viewed January 28, 2017).

[200] David A. Fahrenthold, *Trump will donate his first-quarter salary — $78,333 — to the National Park Service, White House says*, THE WASHINGTON POST (April 3, 2017), available at <https://www.washingtonpost.com/news/post-politics/wp/2017/04/03/trump-will-donate-his-first-quarter-salary-78333-to-the-national-park-service-white-house-says/?utm_term=.ae3971e37756> (last viewed May 29, 2017).

[201] *Constitution Is Cited as Bar to Pension for Reagan*, THE NEW YORK TIMES (August 29, 1987), *available at* <http://www.nytimes.com/1987/08/29/us/constitution-is-cited-as-bar-to-pension-for-reagan.html?pagewanted=print> (last viewed January 28, 2017).

[202] For example, in the third presidential debate in 2012 President Obama said, "Well, my first job as commander in chief, Bob, is to keep the American people safe." Governor Mitt Romney, the challenger in the election, said in the same debate that he saw "the highest responsibility of the president of the United States" to be "to maintain the safety of the American people." *Transcript and Audio: Third Presidential Debate*, NATIONAL PUBLIC RADIO (October 22, 2012), *available at* http://www.npr.org/2012/10/22/163436694/ transcript-3rd-obama-romney-presidential-debate (last viewed April 1, 2015). And in 2007, President George W. Bush said, "As President, my most solemn responsibility is to keep the American people safe." *Transcript: President Bush on Iraq* THE NEW YORK TIMES (July 12, 2007), *available at* http://www.nytimes.com/2007/07/12/washington/12bush_transcript.html?pagewanted=all (last viewed April 1, 2015).

[203] *Bibles and Scripture Passages Used by Presidents in Taking the Oath of Office*, Library of Congress, http://memory.loc.gov/ammem/pihtml/pibible.html (last viewed August 23, 2013).

[204] Press Release, *Grant of Executive Clemency*, The White House (July 2, 2007) *available at* http://georgewbush-whitehouse.archives.gov/news/releases/2007/07/20070702-4.html (last viewed September 9, 2013).

[205] Gregory Korte, *Obama grants 330 more commutations, bringing total to a record 1,715* USA TODAY (Jan. 19, 2017), *available at* <http://www.usatoday.com/story/news/politics/2017/01/19/obama-grants-330-more-commutations-bringing-total-record-1715/96791186/> (last viewed January 28, 2017).

[206] Michael E. O'Hanlon, *New START Shouldn't Be Stopped*, POLITICO (November 18, 2010), *available at* http://www.brookings.edu/research/opinions/2010/11/18-new-start-ohanlon (reprinted by The Brookings Institution) (last viewed March 15, 2014).

[207] *The Senate's Role in Treaties*, senate.gov, <https://www.senate.gov/artandhistory/history/common/briefing/Treaties.htm> (last viewed January 28, 2017).

[208] *Treaties*, senate.gov *available at* http://www.senate.gov/artandhistory/history/common/briefing/Treaties.htm (last viewed September 9, 2013).

[209] David Ackerman, *Withdrawal from the ABM Treaty: Legal Considerations*, CONGRESSIONAL RESEARCH SERVICE (December 31, 2002) p. 1, *available at* http://assets.opencrs.com/rpts/RS21088_20021231.pdf (last viewed September 9, 2013).

[210] *Treaties*, senate.gov *available at* <http://www.senate.gov/artandhistory/history/common/briefing/Treaties.htm> (last viewed September 9, 2013).

[211] James Gerstenzang, *Senate Approves NAFTA on 61-38 Vote: Trade: Passage in upper house had been expected. Pact still faces action in Mexico and Canada*, THE LOS ANGELES TIMES (November 21, 1993), *available at* http://articles .latimes.com/ 1993-11-21/news/mn-59485_1_trade-pact (last viewed September 10, 2013).

[212] Valerie Richardson, *White House defends Obama evading Senate on Paris climate deal*, THE WASHINGTON TIMES (Aug. 29, 2016), *available at* <http:// www.washingtontimes.com/news/2016/aug/29/obama-will-bypass-senate-ratify-paris-climate-acco/> (last viewed January 28, 2017).

[213] Dave Boyer, *Obama, Chinese president ratify climate-change agreement*, THE WASHINGTON TIMES (September 3, 2016), available at < http://www .washingtontimes.com/news/2016/sep/3/obama-xi-ratify-climate-change-agreement/> (last viewed February 6, 2017).

[214] Climate deal must avoid US Congress approval, French minister says, THE GUARDIAN, (1 June 2015), available at < https://www.theguardian.com/world/ 2015/jun/01/un-climate-talks-deal-us-congress> (last viewed February 6, 2017).

[215] Jonathan Weisman, *Parties Do Battle Over U.S. Forces' Future in Iraq*, THE WASHINGTON POST (June 12, 2008), available at < http://www.washington post.com/wp-dyn/content/article/2008/06/11/AR2008061103452.html> (last viewed February 6, 2017).

[216] *Current Executive Branch Nominations and Appointments*, UNITED STATES OFFICE OF GOVERNMENT ETHICS, http://www .oge.gov/open-government/access-records/current-executive-branch-nominations-and-appointments/ (last viewed September 10, 2013).

[217] *How Clinton Treated Hatch*, Thinkprogress.org (July 1, 2005), *available at* http://thinkprogress.org/politics/2005/07/01 /1228/how-clinton-treated-hatch/.

[218] Mahita Gajanan, *A Senator Asked Neil Gorsuch If He'd Rather Fight a Horse-Sized Duck or 100 Duck-Sized Horses*, TIME (March 21, 2017) <http://time.com /4708665/neil-gorsuch-supreme-court-jeff-flake-horse-duck-reddit/> (last viewed May 30, 2017).

[219] Ann Sanner, *Team Jacob or Team Edward? Turns out Elena Kagan would rather talk about legal stuff*, THE CHRISTIAN SCIENCE MONITOR (July 2, 2010), *available at* http://www .csmonitor.com/From-the-news-wires/2010/0702/Team-Jacob-or-Team-Edward-Turns-out-Elena-Kagan-would-rather-talk-about-legal-stuff (last viewed September 10, 2013).

[220] *See* Barry J. McMillion, *Supreme Court Appointment Process: Senate Debate and Confirmation Vote*, CONGRESSIONAL RESEARCH SERVICE (October 19, 2015), *available at https://fas.org/sgp/crs/misc/R44234.pdf (last viewed May 30, 2017).*

[221] Michael Kelly, *Settling In: The President's Day; Clinton Cancels Baird Nomination for Justice Dept.*, THE NEW YORK TIMES (January 22, 1993), *available at* http://www.nytimes.com/ 1993/01/22/us/settling-president-s-day-clinton-cancels-baird-nomination-for-justice-dept.html?pagewanted=all&src=pm (last viewed September 11, 2013).

[222] *Examining the History and Legality of Executive Branch Czars*, Hearing Before the Committee on the Judiciary, United States (October 6, 2009), S. Hrg. 111-562, Serial No. J-111-54, *available at* http://www.gpo.gov/fdsys/pkg/ CHRG-111shrg57708/pdf/CHRG-111shrg57708.pdf (last viewed September 11, 2013).

[223] *See Examining the History and Legality of Executive Branch Czars*, Hearing Before the Committee on the Judiciary, United States (October 6, 2009), S. Hrg. 111-562, Serial No. J-111-54, p. 2 *available at* http://www.gpo.gov/fdsys/pkg/CHRG-111shrg57708/pdf/CHRG-111shrg57708.pdf (last viewed September 11, 2013); Orrin Hatch, *Obama's Czars: Bending the Constitution*, THE DAILY HERALD (June 13, 2012), *available at* http://www.heraldextra.com/news/state-and-regional/obama-s-czars-bending-the-constitution/article_62145e68-216a-52eb-a450-eb202b5d2c98.html (last viewed September 10, 2013).

[224] *Characteristics of Presidential Appointments that do not Require Senate Confirmation*, U.S. Government Accountability Office (March 1, 2013), GAO-13-299R, *available at* http://www .gao.gov/assets/660/652573.pdf (last viewed September 11, 2013).

[225] *Id.*

[226] *SYRIA: U.S. Senate approves Robert Ford as ambassador*, THE LOS ANGELES TIMES (October 4, 2011), http://latimesblogs.latimes.com/world_now/2011/10/syria-us-ambassador-robert-ford-confirmation.html#sthash.EmrRBfeV.dpuf (last viewed September 11, 2013).

[227] Henry B. Hogue, *Recess Appointments: Frequently Asked Questions*, Congressional Research Service (June 7, 2013), *available at* http://www.senate.gov/CRSReports/crs-publish.cfm?pid='0DP%2BP%5CW%3B%20P%20%20%0A (last viewed September 11, 2013).

[228] *Id.*

[229] Henry B. Hogue, *Recess Appointments Made by President Barack Obama*, Congressional Research Service (May 28, 2015), *available at* <https://fas.org/sgp/crs/misc/R42329.pdf> (last viewed January 10, 2017). This figure does not include the four alleged appointments made in January 2012 when President Obama unilaterally declared the Senate to not be in session.

[230] Extraordinary Sessions of Congress – A Brief History, senate.gov, *available at* http://www.senate.gov/artandhistory/history/resources/pdf/ExtraSessions.pdf (last viewed September 11, 2013).

[231] *Woodrow Wilson* MILLER CENTER (University of Virginia) http://millercenter.org/president/wilson/essays/biography/5 (last viewed February 26, 2013)

[232] LeeAnn Ghajar, *Recognition of the Soviet Union* GEORGE MASON UNIVERSITY, http://chnm.gmu.edu/courses/schrag/wiki/index.php?title=Recognition_of_the_Soviet_Union (last viewed September 16, 2013).

[233] *Recognition of the Soviet Union, 1933*, Office of the Historian, U.S. Department of State, http://history.state.gov/ milestones/1921-1936/USSR (last viewed September 16, 2013).

[234] Tahman Bradley, *Obama Proudly Recognizes South Sudan*, ABC News (July 9, 2011), http://abcnews.go.com/blogs/politics /2011/07/obama-proudly-recognizes-south-sudan/ (last viewed September 11, 2013).

[235] Press Release, *Justice Department Refuses to Defend Congress in Legal Battle Over Law Censoring Marijuana Policy Ads*, AMERICAN CIVIL LIBERTIES UNION (January 26, 2005), *available at* https://www.aclu.org/drug-law-reform/justice-department-refuses-defend-congress-legal-battle-over-law-censoring-marijuana (last viewed April 2, 2015).

[236] *Gavett v. Alexander*, 477 F. Supp. 1035 (D.D.C. 1979)

[237] Congressional Research Service, CRS ANNOTATED CONSTITUTION, p. 587 (2000).

[238] 1 Trial of Andrew Johnson, President of the United States on Impeachment, 88, 147 (Washington: 1868)

[239] Gerald Ford's Remarks on the Impeachment of Supreme Court Justice William Douglas, April 15, 1970, page 6; *available at* http://www.fordlibrarymuseum.gov/library/ speeches/700415.pdf (last viewed September 17, 2013).

[240] This is the general definition of "civil officer" on several sites. *See* US Legal Definitions, http://definitions.uslegal.com/ c/civil-officer/

[241] *See* "judicial power" http://definitions.uslegal.com/j/judicial-power/ (last viewed September 30, 2013).

[242] *See* Erwin Chemerinsky, CONSTITUTIONAL LAW (2d. ed.), p. 130 (2005).

[243] *See* Erwin Chemerinsky, CONSTITUTIONAL LAW (2d. ed.), p. 130 (2005).

[244] 29 U.S.C. § 44.

[245] *Judicial Compensation*, USCourts.gov, <http://www.uscourts.gov/judges-judgeships/judicial-compensation> (last viewed February 9, 2017).

[246] *Suits Affecting Ambassadors, Other Public Ministers, and Consuls*, CRS ANNOTATED CONSTITUTION, p. 726-727 (2000).

[247] *Cases of Admiralty and Maritime Jurisdiction*, CRS ANNOTATED CONSTITUTION, p. 728-729 (2000).

[248] *Id.*

[249] *See R.M.S. Titanic, Inc. v. Haver,* 171 F.3d 943 (4th Cir. Va. 1999) and related opinions for a history of the litigation over the Titanic salvage.

[250] 523 U.S. 767 (1998).

[251] *See* Sheldon F. Kurtz and Herbert Hovenkamp, AMERICAN PROPERTY LAW, p. 215-16 (5th ed. 2004).

[252] *See Town of Pallet v. Clark*, 13 U.S. 292 (1815).

[253] CRS ANNOTATED CONSTITUTION, p. 773-74 (2000).

[254] 28 U.S.C. § 1332.

[255] 43 Stat. 936 (1925).

[256] *Frequently Asked Questions*, United States Supreme Court https://www.supremecourt.gov/faq.aspx#faqgi9 (last viewed February 10, 2017).

[257] *The Aaron Burr Treason Trial — Historical Background and Documents*, FEDERAL JUDICIAL CENTER http://www.fjc.gov/ history/home.nsf/page/tu_burr_narrative.html (last viewed October 7, 2013).

[258] 15 Stat. 702 (1868).

[259] Susan Heller Anderson, *Mildred Gillars, 87, of Nazi Radio, Axis Sally to an Allied Audience*, THE NEW YORK TIMES (July 2, 1988), *available at* http://www.nytimes.com/1988/07/02/ obituaries/midred-gillars-87-of-nazi-radio-axis-sally-to-an-allied-audience.html (last viewed October 7, 2013).

[260] Adam Blenford, *Death ends myth of Tokyo Rose*, BBC NEWS (Sep. 28, 2006), http://news.bbc.co.uk/2/hi/americas/5389722.stm (last viewed April 6, 2015).

[261] *Adam Gadahn Fast Facts*, CNN, http://www.cnn.com/2013/ 03/23/us/adam-gadahn-fast-facts/index.html (last viewed October 7, 2013).

[262] 40 Stat. 217; codified at 18 U.S.C. § 792 et seq.

[263] *See* 18 U.S.C. §§ 792-799.

[264] *See* 18 U.S.C. § 793.

[265] *See* Peter Finn and Sari Horwitz, *U.S. charges Snowden with espionage*, THE WASHINGTON POST (June 21, 2013), *available at* http://www.washingtonpost.com/world/national-security/us-charges-snowden-with-espionage/2013/06/21/507497d8-dab1-11e2-a016-92547bf094cc_story.html (last viewed December 3, 2013).

[266] *See* Charlie Savage, *Manning Is Acquitted of Aiding the Enemy*, THE NEW YORK TIMES (July 30, 2013), *available at* http://www.nytimes.com/2013/07/31/us/bradley-manning-verdict.html?_r=1& (last viewed December 3, 2013).

[267] *Attainder*, The Free Dictionary, http://legal-dictionary.thefreedictionary.com/attainder (last viewed December 4, 2013).

[268] *Corruption of Blood*, THE LAW DICTIONARY, http://thelawdictionary.org/corruption-of-blood/ (last viewed December 4, 2013).

[269] *United States v. Monti*, 100 F.Supp. 209 (E.D.N.Y. 1951).

[270] *Best v. United States*, 184 F. 2d 131 (1st Cir. 1950)

[271] *Burgman Is Sentenced to Prison As Traitor*, THE OWOSSO ARGUS-PRESS (December 19, 1949) *available at* http://news.google.co.uk/newspapers?id=TV4iAAAAIBAJ&sjid=ZqoFAAAAIBAJ&pg=2964,2433917&dq=herbert+burgman&hl=en (last viewed December 4, 2013).

[272] *Kawakita v. United States*, 190 F.2d 506 (9th Cir. 1951), *available at* http://uniset.ca/other/cs5/190F2d506.html (last viewed December 4, 2013).

[273] David Rozenzweig, *POW Camp Atrocities Led to Treason Trial*, THE LOS ANGELES TIMES (September 20, 2002), *available at* http://articles.latimes.com/2002/sep/20/local/me-onthelaw20 (last viewed December 4, 2013).

[274] Pub.L. 104–199, 110 Stat. 2419; 1 U.S.C. § 7 and 28 U.S.C. § 1738C.

[275] The Supreme Court completely ignored this Full Faith and Credit clause in its 2015 decision mandating same-sex marriages nationwide. *See Obergefell v. Hodges*, No. 14-556, 576 U.S. ___ (2015) Instead, it focused solely on the 14th Amendment.

[276] Philip Quarles, *Robert F. Kennedy Announces His Senate Candidacy, 1964*, WNYC (November 5, 2012) http://www.wnyc .org/story/192691-robert-kennedy/ (last viewed December 4, 2013).

[277] Adam Nagourney, *In a Kennedy's Legacy, Lessons and Pitfalls For Hillary Clinton; Carpetbagger Issue Has Echoes of '64, But Differences Could Prove Crucial*, THE NEW YORK TIMES (September 10, 2000), *available at* http://www.nytimes .com/2000/09/10/nyregion/kennedy-s-legacy-lessons-pitfalls-for-hillary-clinton-carpetbagger-issue-has.html (last viewed March 15, 2014).

[278] *See, e.g.,* Julie Shaw, *"The Forgotten Constitution"* THE FOUNDRY (September 17, 2012), *available at* http://blog .heritage.org/2012/09/17/the-forgotten-constitution/ (last viewed December 16, 2013).

[279] Alaska Statehood Act (July 7, 1958), section 6; *available at* http://avalon.law.yale.edu/20th_century/ak_statehood.asp (last viewed April 7, 2015).

[280] *See Joint Resolution for Annexing Texas to the United States Approved March 1, 1845*, THE TEXAS STATE LIBRARY AND ARCHIVES, *available at* https://www.tsl.texas.gov/ref/abouttx/ annexation/march1845.html (last viewed April 7, 2015).

[281] *Opinion of Abraham Lincoln on the Admission of West Virginia* (December 31, 1862) West Virginia Archives and History, WEST VIRGINIA DIVISION OF CULTURE AND HISTORY, *available at* http://www.wvculture.org/history/ statehood/ lincolnopinion.html (last viewed December 17, 2013).

[282] Ross W. Gorte et al, *Federal Land Ownership: Overview and Data*, Congressional Research Service (February 8, 2012), *available at* http://www.fas.org/sgp/crs/misc/R42346.pdf (last viewed December 17, 2013).

[283] *Id.*

[284] *Id.*

[285] *See* Justin James Quigley, *Grand Staircase-Escalante National Monument: Preservation or Politics?*, 19 J. LAND RESOURCES & ENVTL. L. 55, 98-99 (1999).

[286] Article V, Mode of Amendment, http://www.gpo.gov/fdsys/pkg/GPO-CONAN-1992/pdf/GPO-CONAN-1992-9-6.pdf (p. 900) (last viewed December 18, 2013).

[287] *Id.*

[288] Thomas V. DiBacco, *Pick a Marble, Choose a President*, THE WALL STREET JOURNAL (April 6, 2015), *available at* http://www.wsj.com/articles/thomas-v-dibacco-pick-a-marble-choose-a-president-1428361352? (last viewed April 13, 2015).

[289] 1 Stat. 23.

[290] *See also Oath of Office*, U.S. Senate, http://www.senate.gov/artandhistory/ history/common/briefing/Oath_Office.htm (last viewed January 2, 2014).

[291] 5 U.S. C. § 3331.

[292] 28 U.S.C. § 453.

[293] *See An Originalist Analysis of the No Religious Test Clause*, 120 HARVARD L. REV. 1649, 1651 (2007), *available at* http://harvardlawreview.org/media/pdf/ no_religious_test_clause.pdf.

[294] *Id.*

[295] *Id.*

[296] *See* WILLIAM H. REHNQUIST, *The True Meaning of the Establishment Clause: A Dissent*, in HOW DOES THE CONSTITUTION PROTECT RELIGIOUS FREEDOM? 106 (Robert A. Goldwin and Art Kaufman, eds., 1987).

[297] The Founders' Constitution, Volume 5, Amendment I (Religion), Document 58, http://press-pubs.uchicago.edu/ founders/documents/amendI_religions58.html (last viewed March 25, 2014. The University of Chicago Press

[298] *See generally* Derek H. Davis, *Thomas Jefferson's Letter to the Danbury Baptist Association*, in THOMAS JEFFERSON AND PHILOSOPHY: ESSAYS ON THE PHILOSOPHICAL CAST OF JEFFERSON'S WRITINGS, M. Andrew Holowchak, ed., 79-90 (Lexington Books, 2014).

[299] *See generally* "From the Danbury Baptist Association, 7 Oct. 1801" THE PAPERS OF THOMAS JEFFERSON, Volume 35: 1 August to 30 November 1801(Princeton University Press, 2008), 407-9, *available at* https:// jeffersonpapers.princeton.edu/ selected-documents/danbury-baptist-association (last viewed July 6, 2015).

[300] *See generally* Congressional Research Service, CRS ANNOTATED CONSTITUTION, p. 969-71 (2000).

[301] *Reynolds v. United States*, 98 U.S. 145 (1878).

[302] 42 U.S.C. §§ 2000bb.

243

[303] *See* Erwin Chemerinsky, CONSTITUTIONAL LAW (2d. ed.), p. 1477-78 (2005).
[304] *See id.* at p. 1045-46.
[305] Lobbying Database, Opensecrets.org, http://www.opensecrets.org/lobby/ (last viewed February 10, 2017).
[306] *See District of Columbia v. Heller*, 554 U.S. 570 (2008).
[307] Paul S. Boyer, Clifford E. Clark, Jr., Karen Halttunen, Joseph F. Kett, Neal Salisbury, Harvard Sitkoff, Nancy Woloch, THE ENDURING VISION: A HISTORY OF THE AMERICAN PEOPLE (7th Edition) p. 835.
[308] John Carney, *Rajaratnam Gets Hit With Highest Bail In US History*, BUSINESS INSIDER, http://www.businessinsider.com/ rajarantam-gets-hit-with-highest-bail-in-us-history-2009-10#ixzz2x2fzxBVO (last viewed March 25, 2014).
[309] *Graduated Driver Licensing Laws*, Governors Highway Safety Association (May 2015), *available at* http://www.ghsa.org/html/stateinfo/laws/license_ laws.html (last viewed May 13, 2015).
[310] *Marriage Laws of the Fifty States, District of Columbia and Puerto Rico*, Cornell University Law School, *available at* https://www.law.cornell.edu/wex/ table_marriage (last viewed April 15, 2015).
[311] Codified at 42 U.S.C. § 1994
[312] *See Fourteenth Amendment and Citizenship* THE LAW LIBRARY OF CONGRESS *available at* http://www.loc.gov/law/ help/citizenship/fourteenth_amendment _citizenship.php; *see also Jones v. Alfred H. Mayer Co.*, 392 US 409, 436 (1968)
[313] *The Slaughterhouse Cases*, 83 U.S. 36 (1872).
[314] David Smolin, *Equal Protection Clause*, THE HERITAGE GUIDE TO THE CONSTITUTION, pp. 398-404 (Edwin Meese and David F. Forte, eds.) (2006).
[315] *See State Criminal Re-enfranchisement Laws (Map)*, American Civil Liberties Union, *available at* https://www .aclu.org/map/state-criminal-re-enfranchisement-laws-map?redirect=maps/map-state-felony-disfranchisement-laws (last viewed February 10, 2017); Daniel Weeks, *Should Felons Lose the Right to Vote?* THE ATLANTIC (January 7, 2014) *available at* http://www.the atlantic.com/politics/archive/2014/01/should-felons-lose-the-right-to-vote/ 282846/ (last viewed January 21, 2014). *See also Disenfranchised Felons* (Editorial) NEW YORK TIMES, July 15, 2012, http://www.nytimes.com/2012/07 /16/opinion/disenfranchised-felons.html?_r=0 (last viewed March 6, 2013).
[316] The Private Act of December 14, 1869, ch.1, 16 Stat. 607.
[317] Ch. 193, 17 Stat. 142.
[318] 30 Stat. 432.
[319] Deborah Solomon, *The 14th Amendment is Obama's Best Option on Debt Ceiling*, BLOOMBERG VIEW, Jan 7, 2013 11:54 AM PT, http://www. bloomberg.com/news/2013-01-07/the-14th-amendment-is-obama-s-best-option-on-debt-ceiling.html (last viewed March 6, 2013); Alexander Bolton, Senate Dems: We'll back Obama if he raises debt limit unilaterally, THE HILL, http://thehill.com/blogs/on-the-money/banking-financial-institutions/276751-senate-dems-well-back-obama-if-he-raises-debt-limit-unilaterally (last viewed March 7, 2013).
[320] Kathleen Hunter, *Senate Democrats Urge Obama to Act on Debt If Needed*, BLOOMBERG, http://www.businessweek.com /news/2013-01-11/senate-democrats-urge-obama-to-act-on-debt-if-needed (last viewed March 6, 2013).
[321] Codified at 42 U.S.C. § 1983,
[322] *Berg et al v. NYPD et al*, 12 CIV 3391 (S.D.N.Y. April 30, 2012).

[323] Sari Horwitz, *Eric Holder vows to aggressively challenge voter ID laws*, THE WASHINGTON POST (July 10, 2012), *available at* http://www.washington post.com/world/national-security/eric-holder-vows-to-aggressively-challenge-voter-id-laws/2012/07/10/gJQApOASbW_story.html (last viewed March 29, 2014).

[324] Charlie Savage and Manny Fernandez, *Court Blocks Texas Voter ID Law, Citing Racial Impact*, THE NEW YORK TIMES, (August 30, 2012), *available at* http://www.nytimes.com/2012/ 08/31/us/court-blocks-tough-voter-id-law-in-texas.html (last viewed March 29, 2014).

[325] Press Release, *Court Blocks South Carolina's Discriminatory Voter ID Law for 2012 Election*, American Civil Liberties Union (October 10, 2012), *available at* http://www.aclu.org/voting-rights/court-blocks-south-carolinas-discriminatory-voter-id-law-2012-election (last viewed March 29, 2014).

[326] *Shelby County v. Holder*, 570 U.S. 2 (2013).

[327] Chuck Marr and Chye-Ching Huang, *Misconceptions and Realities About Who Pays Taxes*, Center on Budget and Policy Priorities, Updated September 17, 2012, *available at* http:// www.cbpp.org/files/5-26-11tax.pdf (last viewed March 11, 2013). Also at http://www.cbpp.org/cms/index.cfm?fa=view& id=3505#_ftnref6

[328] Roberton Williams, *And Now for the Movie: Fewer Americans Pay No Federal Income Tax*, Tax Policy Center, Urban Institute and Brookings Institution (August 29, 2013), *available at* http://taxvox.taxpolicycenter.org/ 2013/08/29/and-now-for-the-movie-fewer-americans-pay-no-federal-income-tax/

[329] Roberton Williams, *New Estimates Of How Many Households Pay No Federal Income Tax*, FORBES (Oct. 6, 2015), *available at* http://www.forbes .com/sites/beltway/2015/10/06/new-estimates-of-how-many-households-pay-no-federal-income-tax/#4ac7ae423cf4 (last viewed February 10, 2017).

[330] Jay S. Bybee, *Ulysses at the Mast: Democracy, Federalism, and the Sirens' Song of the Seventeenth Amendment* 91 Nw. U. L. Rev. 500, 536. (1997)

[331] *Id.* at 542.

[332] *Id.*

[333] *Direct Election of Senators* U.S. Senate (senate.gov) *available at* http://www.senate.gov/artandhistory/history/ common/briefing/Direct_Election_Senators.htm (last viewed January 30, 2014).

[334] Editorial, *Mass. Democrats shouldn't change laws on U.S. Senate openings,* BOSTON GLOBE (December 4, 2012) http://www.bostonglobe.com/opinion/editorials/2012/12/04/massachusetts-democrats-shouldn-change-laws-senate-openings/EySECF1XbycCfrCw9dtUKP/story.html (last viewed May 7, 2016).

[335] *Appointed Senators*, U.S. Senate (senate.gov), <https://www.senate.gov/ artandhistory/history/common/briefing/senators_appointed.htm> (last viewed May 30, 2017).

[336] Carl Hulse, *New Idea on Capitol Hill: To Join Senate, Get Votes* N.Y. TIMES (March 10, 2009) *available at* http://www. nytimes.com/2009/03/11/us/politics/ 11senate.html?_r=1& (last viewed June 10, 2015).

[337] Thomas H. Neale, *U.S. Senate Vacancies: Contemporary Developments and Perspectives*, CONGRESSIONAL RESEARCH SERVICE (March 10, 2017), *available at* < https://fas.org/sgp/crs/misc/R44781.pdf> (last viewed May 30, 2017).

[338] *Id.*

245

[339] *See* Richard Worth, *Teetotalers and Saloon Smashers: The Temperance Movement and Prohibition* (2009), pp. 82-88.

[340] 41 Stat. 305 (chapter 83)

[341] Jessica Leving, *Beer with extra buzz on tap up to 16%*, USA TODAY (November 4, 2009) http://usatoday30.usatoday.com/news/nation/2009-11-03-beer_N.htm (last viewed January 30, 2014).

[342] *See* Kristin Thoennes Keller, *The Women Suffrage movement, 1848-1920* (2003) (map on page 33).

[343] James Buchanan, *Fourth Annual Message to Congress on the State of the Union*, (December 3, 1860). Online by Gerhard Peters and John T. Woolley, THE AMERICAN PRESIDENCY PROJECT. http://www.presidency.ucsb.edu/ws/?pid= 29501 (last viewed April 1, 2014).

[344] *First Innaugrual Address of Abraham Lincoln* (March 4, 1861) *available at* http://avalon.law.yale.edu/19th_century/ lincoln1.asp (last viewed April 1, 2014).

[345] *See* Ted Widmer, *Lincoln Declares War*, THE NEW YORK TIMES (April 14, 2011), *available at* http://opinionator.blogs.nytimes.com/2011/04/14/lincoln-declares-war/ (last viewed April 1, 2014).

[346] Richard S. Beth and Jessica Tollestrup, *Lame Duck Sessions of Congress, 1935-2010 (74th-111th Congresses)*, Congressional Research Service (August 30, 2011) *available at* http://www.senate.gov/reference/resources/pdf/ RL33677.pdf (last viewed February 3, 2014).

[347] *Local Option Elections*, Texas Alcoholic Beverage Commission, http://www.tabc.state.tx.us/local_option_elections/ (last viewed February 10, 2017).

[348] *See Local Options: List of Dry Towns and Partially Dry Towns*, STATE OF NEW YORK LIQUOR AUTHORITY (February 27, 2013), *available at* https://www.sla.ny.gov/system/files/2012-3-LocalOptions.pdf (last viewed February 10, 2017); Joseph Spector, NY is down to just eight "dry" towns, Democrat & Chronicle (Nov. 5, 2015), *available at* http://www.democratand chronicle.com/story/news/politics/blogs/vote-up/2015/11/05/ny-is-down-to-just-eight-dry-towns/75214064/ (last viewed February 10, 2017).

[349] Brenda van Dyck, *The History of 0.08 Percent Alcohol Concentration in Minnesota*, Information Brief, Minnesota House of Representatives Research Department (November 2003), *available at* http://www.house.leg.state.mn.us/ hrd/pubs/ aceight.pdf (last viewed April 1, 2014).

[350] Lee Davidson, *Hatch helps bring D.C.-Utah House seat bill to Senate floor*, THE DESERET NEWS (January 7, 2009), *available at* http://www.deseret news.com/article/705275644/Hatch-helps-bring-DC-Utah-House-seat-bill-to-Senate-floor.html?pg=all (last viewed February 3, 2014).

[351] Press Release, *Senator Murkowski Introduces D.C . Voting Rights Constitutional Amendment*, PROJECT VOTE SMART, (February 25, 2009), *available at* http://votesmart.org/public-statement/410263/senator-murkowski-introduces-dc-voting-rights-constitutional-amendment#.UzuX9T2wJtA (last viewed April 1, 2014).

[352] *See* Sari Horwitz, *Eric Holder vows to aggressively challenge voter ID laws*, THE WASHINGTON POST (July 10, 2012), *available at* http://www.washington post.com/world/national-security/eric-holder-vows-to-aggressively-challenge-voter-id-laws/2012/07/10/gJQApOASbW_story.html (last viewed April 1, 2014).

[353] *John Tyler, 10th Vice President (1841)*, US SENATE, http://www.senate.gov/
artandhistory/history/common/generic/VP_John_Tyler.htm (last viewed April 1,
2014).

[354] *Ike's agreement with Nixon*, LEWISTON EVENING JOURNAL (March 6, 1958)
p. 4 (Lewiston-Auburn, Maine) http://news.google.com/newspapers?nid=1913
&dat=19580306&id=ynEgAAAAIBAJ&sjid=RGcFAAAAIBAJ&pg=936,46025
9/ (last viewed February 5, 2014).

[355] Thomas H. Neale, *The Eighteen year Old Vote: The Twenty-Sixth Amendment
and Subsequent Voting Rates of Newly Enfranchised Age Groups*, Congressional
Research Service (May 20, 1983), p. 16 n. 33 *available at* http://digital.library
.unt.edu/ark:/67531/metacrs8805/m1/1/high_res_d/83-103GOV_
1983May20.pdf (last viewed February 5, 2014).

[356] Zeke J. Miller, *The Politics of the Millennial Generation*, THE NEW YORK
TIMES (May 9, 2013), *available at* http://swampland.time.com/2013/05/09/
millennial-politics/ (last viewed February 5, 2014).

[357] Ida A. Brudnick, *Salaries of Members of Congress: Recent Actions and
Historical Tables*, Congressional Research Service (June 21, 2016) *available at*
https://fas.org/sgp/crs/misc/97-1011.pdf (last viewed February 10, 2017); Ida A.
Brudnick, *Salaries of Members of Congress: Congressional Votes, 1990-2015*
Congressional Research Service (April 15, 2015) *available at* https://www.fas
.org/sgp/crs/misc/97-615.pdf (last viewed June 15, 2015).

[358] *Id. See also* Summary of President and congressional Pay Data
http://oregonstate.edu/cla/polisci/faculty-research/sahr/ sumprpay.pdf

[359] The Founders' Constitution, Volume 4, Article 7, Document 3, http://press-
pubs.uchicago.edu/founders/documents/a7s3.html The University of Chicago
Press.

[360] *The Charters of Freedom, Questions and Answers*, The National Archives
http://www.archives.gov/exhibits/charters/ constitution_q_and_a.html